PELICAN BOOKS

A517

STRAVINSKY
IN CONVERSATION WITH
ROBERT CRAFT

STRAVINSKY

IN CONVERSATION WITH

ROBERT CRAFT

With Eight Plates

PENGUIN BOOKS

Penguin Books Ltd, Harmondsworth, Middlesex
AUSTRALIA : Penguin Books Pty Ltd, 762 Whitehorse Road,
Mitcham, Victoria

—

Conversations with Igor Stravinsky first published in U.S.A. 1958
First published in Great Britain by Faber and Faber 1959
Memories and Commentaries first published in U.S.A. 1959
First published in Great Britain by Faber and Faber 1960
Published in Pelican Books as *Stravinsky in Conversation with Robert Craft* 1962

—

—

Made and printed in Great Britain
by C. Nicholls & Company Ltd
Set in Monotype Perpetua

The books in this volume are the first two of a series by Igor Stravinsky and Robert Craft published in hardback edition by Faber & Faber. The third volume in the series, Expositions and Developments, *is being published by Faber & Faber simultaneously with this Pelican edition.*

Contents

IGOR STRAVINSKY: MEMORIES AND COMMENTARIES

Acknowledgements

Acknowledgements and thanks are due to Madame de Tinan for permission to reprint letters by Claude Debussy; to Madame Jacques Rivière for letters by Jacques Rivière; to Monsieur Édouard Ravel for letters by Maurice Ravel: and to the Trustees for the copyrights of the late Dylan Thomas for letters by Dylan Thomas.

Preface

WHEN it was heard that the great Poet would be passing through the town, a request was sent that he should address the public in the market-place on the subject of his works and ideals. The town was in a remote and little visited part of the provinces, and books were hard to come by in those days before the revolution. The local Scribe, who was known to have literary tastes, was asked to speak a few words of introduction in order that the townspeople should not be blind to the greatness of their visitor and the honour that was being done them.

When the day and the hour had arrived, a number of the inhabitants were gathered in the market-place, and the great Poet made his way to the platform, accompanied by prominent persons of the town. The Scribe bowed to the Poet and began his words of introduction. Soon, inspired by the majesty of his theme, he put aside his few notes and spoke of all that the work of the great Poet had taught him, which indeed was almost all he knew and cared for. He explained in words of many syllables how the Poet had shown the great uses of little words, and how he opened the eyes and souls of all who read him. He spoke of the problems of versification, but also of the sacred fires of inspiration, and the power of the artist to change the past, the present, and the future. (Few believed him.) The Scribe had pondered much on these things in quiet moments at his desk in the Council House, and had often been heard to complain that fate had denied him sufficient leisure to write verses of his own.

All the while, the crowd in the market-place grew, and many who had just arrived and knew no better remarked with disappointment, 'This must be the great Poet speaking.' The time passed, but from the heights of his discourse the Scribe did not notice that his audience had grown very restive. If the sun had not begun to sink behind the mountains and if a cold shadow had not fallen on the market-place, the Scribe might never have found his ending. But the going of the sun reminded him of his humble duty, and he stopped.

The great Poet rose to his feet, and thanking the Scribe gracefully, said that there had been much food for thought in his words. Those who sold rice were seldom as hungry as those who grew it. And with that single remark – which few on the platform understood – he called for his belongings and went on his journey much relieved. For in truth he never liked to speak about his works or his ideals, preferring to let others come and find them.

*

After half a century of music appreciation, music has never been less appreciated. From all sides came people anxious to describe what is audible to all but the very deaf. Like the commentators in the old technicolour travelogues who told us, as the camera surveyed the pink coral reef, that it was pink and a coral reef, they were perfectly redundant. Worse than redundant were the lower analysts, who fled in terror from the indescribable, and sought refuge in proclaiming the exact number of bricks in the cathedral, the exact number of man-hours spent in its completion, and the height and breadth of every wall and buttress, to the last inch. The perfect extra-mural activity: music from beyond the walls, 'music in the head'.

*

Within the conclave it is not always different. We have now reached the age of the symphonic programme note, which the composer conceives even before the actual work, its illustration. The note, or the article, takes longer to read than the work itself takes to play, and is as little comprehended. The International Society for the Performance of Contemporary Programme Notes has its own special Festival.

*

The real composer is seldom eager to write about his work. Not only because it brings him into bad company – though that is painful enough – but also for reasons that reflect on his own vocation. The composer who refuses to write copiously about his works recognizes the danger of implying that they leave something to be 'said': even that music itself, the purest, the most explicit and the most nearly autonomous of the arts, leaves something to be 'said'.

Still more disturbing is the fear that verbalization may distort or dispel a tension that is more fully and more truly resolved in a work of art. The very act of his examining what is *natural* to him threatens to make it unnatural. We remember with grief the bearded man who did not know the answer when asked if he slept with his beard outside or inside the sheets. Experimenting with his beard one way and then the other, he fell victim to insomnia and wasted away. He was an unwise man and would not have made a good composer. Satie went to the Schola Cantorum in his fortieth year to examine the same question. But he was a wise man and his beard was well trimmed. He managed to sleep quite as soundly thereafter.

*

The composer as somnambulist: 'I wish people would let me have the privilege of being a little bit unconscious. It is so nice sometimes to go blind, just with the *feeling* for the right thing.'*

*

Theoretically, we cannot ask the somnambulist questions. But the daily office-worker in us all resents the artist's nocturnal activity. We wish to discover the secret. Of late, more than one book has flounced on to the market, offering, like some matrimonial gazette, 'Meetings' with X or Y, the well-known composer. The promise of intimacy is of course never kept. We can't 'meet' the composer because the gesticulating bulk of his questioner stands in front of him in attitudes of admiration that are barely distinguishable from self-admiration, and asks questions which are either ignored or returned empty-handed. There is only one advantage in reading a book of that kind. It sharpens one's appreciation of the extraordinary quality of contact which informs the two volumes of Stravinsky-Craft conversations. There is only one question in the whole series which Stravinsky does not answer, and that omission, whether intentional or not, is as precise and as eloquent as an answer. There is never any waste. A sentence takes the place of an essay, a paragraph stands where a book might have fallen. There are times when it seems that 'everything takes place by abridgement, hypothetically: one avoids the narration'. There are other times when narration is not avoided, but only in order that it may contract back again into commentary. These dialogues may be 'disguised monologue', but they discover a drama of their own. The last two sentences of the opening section of 'Memories and Commentaries' are as characteristic of Stravinsky's 'coda feeling' as, say, the final pages of the Symphony in C. Whatever Mr Craft's contributions to these Conversations, the final triumph is that they are, as a whole, quintessentially

* Stravinsky, quoted by Sol Babbit in *Modern Music* (Summer 1946)

Stravinskian. Only someone who has lived long and well in Stravinsky's music would know how to get out of it and what to get out of it with mere words.

*

The end of a book, like the end of a musical work, should be the epitome of all the reasons for starting it. The last five sentences of Stravinsky's *Chronicle of My Life* (1935) and the last five of his *Poetics of Music* (1940) were no less than that. The *Chronicle*, that remarkable exercise in *secco* recitative, belonged to '*le vierge, le vivace, et le bel aujourd'hui*'. Living with some intensity in the present (despite the chronicling) it ended there. The *Poetics*, as the title says, go beyond the material, and so come to rest on the timeless plane of Faith. Turn now to the close of the first series of Conversations: a youthful close, looking with hope and a touch of useful irony at the future. By comparison the ending of the second series (discounting the section on the three operas) is neither young nor old, but ageless: '"Our heritage was left to us by no will." ... At the same time, however, the artist feels his "heritage" as the grip of a very strong pair of pincers.' With that grip, we can begin all our journeys to Stravinsky.

*

The composer as captive ... Every artist born into one of the marginal cultures – Russian, British, Iberian, American – looks with envy at Central Europe. Only those menaced by proximity must also look with enmity. The Frenchman retires behind his Maginot Line and tries to live on the provisions left by the Renaissance polyphonists, the clavevinistes, and Debussy. The Italian is more secure, because the Great Tradition of Central Europe that stretches from Schütz to Schoenberg and unites the Rhine and the Danube in one vast flow of continuity also has tributaries that run down to the Mediterranean. Wherever the Central European composer may choose to join the current, the whole continent of music – polyphony, monody, homophony, the modal, the diatonic, the chromatic – is theoretically within his reach. However slight his talent, he is almost certain to be carried *somewhere*; whereas the Englishman can only stand on a ledge and try to grasp the end of a broken thread, while the Russian gropes in a snowstorm for a few green shrubs planted in shallow soil. In this predicament, outstanding talent may never find the peace to achieve real greatness.

Stravinsky's generation was dominated by the Russian Five, those none too stalwart precursors of the afforestation policy in Soviet music. Stravinsky soon rejected them for The Two: Glinka and Tchaikovsky. Glinka has been a lifelong love, but he was too small and, despite *Mavra*, too far from the music of our time to be a lifelong inspiration.

Tchaikovsky was more formidable. Before Stravinsky could face up to him, he had to rid himself of the few supports he had used in *Firebird*, *Petrushka*, and *The Rite*. Rimsky's demon, the tritone, had its last fling in *Petrushka*. (Not only the tritone: without the example of *Coq d'Or*, those apocalyptic masqueraders would have made a different musical entry in the last scene.) *The Rite's* 'pagan night' had been a Debussyan night, and that kind of mystery was transcended a few years later by the finer Mystery of the *Symphonies of Wind Instruments*, in memory of Debussy: a sacred night. Stravinsky's first purely Russian music – *Les Noces* and *Renard* – was achieved at the cost of his first and only real revolution. With inspired rudeness, these works turned a peasant back on the West, denying not only a whole harmonic tradition, but through that and the subject matter, a whole system of bourgeois and aristocratic culture. Ideology apart, they are closer to the psychology of the

October revolution than the defenestrated Tsarist Symphonies officially prescribed in Soviet Russia. Yet their kind of revolution is only a violently accelerated form of evolution. The waste products of the Russian tradition, and the foreign matter which was embedded in it, were together destroyed in a single conflagration, so that a simpler and stronger process of evolution could begin again. *Les Noces* and *Renard* cleared the muddy snow from the soil, and gave *Stravinsky* a solid ground from which he could set out once again for the West. His physical migration to Paris after the First World War had a logic of its own, for it was the most direct route from a purely Russian musical culture towards a Central European one.

*

From the periphery to an adjacency ... The *Chronicle of My Life* records among other things Stravinsky's engagement with French musical culture. Only the looming shadow of Beethoven (which looms still in Stravinsky's musical cosmos) was there to act as reminder of what lay across the border. Delibes, Chabrier, Gounod, and Bizet – the composers mentioned with affectionate respect in the *Chronicle* and still remembered in the *Poetics* – figured primarily as representatives of the French melodic genius, for melody was then one of Stravinsky's necessary preoccupations. That was one of the reasons why Debussy's essentially *harmonic* style held less attraction for him. Another reason was that Debussy at that time seemed to have encouraged the invasion of music by literary and pictorial elements. Although Debussy wisely put the titles of his piano *Préludes* at the *end* of each piece, and although many of them are quite as obviously 'absolute' music as the still more remarkable *Études* of his late years, it has been the latter which have acquired a snob *cachet* on the hollow ground that they are less 'expressive', in the bad literary sense. But forty years ago, it was necessary to stand guard over *espressivo*, lest it should come to express nothing, musically.

*

'I consider that music is, by its very nature, essentially powerless to *express* anything at all, whether a feeling, an attitude of mind, a psychological mood, a phenomenon of nature, etc. ...' That sentence in Stravinsky's *Chronicle* provoked, and still provokes, more bad temper and more defensive philosophization than any of his music. Indeed, it is hard to see how so innocuous a remark could have troubled anyone who has heard and felt Stravinsky's own music. Admittedly, the formulation is not quite precise. The word 'essentially' also requires emphasis: '*essentially* powerless' – that is, 'in its essence', which is the articulation of sound in auditory space and time. Unless we include Straussian onomatopoeia, the entire field of musical experience supports Stravinsky's contention. The expressive significances in classical Greek or Indian modal theory are an obvious fiction, and our own impoverished modal theory – the 'tragic' minor and the 'bright' major – is not only a fiction, but also something that is contradicted by the fact of innumerable masterpieces (and folksongs) of all periods. Even on the simplest emotive level, the interpretations given to many standard masterpieces are so widely varied as to be useless as a yardstick of objective judgement. Music is a language only by consent (Stravinsky does not deny the possibility or the value of that consent), but its peculiar communicability depends at its highest on an irreducible ambiguity. That ambiguity is the very life-blood of music-drama, explaining the precious paradox that the finest opera, which in theory should be the most literary of all forms of music, is in fact as 'absolute' as the symphony or quartet. If music's power of expressing things beyond itself were inherent rather than an attribute, the Handel who continually transferred and adapted music from one opera or oratorio to another, making it 'express' quite different and even opposite things, would have been guilty of a massive deceit. Wagner's *Leitmotiv* technique, after the primitive early stage, becomes an essentially symphonic device, and the structure of the motives themselves is adapted accordingly. At its most developed, his whole *Leitmotiv* technique depends on a complete fluidity of associations which would be impossible if a literary idea were part of the essence of the musical shape. The same is true of the so-called impressionism of Debussy. Suppose *La Mer* were renamed *Le Pays*, and the first movement called 'An Afternoon in the Mountains' instead of 'From Dawn to Midday on the Sea'. The music would not be less, or differently, comprehensible. Whatever its title, *La Mer* is arguably the best and most original French symphony. The 'waves' communicate as music. So do Strauss's Critics (in *Heldenleben*). But his Sheep don't.

*

'Art postulates communion, and the artist has an imperative need to make others share the joy which he experiences himself.'* For Stravinsky, this 'imperative need' was inseparable from another one: to build, single-handed, the musical history that Russia lacked. The guide-books point excitedly at the beginning of the process, which they call Stravinsky's 'Back to Bach' period; and the tourists say 'yes, yes' without looking up from the pages. In fact most of the great Central European composers from Mozart to Schoenberg have gone 'back to Bach' at some point or other. But that precedent has little or nothing to do with the works of Stravinsky's early Parisian years – the Piano

* Stravinsky, *Chronicle of My Life*

Sonata and Concerto, the Serenade in A – which are usually cited in this context. Nor has the old gibe 'Bach with wrong notes'. In Stravinsky, the notes are not wrong, and it is not Bach – or even Telemann. In listening to those three works, it is better to forget all about neo-classicism and other slogans which are exploited as a convenient substitute for listening. If slogans continue to block the way, measures can be taken against them. For instance, try playing Chopin's A flat Prelude – the one without opus number – before the Rondoletto of the Serenade in A: not to suggest a source, but to clear the ears and widen the perspective. Similarly, Bach or Handel are the least useful way to the opening *Allegro* of the Piano Concerto. We don't think of the Russian Dance in *Petrushka* as 'neo-classical' even though the melodic and rhythmic shape of the main idea might – out of context – be taken for a fragment from a Vivaldi Concerto. Yet it is the Russian Dance rather than the classics which we should hear 'behind' the Concerto's *allegro*. The same applies to those parts of the Pergolesi-inspired *Pulcinella* which Stravinsky has most completely made his own – for instance the finale, which crosses pandiatonic with guitar harmony, putting Pergolesi out of sight and mind.

The features of rhythm and texture in Stravinsky's early Parisian music which suggest an affinity with the baroque period are no more than a stabilizing framework, within which Stravinsky continued to evolve a new and quite unclassical type of harmony. This search for a fresh harmonic order had been made necessary after the scorched-earth campaign of *Les Noces* and *Renard*, and it is far more fundamental to the early Parisian works than any external stylistic features. The order was finally established in *Oedipus Rex* (1927). The dramatic form is quasi-Handelian but the musical materials are worlds apart from neo-baroque antiquarianism. Where the *melos* is not demonstrably

Russian, it is if anything Verdian – note for instance the origins of the wonderful 'Invidia fortunam odit' passage in the Verdi Requiem.

Despite the many marvels in Stravinsky's earlier music, *Oedipus Rex* is, I think, his first wholly great work. And from that summit he was at last able to face up to the challenge of the broadest and most cosmopolitan of his Russian forebears, Tchaikovsky. The ballet *Apollon Musagète* (1927) meets Tchaikovsky on Stravinsky's own terms. *The Fairy's Kiss* (1928) does the same thing, more daringly, on Tchaikovsky's. *The Fairy's Kiss* was a necessary but affectionate embrace, and it ended in a conquest. Stravinsky's development of 'None but the lonely heart' achieves a harmonic and dynamic climax which for sheer concentration of tensions surpasses anything of the kind in Tchaikovsky. After this Stravinsky could say farewell with a clear conscience.

Now at last Stravinsky could afford to go 'back to Bach'. The double fugue of the *Symphony of Psalms* (1930) and the Arias of the Violin Concerto (1931) acknowledge Bach in order to make possible the more Beethovenian style of the Concerto for Two Pianos (1935). As the line of development extends it is seen to twist and turn in many directions, sometimes curling back on itself to leave an isolated pocket – like the melodrama *Persephone* of 1934; a consummate farewell to French lyricism and especially to Gounod. (To-day Gounod's music rests in the poorhouse, but that is not entirely his fault: we do not malign *Persephone* by associating him with it.)

One can understand how puzzling the line of Stravinsky's career must have seemed in the early stages. There was a time when people used to speak of the 'journeys' of Stravinsky, and the first glimmer of understanding came only when it was seen to be a single journey. But it still appeared to have been drawn across the historical and geographical map of European music, and that made the line hard to read. But take the map away, and the tracing of Stravinsky's career is shown as something quite different from an explorer's chart: more like one of those drawings Picasso makes with a single unbroken line and its adventures (one of them is reproduced on the cover of the piano score of Ragtime). Clouzot has let us watch Picasso execute one of these single-line drawings in forty seconds. The graph of Stravinsky's career from *Renard* to the present day has taken forty years to evolve, and for the first fifteen years or so it may have meant as little to 'outsiders' as Picasso's drawing after fifteen seconds. At least a few of Stravinsky's early critics can be forgiven.

The Stravinskian line continues still, but the landscape is clear and the monuments are there. The line was always centripetal, and now it has reached its centre. Stravinsky's encounter with the music of Anton Webern was the astounding yet now seemingly inevitable outcome of his historical and geographical search. His discovery of the past has led to the present, his journey from Russia has led to the most exclusively Central European composer he has yet acknowledged.

Webern's exclusiveness goes further and finer than that. His is the opposite pole to Schoenberg, the last of music's great inclusives. Schoenberg comprehended so much, and on such a scale, that he had no time or need to discard once his first great sacrifice had been made. Webern discarded all he dared. So it is fitting that he should be saluted by Stravinsky, whose own magnificent survival depended on rejecting so much, and selecting so carefully. Webern and Stravinsky have always – not just today – been alike in this one thing: their music is a relentless exercise in practical criticism. It marks a sustained triumph of the puritan conscience.

*

The composer as critic: we speak too easily of styles and tendencies. Look at the materials. Music is composed of intervals arranged horizontally and vertically. As the tonal system grew old, those intervals aged with it, became less athletic. The increasingly frequent substitution of simple by compound intervals was partly a reaction to that hardening of the intervallic arteries, but the life that device could bring to a tonal context was not inexhaustible. So when Stravinsky began to build a new tonality, he subjected the phenomenon of *interval* to an extreme scrutiny. Gradually, in each work, he built up a vocabulary that was wholly new, yet based on the old simple things. One can think of a major or minor third, or a sixth, or an octave, and immediately some passage in Stravinsky comes to mind by virtue of the special life it gave that interval. (Even the 'modern' fourth, beaten to death by Hindemith pupils the world over, is miraculously resurrected in the Gigue of Stravinsky's *Duo concertant*.) As with intervals, so with chords. *The Symphony of Psalms* gave us the most famous, and in a sense the first, triad in modern music. Other basic terms, as well worn as diminished and dominant sevenths, find new substance through Stravinsky; and something as old-whorish as the *sixte ajoutée* is made to hold its head proudly in honest harmonic company. The scrutiny of individual intervals eventually led Stravinsky to the most intensive form of that scrutiny, the series. Equally, his harmonic sense must drive him towards that hard problem, the harmonic aspect of the series.

These are 'critical' problems. And they have been, and are, the responsibility of a composer whose self-criticism is one of the great artistic examples of our time. Probably, Stravinsky does not compose easily, though it is hard to define ease in composition – except when it has been the cause of failure. That Schoenberg writes a great, large, work in a fortnight, while Stravinsky takes a year to write a great small one, does not mean it was any easier for Schoenberg.

*

The true craftsman must at some point be a fanatic (and the fanatic who is a bad craftsman is an impostor or a lunatic). 'We throw our failures away. They, who are failures, throw themselves away.'* The pain of creation is not an easy school for learning to understand the creative pains of those who belong to a different party. In his Conversations, Stravinsky speaks of the 'turgid and graceless Brahms'. If this is found shocking, try to imagine how a Brahms Symphony sounds to the sharp fox's ears of *Renard*, try to act out Brahms's kind of movement-in-time with muscles tensed for the Spartan exercises of *Agon*. Of course Brahms seems impossible, impassable. He is for Britten too – and that is no accident either. To have to deny a work like the Brahms Clarinet Quintet is perhaps a necessary sacrifice for those who must go in the opposite direction. Only the rabbit has ears in the back of his head.

A composer is responsible to himself alone in these matters, and it is dangerous to follow him. It is easier to echo dumbly Stravinsky's hatred of the 6/4 chords in Strauss's *Ariadne* than to consider why they are different from the 6/4 chords in *Persephone*. And those who believe that Stravinsky has *given* them the right to think little of Brahms or late Schoenberg commit the silliest imposture. They lay claim to Stravinsky's own ears, and try to pawn his supreme privileges in the market of second-hand values.

*

The critical market-place: 'How was the Stravinsky work?', asked the famous critic, who had only reached the concert

* Brecht: *The Exception and the Rule*

in time for a novelty from the Riviera. 'Oh nothing,' replied his equally distinguished colleague. 'Just as I thought,' said the first, much gratified. The work in question was the Concerto for two solo pianos, which assuredly is one of the masterpieces of the literature.

That dialogue of a few years ago seemed nothing out of the ordinary at the time. It was the end of a wretched era. For about thirty years, Stravinsky's reputation (like Schoenberg's) had been the plaything of persons who neither knew nor wished to know his most characteristic works. So long as these works were not heard, everything spoken in their defence and every declaration by the composer himself was a feather without a bird, blown in the wind, stuck in some journalist's cap, made into pillows for the lazy. And anyway, forgotten.

*

Some years after the revolution, the great Poet happened to pass through the town unannounced. He inquired repeatedly for the Scribe, but no one could say what had become of him, or even remembered his name. The Poet's disappointment was not too grave, and besides, he was happy to notice that he was recognized by many as he walked through the town. And in the market-place he saw that his books were well displayed, and that the buyers were not only the old and learned.

Observing that his books had now found appreciation even in the remotest regions, he decided that at last he could safely publish certain reflections on his life and work which he had hitherto preferred to keep to himself.

DAVID DREW

London
August 1961

CONVERSATIONS WITH
IGOR STRAVINSKY

In the Kingdom of the Father there is no drama but only dialogue, which is disguised monologue.

RUDOLPH KASSNER

TO

ISAIAH BERLIN

About Composing and Compositions

R.C. When did you become aware of your vocation as a composer?

I.S. I do not remember when and how I first thought of myself as a composer. All I remember is that these thoughts started very early in my childhood, long before any serious musical study.

R.C. The musical idea: when do you recognize it as an idea?

I.S. When something in my nature is satisfied by some aspect of an auditive shape. But long before ideas are born I begin work by relating intervals rhythmically. This exploration of possibilities is always conducted at the piano. Only after I have established my melodic or harmonic relationships do I pass to composition. Composition is a later expansion and organization of material.

R.C. Is it always clear in your mind from the inception of the idea what form of composition will develop? And the idea itself: is it clear what instrumental sound will produce it?

I.S. You should not suppose that once the musical idea is in your mind you will see more or less distinctly the form your composition may evolve. Nor will the sound (timbre) always be present. But if the musical idea is merely a group of notes, a motive coming suddenly to your mind, it very often comes together with its sound.

R.C. You say that you are a doer, not a thinker; that composing is not a department of conceptual thinking; that your nature is to compose music and you compose it naturally, not by acts of thought or will. A few hours of work on about one-third of the days of the last fifty years have produced a catalogue which testifies that composing is indeed natural to you. But how is nature approached?

I.S. When my main theme has been decided I know on general lines what kind of musical material it will require. I start to look for this material, sometimes playing old masters (to put myself in motion), sometimes starting directly to improvise rhythmic units on a provisional row of notes (which can become a final row). I thus form my building material.

R.C. When you achieve the music you have been working to create, are you always sure of it, do you always instantly recognize it as finished, or do you sometimes have to try it for a greater period of time?

I.S. Usually I recognize my find. But when I am unsure of it I feel uncomfortable in postponing a solution and in relying on the future. The future never gives me the assurance of reality I receive from the present.

R.C. What is theory in musical composition?

I.S. Hindsight. It doesn't exist. There are compositions from which it is deduced. Or, if this isn't quite true, it has a by-product existence that is powerless to create or even to justify. Nevertheless, composition involves a deep intuition of theory.

R.C. Do musical ideas occur to you at random times of the day or night?

I.S. Ideas usually occur to me while I am composing, and only very rarely do they present themselves when I am away from my work. I am always disturbed if they come to my ear when my pencil is missing and I am obliged to keep them in my memory by repeating to myself their intervals and rhythm. It is very important to me to remember the pitch of the music at its first appearance: if I transpose it for some reason I am in danger of losing the freshness of first contact and I will have difficulty in recapturing its attractiveness. Music has sometimes appeared to me in dreams, but only on one occasion have I been able to write it down. This was during the composition of *L'Histoire du soldat*, and I was surprised and happy with the result. Not only did the music appear to me but the person performing it was present in the dream as well. A young gipsy was sitting by the edge of the road. She had a child on her lap for whose entertainment she was playing a violin. The motive she kept repeating used the whole bow, or, as we say in French, '*avec toute la longueur de l'archet*'. The child was very enthusiastic about the music and applauded it with his little hands. I, too, was very pleased with it, was especially pleased to be able to remember it, and I joyfully included this motive in the music of the *Petit Concert*.

R.C. You often speak of the weight of an interval. What do you mean?

I.S. I lack words and have no gift for this sort of thing anyway, but perhaps it will help if I say that when I compose an interval I am aware of it as an object (when I think about it in that way at all, that is), as something outside me, the contrary of an impression.

Let me tell you about a dream that came to me while I was composing *Threni*. After working late one night I retired to bed still troubled by an interval. I dreamed about this interval. It had become an elastic substance stretching exactly between the two notes I had composed, but underneath these notes at either end was an egg, a large testicular egg. The eggs were gelatinous to the touch (I touched them), and warm, and they were protected by nests. I woke up knowing that my interval was right. (For those who want more of the dream, it was pink – I often dream in colour. Also, I was so surprised to see the eggs I immediately understood them to be symbols. Still in the dream I went to my library of dictionaries and looked up 'interval', but found only a confusing explanation which I checked the next morning in reality and found to be the same.)

R.C. While composing do you ever think of any audience? Is there such a thing as a problem of communication?

I.S. When I compose something, I cannot conceive that it should fail to be recognized for what it is, and understood. I use the language of music, and my statement in my grammar will be clear to the musician who has followed music up to where my contemporaries and I have brought it.

R.C. Have you ever thought that music is as Auden says 'a virtual image of our experience of living as temporal, with its double aspect of recurrence and becoming'?

I.S. If music is to me an 'image of our experience of living as temporal' (and however unverifiable, I suppose it is), my saying so is the result of a reflection, and as such is independent of music itself. But this kind of thinking about music is a different vocation altogether for me: I cannot *do* anything with it as a truth, and my mind is a *doing* one. Auden means 'Western' music or, as he would say, 'music as history'; jazz improvization is the dissipation of the time image and, if I understand 'recurrence' and 'becoming', their aspect is greatly diminished in serial music. Auden's 'image of our experience of living as temporal' (which is also an image) is above music, perhaps, but it does not obstruct or contradict the purely musical experience. What shocks me, however, is the discovery that many people think below music. Music is merely something that reminds them of something else – of landscapes, for example; my *Apollo* is always reminding someone of Greece. But in even the most

32

specific attempts at evocation, what is meant by being 'like', and what are 'correspondences'? Who, listening to Liszt's precise and perfect little *Nuages gris*, could pretend that 'grey clouds' are a musical cause and effect?

R.C. Do you work with a dialectical conception of form? Is the word meaningful in musical terms?

I.S. Yes to both questions, in so far as the art of dialectics is, according to the dictionaries, the art of logical discussion. Musical form is the result of the 'logical discussion' of musical materials.

R.C. I have often heard you say 'an artist must avoid symmetry but he may construct in parallelisms'. What do you mean?

I.S. The mosaics at Torcello of the Last Judgement are a good example. Their subject is division, division, moreover, into two halves suggesting equal halves. But, in fact, each is the other's complement, not its equal nor its mirror, and the dividing line itself is not a perfect perpendicular. On the one side skulls with, in the sockets, lightning-shaped snakes, and on the other, Eternal Life (those white figures, I wonder if Tintoretto didn't know them), are balanced, but not equally balanced. And, the sizes and proportions, movements and rests, darks and lights of the two sides are always varied.

Mondrian's *Blue Façade* (*composition 9, 1914*) is a nearer example of what I mean. It is composed of elements that tend to symmetry but in fact avoids symmetry in subtle parallelisms. Whether or not the suggestion of symmetry is avoidable in the art of architecture, whether it is natural to architecture, I do not know. However, painters who paint architectural subject matter and borrow architectural designs are often guilty of it. And only the master musicians have managed to avoid it in periods whose architecture has embodied aesthetic idealisms, i.e., when architecture was symmetry and symmetry was confused with form itself. Of all the musicians of his age Haydn was the most aware, I think, that to be perfectly symmetrical is to be perfectly dead. We are some of us still divided by an illusory compulsion towards 'classical' symmetry on the one hand, and by the desire to compose as purely non-symmetrically as the Incas, on the other.

R.C. Do you regard musical form as in some degree mathematical?

I.S. It is at any rate far closer to mathematics than to literature – not perhaps to mathematics itself, but certainly to something like mathematical thinking and mathematical relationships. (How misleading are all literary descriptions of musical form!) I am not saying that composers think in equations or charts of numbers, nor are those things more able to symbolize music. But the way composers think, the way I think, is, it seems to me, not very different from mathematical thinking. I was aware of the similarity of these two modes while I was still a student; and, incidentally, mathematics was the subject that most interested me in school. Musical form is mathematical because it is ideal, and form is always ideal, whether it is, as Ortega y Gasset wrote 'an image of memory or a construction of ours'. But though it may be mathematical, the composer must not seek mathematical formulae.

R.C. You often say that to compose is to solve a problem. Is it no more than that?

I.S. Seurat said: 'Certain critics have done me the honour to see poetry in what I do, but I paint by my method with no other thought in mind.'

R.C. In your Greek-subject pieces *Apollo, Oedipus, Orpheus, Persephone*, dotted rhythms are of great importance (the opening of *Apollo*; the canonic interlude in *Orpheus*; the 'Underworld' music in *Persephone*; the *Oedipus* 'Nonne Monstrum' aria). Is the use of these rhythms conscious stylistic reference to the eighteenth century?

I.S. Dotted rhythms are characteristic eighteenth-century rhythms. My uses of them in these and other works of that period, such as the introduction to my Piano Concerto, are conscious stylistic references. I attempted to build a new music on eighteenth-century classicism using the constructive principles of that classicism (which I cannot define here) and even evoking it stylistically by such means as dotted rhythms.

R.C. Valéry said: 'We can construct in orderly fashion only by means of conventions.' How do we recognize those conventions in, say, Webern's songs with clarinet and guitar?

I.S. We don't. An entirely new principle of order is found in the Webern songs which in time will be recognized and conventionalized. But Valéry's essentially classical *dicta* do not foresee that new conventions can be created.

R.C. A novelist (Isherwood) once complained to you of his difficulties in a technical question of narration. You advised him to find a model. How do you model in music?

I.S. As I have just described in the case of eighteenth-century dotted rhythms; I have modelled this conventional rhythmic device so that I could 'construct in orderly fashion'.

R.C. Why did you dispense with bar lines in the *Diphonas* and *Elegias* of the *Threni*?

I.S. The voices are not always in rhythmic unison. Therefore, any bar lines would cut at least one line arbitrarily. There are no strong beats in these canons, in any case, and the conductor must merely count the music out as he counts out a motet by Josquin. For the same reasons I have also written half notes rather than tied notes over bars. This is perhaps more difficult to read, but it is a truer notation.

R.C. Did you model your *Threni* on the *Lamentations* of any old master, as, for example, you modelled some dances for *Agon* from de Lauze's *Apologie de la danse* and from Mersenne's musical examples?

I.S. I had studied Palestrina's complete service, and the *Lamentations* of Tallis and Byrd but I don't think there is any 'influence' of these masters in my music.

R.C. Why do contemporary composers tend to use smaller note values for the beat than did nineteenth-century composers, quaver beats instead of crochet, and semiquavers instead of quavers? Your music contains many examples of this tendency (the second movement of the *Symphony in C* which is in quaver and semiquaver beats, and the final piece of the *Duo concertant* which is in semiquaver beats). If you were to double the note values of this music, rewrite it in crochets and quavers, how would it affect the music in your mind? Also, do you always think or see the note unit as you compose, and have you ever rewritten anything in different note values after it was composed? Your 1943 revision of the *Danse sacrale* from the *Sacre du printemps* doubles the values from semiquavers to quavers; was this done to facilitate reading (does it facilitate reading)? Do you believe the size of the note has a relation to the character of the music?

I.S. 'I don't think you are entirely correct in assuming an evolution from minim to crotchet to quaver pulsations. Contemporary music has created a much greater range and variety of tempi and a vastly greater rhythmic range, therefore the greater range and variety of rhythmic unit (see any table of notation and compare the types of rhythmic unit in use in the last five centuries with those in use today). We write fast tempo music or slow tempo music in large or small note values depending on the music. That is my only explanation.

As a composer I associate a certain kind of music, a certain tempo of music, with a certain kind of note unit. I compose directly that way. There is no act of selection or translation, and the unit of the note and the tempo appear in my imagination at the same time as the interval itself. Only rarely, too, have I found that my original beat unit has led me into notation difficulties. The *Dithyrambe* in the *Duo concertant*, however, is one such example.

It is difficult for me to judge whether a work of mine translated into larger or smaller note units but played in the same tempo would make an aural difference to me. However, I know that I could not look at the music in its translated state, for the shape of the notes as one writes them is the shape of the original conception itself. (Of course the performer with his different approach will regard the whole problem of notation as a matter of choice, but this is wrong.)

I *do* believe in a relation between the *character* of my music and the kind of note unit of the pulsation, and I do not care that this may be undemonstrable – it is demonstrable to me on the composer's side simply because I think that way. And, conventions have not worked universally for so long that we may deny that there is any relation of ear and eye. Who can take from dictation a passage of contemporary music in 6/4 and tell whether in fact it is not 6/8 or 6/16?

The point of legibility. I did translate my *Danse sacrale* into larger note values to facilitate reading (of course it is more readable, the reduction in rehearsal time proves that).* But legibility and larger note values go together only up to a point. This idea of fast music in white notes applies only to certain types of music (the first movement of my *Symphony in C*, for example, and the *Gloria Patri* in Monteverdi's *Laudate Pueri* from the *Vespers*), but this question cannot be dissociated from the question of bar

* I was also obliged to recopy the first movement of my *Ebony Concerto* in quavers, when the 'jazz' musicians, for whom it was written, proved themselves unable to read semiquavers.

units and of the rhythmic construction of the music itself.

Perhaps the present lack of universal conventions may be interpreted as a blessing; the performer can only profit from a situation in which he is obliged to review his prejudices and develop reading versatility.

R.C. Metres. Can the same effect be achieved by means of accents as by varying the metres? What are bar lines?

I.S. To the first question my answer is, up to a point, yes, but that point is the degree of real regularity in the music. The bar line is much much more than a mere accent and I don't believe that it can be simulated by an accent, at least not in my music.

R.C. In your own music, identity is established by melodic, rhythmic, and other means, but especially by tonality. Do you think you will ever abandon the tonal identification?

I.S. Possibly. We can still create a sense of return to exactly the same place without tonality: musical rhyme can accomplish the same thing as poetic rhyme. But form cannot exist without identity of some sort.

R.C. What is your feeling now about the use of music as accompaniment to recitation (*Persephone*)?

I.S. Do not ask. Sins cannot be undone, only forgiven.

THE SERIES

R.C. Do you think of the intervals in your series as tonal intervals; that is, do your intervals always exert tonal pull?

I.S. The intervals of my series are attracted by tonality; I compose vertically and that is, in one sense at least, to compose tonally.

R.C. How has composing with a series affected your own harmonic thinking? Do you work in the same way — that is, hear relationships and then compose them?

I.S. 'I hear certain possibilities and I choose. I can create my choice in serial composition just as I can in any tonal contrapuntal form. I hear harmonically, of course, and I compose in the same way I always have.

R.C. Nevertheless, the Gigue from your *Septet* and the choral canons in the *Canticum sacrum* are much more difficult to hear harmonically than any earlier music of yours. Hasn't composing with a series therefore affected your harmonic scope?

I.S. It is certainly more difficult to hear harmonically the music you speak of than my earlier music; but any serial music intended to be heard vertically is more difficult to hear. The rules and restrictions of serial writing differ little from the rigidity of the great contrapuntal schools of old. At the same time they widen and enrich harmonic scope; one starts to hear more things and differently than before. The serial technique I use impels me to greater discipline than ever before.

R.C. Do you think your time world is the same for the kind of music you are now composing and for your music of thirty-five years ago (*Mavra*, Piano Sonata, Piano Concerto, *Apollo*)?

I.S. My past and present time worlds cannot be the same. I know that portions of *Agon* contain three times as much music for the same clock length as some other pieces of mine. Naturally, a new demand for greater in-depth listening changes time perspective. Perhaps also the operation of memory in a non-tonally developed work (tonal, but not eighteenth-century tonal system) is different. We are located in time constantly in a tonal-system work, but we may only 'go through' a polyphonic work, whether Josquin's *Duke Hercules Mass* or a serially composed non-tonal-system work.

R.C. Do you find any similarity in the time worlds of oriental music and of certain recent examples of serial music?

I.S. I do not think anything in the nature of the serial idea makes series in essence 'oriental'. Schoenberg himself was a cabalist, of course, but that is merely a personal preoccupation. We have all remarked a monotony (not in any pejorative sense) that we call 'oriental' in serial works, in Boulez's *Le Marteau sans maître* for instance. But the kind of monotony we have in mind is characteristic of many kinds of polyphonic music. Our notion of what is oriental is an association of instrumentation chiefly, but also of rhythmic and melodic designs – a very superficial kind of association indeed. I myself have no habit of anything oriental, and especially no measure of time in oriental music. In fact, my attitude resembles that of Henri Micheaux: in the Orient I recognize myself as a barbarian – that excellent word invented by Attic Greeks to designate a people who could not answer them in Attic Greek.

TECHNIQUE

R.C. What is technique?

I.S. The whole man. We learn how to use it but we cannot acquire it in the first place; or, perhaps I should say that we are born with the ability to acquire it. At present it has come to mean the opposite of 'heart', though, of course, 'heart' is technique too. A single blot on a paper by my friend Eugene Berman I instantly recognize as a Berman blot. What have I recognized – a style or a technique? Are they the same signature of the whole man? Stendhal (in the *Roman Promenades*) believed that style is 'the manner that each one has of saying the same thing'. But, obviously, no one says the same thing because the saying is also the thing. A technique or a style for saying something original does not exist *a priori*, it is created by the original saying itself. We sometimes say of a composer that he lacks technique. We say of Schumann, for example, that he did not have enough orchestral technique. But we do not believe that more technique would change the composer. 'Thought' is not one thing and 'technique' another, namely, the ability to transfer, 'express', or develop thoughts. We cannot say 'the technique of Bach' (I never say it), yet in every sense he had more of it than anyone; our extraneous meaning becomes ridiculous when we try to imagine the separation of Bach's musical substance and the making of it. Technique is not a teachable science, neither is it learning, nor scholarship, nor even the knowledge of how to do something. It is creation, and, being creation, it is new every time. There are other legitimate uses of the word, of course. Painters have water-colour and gouache techniques, for example, and there are technological meanings; we have techniques of bridge-building and even 'techniques for civilization'. In these senses one may talk of composing techniques – the writing of an academic fugue. But in my sense, the original composer is still his own and only technique. If I hear of a new composer's 'technical mastery' I am always interested in the composer (though critics employ the expression to mean 'but he hasn't got the more important thing'). Technical mastery has to be *of* something, it has to *be* something. And since we can recognize technical skill when we can recognize nothing else, it is the only manifestation of 'talent' I know of; up to a point technique and talent are the same. At present all of the arts, but especially music, are engaged in 'examinations of technique'. In my sense such an examination must be into the nature of art itself – an examination that is both perpetual and new every time – or it is nothing.*

* In the case of my own music I know that my first works, the *Faune et Bergère* and the Symphony in E flat lack personality while at the same time they demonstrate definite technical ability with the musical materials. The *Faune* sounds like Wagner in places, like Tchaikovsky's *Romeo and Juliet* in other places (but never like Rimsky-Korsakov, which must have troubled that master), and like Stravinsky not at all, or only through thickly bespectacled hindsight.

R.C. Your music always has an element of repetition, of *ostinato*. What is the function of *ostinato*?

I.S. It is static – that is, anti-development; and sometimes we need a contradiction to development. However, it became a vitiating device and was at one time overemployed by many of us.

INSTRUMENTATION

R.C. What is good instrumentation?

I.S. When you are unaware that it *is* instrumentation. The word is a gloss. It pretends that one composes music and then orchestrates it. This is true, in fact, in the one sense that the only composers who can be orchestrators are those who write piano music which they transcribe for orchestra; and this might still be the practice of a good many composers, judging from the number of times I have been asked my opinion as to which instruments I think best for passages the composers play on the piano. As we know, real piano music, which is what these composers usually play, is the most difficult to instrumentate. Even Schoenberg, who was always an instrumental master (one could make a very useful anthology of instrumental practice in his music from the first song of op. 22 to *Von Heute auf Morgen* with its extraordinary percussion, piano, and mandoline), even Schoenberg stumbled in trying to transfer Brahms's piano style to the orchestra (his arrangement of Brahms's G minor pianoforte quartet for orchestra), though his realization of the cadenza in the last movement with arpeggiated pizzicatos is a masterstroke. It is not, generally, a good sign when the first thing we remark about a work is its instrumentation; and the composers we remark it of – Berlioz, Rimsky-Korsakov, Ravel – are not the best composers. Beethoven, the greatest orchestral master of all in our sense, is seldom praised for his instrumentation; his symphonies are too good music in every way and the orchestra is too integral a part of them. How silly it sounds to say of the trio of the Schèrzo of the Eighth Symphony: 'What splendid instrumentation' – yet, what incomparable instrumental thought it is. Berlioz's reputation as an orchestrator has always seemed highly suspect to me. I was brought up on his music; it was played in the St Petersburg of my student years as much as it has ever been played anywhere in the world,* so I dare say this to all the literary-minded people responsible for his revival. He was a great innovator, of course, and he had the perfect imagination of each new instrument he used, as well as the knowledge of its technique. But the music he had to instrumentate was often poorly constructed harmonically. No orchestral skill can hide the fact that Berlioz's basses are sometimes uncertain and the inner harmonic voices unclear. The problem of orchestral distribution is therefore insurmountable and balance is regulated superficially, by dynamics. This is in part why I prefer the small Berlioz to the grandiose.

Many composers still do not realize that our principal instrumental body today, the symphony orchestra, is the creation of harmonic-triadic music. They seem unaware that the growth of the wind instruments from two to three

---

* I remember a description of Berlioz by Rimsky-Korsakov who had met the French master after one of the famous Berlioz concerts in St Petersburg in the late sixties. Rimsky-Korsakov, who was then twenty-three or twenty-four, had attended the concert with other young composers of the group. They saw Berlioz – in a tail-coat cut very short in the back, Rimsky said – conduct his own music and Beethoven's. Then they were shepherded backstage by Stassov, the patriarch of St Petersburg musical life. They found a small man, Rimsky's words were 'a little white bird with pince-nez', shivering in a fur coat and huddled under a hot pipe which crossed the room just over his head. He addressed Rimsky very kindly: 'And you compose music too?', but kept his hands in his coat sleeves as in a muffler.

to four to five of a kind parallels a harmonic growth. It is extremely difficult to write polyphonically for this harmonic body, which is why Schoenberg in his polyphonic *Variations for Orchestra* is obliged to double, treble, and quadruple the *lines*. The bass, too, is extremely difficult to bring out acoustically and harmonically in the *Variations* because it is the lowest line, merely, and not bass-ic. Though the standard orchestra is not yet an anachronism, perhaps, it can no longer be used standardly except by anachronistic composers. Advances in instrumental technique are also modifying the use of the orchestra. We all compose for solo, virtuoso instrumentalists today, and our soloistic style is still being discovered. For example, harp parts were mostly glissandos or chords as recently as Ravel. The harp can glissando and arpeggiate *en masse*, but it can't play *en masse* as I have used it in my *Symphony in Three Movements*. And, for another example, we are just discovering the orchestral use of harmonics, especially bass harmonics (one of my favourite sounds incidentally; make your throat taut and open your mouth half an inch so that the skin of your neck becomes a drum-head, then flick your finger against it: that is the sound I mean).

At the beginning of my career the clarinet was considered incapable of long fast-tongue passages. I remember my Chopin instrumentations for *Les Sylphides* in Paris in 1910 and an ill-humoured clarinet player telling me after he had stumbled on a rapid staccato passage (the only way I could conceive Chopin's pianism): '*Monsieur, ce n'est pas une musique pour la clarinette.*' What instruments do I like? I wish there were more good players for the bass clarinet and the contra-bass clarinet, for the alto trombone (of my *Threni* and Berg's *Altenberg Lieder*), for the guitar, the mandoline, and the cymbalom. Do I dislike any instrument? Well, I am not very fond of the two most conspicuous instruments

44

of the *Lulu* orchestra, the vibraphone and the alto saxophone. I do admit, however, that the vibraphone has amazing contrapuntal abilities; and the saxophone's juvenile-delinquent personality floating out over all the vast decadence of *Lulu* is the very apple of that opera's fascination.

R.C. Are you attracted by any new instruments – electric, oriental, exotic, jazz, whatever?

I.S. Of course, I am attracted by many non-standard orchestral instruments, percussion ones especially, but also stringed instruments like those Japanese ones I have heard in Los Angeles whose bridges are moved during the performance. And let us not forget the fact that traditional symphonic instruments like trumpet and trombone are not the same when played by jazz musicians. The latter people demonstrate greater variety in articulation and tone colour, and on some instruments, the trumpet for instance, they appear to be at home in a higher range than the symphonic player – the jazz trumpeter's high lip-trills. We neglect not only the instruments of other ethnographies, however, but those of our greatest European composer as well. This neglect is one reason why Bach's cantatas, which should be the centre of our repertoire, if we must have a repertoire, are comparatively unperformed. We don't have the instruments to play them. Bach had families where we have single instruments: trumpet families, trombone families, oboe families, families for all sorts of the strings. We have simplifications and greater resonance; where he had the lute, perhaps the most perfect and certainly the most personal instrument of all, we have the guitar. I myself prefer Bach's string orchestra with its gambas, its violino and cello piccolo, to our standard quartet in which the cello is not of the same family as the viola and bass. And, if oboes d'amore and da caccia were common I would compose for them. What incomparable instrumental writing is Bach's. You can smell the resin in his violin parts, taste the reeds in the oboes. I am always interested and attracted by new instruments (new to me) but until the present I have been more often astonished by the new resources imaginative composers are able to discover in 'old' instruments. An entry in Klee's *Tage-bücher* says (under May 1913): '*Und das Mass ist noch nicht voll. Man führt sogar Schönberg auf, das tolle Melodram Pierrot Lunaire.*' And not yet full now either. For example, Boulez's third piano sonata is quite as purely 'pianistic' as an *étude* by Debussy, yet it exploits varieties of touch (attack) untried by Debussy, and exposes in its harmonics a whole region of sound neglected until now. (These aspects of the piece are secondary, however, to the aspect of its form; always close to Mallarméan ideas of permutation, Boulez is now nearing a concept of form not unlike that of the idea of *Un Coup de dés*; not only does the pagination of the score of his third piano sonata resemble the *Coup de dés* 'score', but Mallarmé's own preface to the poem seems as well to describe the sonata: '... the fragmentary inter-ruptions of a capital phrase introduced and continued ... everything takes place by abridgement, hypothetically; one avoids the narration . . .'; Mallarmé thought he was borrow-ing ideas from music, of course, and would no doubt be surprised to know that sixty years later his poem had cross-pollinated the two arts; the recent publication of *Le Livre de Mallarmé*** with its startling diagrams of the mathematics of form must have been an uncanny confirmation to Boulez.)

Thus an 'old' instrument, the piano, interests me more than an Ondes Martinot, for instance, though this statement is in danger of giving the impression that I am thinking of instrumentalism as something apart from musical thoughts.

---

* By Jacques Schérer (Gallimard), the first study of Mallarmé's un-published note-books and papers.

GESUALDO

R.C. What motivated you to compose new sextus and bassus parts for the lost ones in Gesualdo's motet *a sette*?

I.S. When I had written out the five existing parts in score, the desire to complete Gesualdo's harmony, to soften certain of his *malheurs* became irresistible to me. One has to play the piece without any additions to understand me, and 'additions' is not an exact description; the existing material was only my starting point: from it I recomposed the whole. The existing parts impose definite limits in some cases, and very indefinite ones in others. But even if the existing parts did not rule out academic solutions, a knowledge of Gesualdo's other music would. I have not tried to guess 'what Gesualdo would have done', however – though I would like to see the original; I have even chosen solutions that I am sure are not Gesualdo's. And though Gesualdo's seconds and sevenths justify mine, I don't look at my work in that light. My parts are not attempts at reconstruction. I am in it as well as Gesualdo. The motet would have been unusual, I think, with or without me. Its form of nearly equal halves is unusual, and so is its consistent and complex polyphony: many of the motets employ a more simple chordal style, and with so many parts so close in range one would expect a treatment of that sort: Gesualdo's music is never dense. The bass part is unusual too. It is of bass-ic importance as it seldom is in Gesualdo. His madrigals are almost all top heavy and even in the motets and responses the bass rests more than any other part. I don't think I am reading myself into Gesualdo in this instance, though my musical thinking is always centred around the bass (the bass still functions as the harmonic root to me even in the music I am composing at present). But this motet which might be Gesualdo's ultimate opus would lead him to unusual things by the mere fact of its being his unique piece in seven parts.

(By the same reasoning I contend that the lost volume of six-voice madrigals contains more complex, more 'dissonant' music than the five-voice volumes, and the one reference we have to any of the madrigals in that book, to *Sei disposto*, bears me out; even his early six-part madrigal, *Donna, se m'ancidete*, has a great number of seconds besides those which are editors' errors.)

I would like to point out the very dramatic musical symbolization of the text that occurs at the dividing point of the form. The voices narrow to three (I am sure Gesualdo has done something similar), then at the words 'seven-fold grace of the paraclete' spread to seven full polyphonic parts.

I hope my little homage to Gesualdo and my own interest in that great musician will help excite the cupidity of other Gesualdines to the search for his lost work, the trio for the three famous ladies of Ferrara, the arias mentioned in Fontanelli's letters, and, above all, the six-part madrigals. This music must be in the Italian private libraries. (When Italy has been catalogued everything will reappear; recently Hotson, the Shakespearian, found a letter in an Orsini library describing an Orsini ancestor's impressions of a performance in Elizabeth's court of what must have been the first night of *Twelfth Night*.) Gesualdo was well related in Naples, in Ferrara, in Modena, in Urbino, even in Rome (his daughter married the Pope's nephew). Let us begin there.

TRANSLATION

R.C. No composer has been more directly concerned with the problems of musical texts sung in translation. Would you say something about the matter?

I.S. Let librettos and texts be published in translation, let synopses and arguments of plots be distributed in advance, let imaginations be appealed to, but do not change the sound and the stress of words that have been composed to precisely certain music at precisely certain places.

Anyway, the need to know 'what they are singing about' is not always satisfied by having it sung in one's own language, especially if that language happens to be English. There is a great lack of schools for singing English, in America at any rate; the casts of some American productions of opera-in-English do not all seem to be singing the same language. And 'meaning', the translator's *argument d'être*, is only one item. Translation changes the character of a work and destroys its cultural unity. If the original is verse, especially verse in a language rich in internal rhymes, it can only be adapted in a loose sense, not translated (except perhaps by Auden; Browning's lines beginning 'I could favour you with sundry touches' are a good example of just how extraordinary double-rhymed verse sounds in English). Adaptation implies translation of cultural locale, and results in what I mean by the destruction of cultural unity. For example, Italian prestos in English can hardly escape sounding like Gilbert and Sullivan, though this may be the fault of my Russian-born, naturalized-American ears and of my unfamiliarity with other periods of English opera (if after Purcell and before Britten there were other periods of English opera).

An example of translation destroying text and music occurs in the latter part of my *Renard*. The passage I am referring to – I call it a *pribaoutki** – exploits a speed and an accentuation that are natural to Russian (each language has characteristic tempi which partly determine musical tempi and character). No translation of this passage can translate what I have done musically with the language. But there are

* A kind of droll song, sometimes to nonsense syllables, sometimes in part spoken. (I.S.)

many such instances in all of my Russian vocal music; I am so disturbed by them I prefer to hear those pieces in Russian or not at all. Fortunately Latin is still permitted to cross borders – at least no one has yet proposed to translate my *Oedipus*, my *Psalms*, my *Canticum*, and my *Mass*.

The presentation of works in their original language is a sign of a rich culture in my opinion. And, musically speaking, Babel is a blessing.

About Musicians and Others

R.C. Do you remember your first attendance at a concert?

I.S. My first experience of a public musical performance was at the Mariinsky Theatre in St Petersburg. My impressions of it are mixed with what I have been told, of course, but as a child of seven or eight I was taken to see *A Life for the Tsar*. We were given one of the official *loges* and I remember that it was adorned with gilt 'winged amours'. The spectacle of the theatre itself and of the audience bewildered me and my mother said later that as I watched the stage, carried away by the sound of the orchestra (perhaps the greatest thrill of my life was the sound of that first orchestra) I asked her, as in Tolstoy: 'Which one is the theatre?' I remember also that Nápravník conducted the opera in white gloves.

The first concert of which I have any recollection was the occasion of a *première* of a symphony by Glazunov. I was nine or ten years old and at this time Glazunov was the heralded new composer. He *was* gifted with extraordinary powers of ear and memory, but it was going too far to assume from this that he must be a new Mozart: the sixteen-year-old prodigy was already a cut-and-dried academician. I was not inspired by this concert.

R.C. Were you impressed by any visiting foreign musicians in your student days in St Petersburg?

I.S. In the early years of this century most of the distinguished foreign artists who came to St Petersburg made calls of homage to Rimsky-Korsakov. I was in his home almost every day of 1903, 1904, and 1905, and therefore met many composers, conductors, and virtuosi there. Rimsky could speak French and English, the latter language having been acquired during his term as a naval officer, but he did not know German. As I spoke the language fluently from my childhood he sometimes asked me to translate for him and a German-speaking guest. I remember meeting the conductors Arthur Nikisch and Hans Richter in this way. The latter knew no word of any language but German, and Rimsky, with no German-speaking member of his family present had to send for me. When Richter saw me he scowled and asked: '*Wer ist dieser Jüngling*?' I remember meeting Max Reger in those years, at a rehearsal I think. He and his music repulsed me in about equal measure. Alfredo Casella also came to Russia then, at the beginning of his career. I did not meet him at that time, but heard about him from Rimsky: 'A certain Alfredo Casella, an Italian musician, came to see me today. He brought me a complicated score of incredible size, his instrumentation of Balakirev's *Islamey*, and asked me to comment on it and to advise him. What could one say about such a thing? I felt like a poor little child' – and saying so he seemed humiliated.

I remember seeing Mahler in St Petersburg, too. His concert there was a triumph. Rimsky was still alive, I believe, but he wouldn't have attended because a work by Tchaikovsky was on the programme (I think it was *Manfred*, the dullest piece imaginable). Mahler also played some Wagner fragments and, if I remember correctly, a symphony of his own. Mahler impressed me greatly, himself and his conducting.

R.C. Would you describe Rimsky-Korsakov as a teacher?

I.S. He was a most unusual teacher. Though a professor at the St Petersburg Conservatory himself, he advised me not to enter it; instead he made me the most precious gift of his unforgettable lessons (1903–6). These usually lasted a little more than an hour and took place twice a week. Schooling and training in orchestration was their main subject. He gave me Beethoven piano sonatas and quartets and Schubert marches to orchestrate, and sometimes his own music, the orchestration of which was not yet published. Then as I brought him the work I did, he showed me his own orchestra score, which he compared with mine, explaining his reasons for doing it differently.

In addition to these lessons I continued my contrapuntal exercises, but by myself, as I could not stand the boring lessons in harmony and counterpoint I had had with a former pupil of Rimsky-Korsakov.

R.C. What music of yours did Rimsky-Korsakov know? What did he say about it? What were his relations with new music: Debussy, Strauss, Scriabin?

I.S. When asked to go to a concert to hear Debussy's music he said: 'I have already heard it. I had better not go: I will start to get accustomed to it and finally like it.' He hated Richard Strauss but probably for the wrong reasons. His attitude towards Scriabin was different. He didn't like Scriabin's music at all, but to those people who were indignant about it his answer was: 'I like Scriabin's music very much.'

He knew well my Symphony in E flat, op. 1, dedicated to him, and also my vocal suite, *Faune et bergère*, both performed in a concert arranged with his help and supervision. He had seen the manuscript of my *Scherzo fantastique*, but his death prevented him from hearing it. He never complimented me; but he was always very close-mouthed and stingy in praising his pupils. But I was told by his friends after his death that he spoke with great praise of the *Scherzo* score.

R.C. Did you have Maeterlinck's *La Vie des abeilles* in mind as a programme for your *Scherzo fantastique*?

I.S. No, I wrote the *Scherzo* as a piece of 'pure' symphonic music. The bees were a choreographer's idea as, later, the bee-like creatures of the ballet (to my string concerto in D), *The Cage*, were Mr Robbins's. I have always been fascinated by bees, awed by them after von Fritsch's book, and terrified after my friend Gerald Heard's *Is Another World Watching*, but I have never attempted to evoke them in my work (as, indeed, what pupil of the composer of the *Flight of the Bumble Bee* would?), nor have I been influenced by them except that, defying Galen's advice to elderly people (to Marcus Aurelius?), I continue to eat a daily diet of honey.

Maeterlinck's bees nearly gave me serious trouble, however. One morning in Morges I received a startling letter from him, accusing me of intent to cheat and fraud. My *Scherzo* had been entitled *Les Abeilles* – anyone's title, after all – and made the subject of a ballet then performing at the Paris Grand Opera (1917). *Les Abeilles* was unauthorized by me and, of course, I had not seen it; but Maeterlinck's name was mentioned in the programme. The affair was settled and, finally, some bad literature about bees was published on the fly-leaf of my score, to satisfy my publisher, who thought a 'story' would help to sell the music. I regretted the incident with Maeterlinck because I had considerable respect for him in Russian translation.

Sometime later I recounted this episode to Paul Claudel. Claudel considered Maeterlinck to have been unusually polite to me: 'He often starts suits against people who say *bonjour* to him. You were lucky not to have been sued for the "bird" part of the *Firebird*, since Maeterlinck had written the *Bluebird* first.'*

* Since writing this I have conducted three performances of the *Scherzo* ('whether or not it is "Fantastique" is up to us to decide,'

This bee-ology reminds me of Rachmaninov, of all people, for the last time I saw that awesome man he had come to my house in Hollywood bearing me the gift of a pail of honey. I was not especially friendly with Rachmaninov at the time, nor, I think, was anyone else: social relations with a man of Rachmaninov's temperament require more perseverance than I can afford: he was merely bringing me honey. It is curious, however, that I should meet him not in Russia, though I often heard him perform there in my youth, nor later when we were neighbours in Switzerland, but in Hollywood.

Some people achieve a kind of immortality just by the totality with which they do or do not possess some quality or characteristic. Rachmaninov's immortalizing totality was his scowl. He was a six-and-a-half-foot-tall scowl.

I suppose my conversations with him, or rather, with his wife, for he was always silent, were typical:

---

one French critic wrote after its *première* in St Petersburg under the baton of Alexander Ziloti), and was surprised to find that the music did not embarrass me. The orchestra 'sounds', the music is light in a way that is rare in compositions of the period, and there are one or two quite good ideas in it such as the flute and violin music at no. 63 and the chromatic movement of the last page. Of course the phrases are all four plus four plus four, which is monotonous, and, hearing it again, I was sorry that I did not more exploit the alto flute. It is a promising opus three, though.

I see now that I did take something from Rimsky's Bumblebee (numbers 49–50 in the score), but the *Scherzo* owes much more to Mendelssohn by way of Tchaikovsky than to Rimsky-Korsakov.

The progress of instrumental technique was illustrated to me by these recent performances in an interesting detail. The original score – written more than fifty years ago – employs three harps. I remember very well how difficult all three parts were for the harpists in St Petersburg in 1908. In 1930 I reduced the three parts to two for a new edition of the orchestral material. Now I see that with a few adjustments the same music can be performed by one player, so much quicker are harpists at their pedals.

Mme Rachmaninov: 'What is the first thing you do when you rise in the morning?' (This could have been indiscreet, but not if you had seen how it was asked.)

Myself: 'For fifteen minutes I do exercises taught me by a Hungarian gymnast and Kneipp Kur maniac, or, rather, I did them until I learned that the Hungarian had died very young and very suddenly, then I stand on my head, then I take a shower.'

Mme Rachmaninov: 'You see, Serge, *Stravinsky* takes showers. How extraordinary. Do you still say you are afraid of them? And you heard Stravinsky say that he exercises? What do you think of that? Shame on you who will hardly take a walk.'

Rachmaninov: (Silence.)

I remember Rachmaninov's earliest compositions. They were 'water-colours', songs and piano pieces freshly influenced by Tchaikovsky. Then at twenty-five he turned to 'oils' and became a very old composer indeed. Do not expect me to spit on him for that, however: he was, as I have said, an awesome man, and besides, there are too many others to be spat upon before him. As I think about him, his silence looms as a noble contrast to the self-approbations which are the only conversation of all performing and most other musicians. And, he was the only pianist I have ever seen who did not grimace. That is a great deal.

R.C. When you were a pupil of Rimsky-Korsakov, did you esteem Tchaikovsky as much as you did later, in the twenties and thirties?

I.S. Then as later in my life I was annoyed by the too frequent vulgarity of his music – annoyed in the same measure as I enjoyed the real freshness of Tchaikovsky's talent (and his instrumental inventiveness), especially when I compared it with the stale naturalism and amateurism of the 'Five' (Borodin, Rimsky-Korsakov, Cui, Balakirev, and Mussorgsky).

R.C. What was Rimsky-Korsakov's attitude to Brahms and when did you yourself first encounter Brahms's music?

I.S. I remember reading the notice of Brahms's death in *New Time* (the St Petersburg conservative newspaper; I subscribed to it for Rozanov's articles) and the impression it made on me. I know that at least three years prior to it I had played quartets and symphonies by the Hamburg master.

Brahms was the discovery of my 'uncle' Alexander Ielatchich, husband of my mother's sister, Sophie. This gentleman, who had an important role in my early development, was a civil service general and a wealthy man. He was a passionate musical amateur who would spend days at a time playing the piano. Two of his five sons were musical, too, and one of them or myself was always playing four-hand music with him. I remember going through a Brahms quartet with him this way in my twelfth year. Uncle Alexander was an admirer of Mussorgsky and as such he had little use for Rimsky-Korsakov. His house was just around the corner from Rimsky's, however, and I would often go from one to the other, finding it difficult to keep a balance between them.

Rimsky did not like Brahms. He was no Wagnerite either, but his admiration for Liszt kept him on the Wagner–Liszt side of the partisanship.

R.C. What opinion did you have of Mussorgsky when you were Rimsky-Korsakov's student? Do you remember anything your father may have said about him? How do you consider him today?

I.S. I have very little to say about Mussorgsky in connexion with my student years under Rimsky-Korsakov. At that time, being influenced by the master who recomposed almost the whole work of Mussorgsky, I repeated what was usually said about his 'big talent' and 'poor musicianship', and about the 'important services' rendered by Rimsky to his 'embarrassing' and 'unpresentable' scores. Very soon I realized the partiality of this kind of mind, however, and changed my attitude toward Mussorgsky. This was before my contact with the French composers who, of course, were all fiercely opposed to Rimsky's 'transcriptions'. It was too obvious, even to an influenced mind, that Rimsky's Meyer-beerization of Mussorgsky's 'technically imperfect' music could no longer be tolerated.

As to my own feeling (although I have little contact with Mussorgsky's music today) I think that in spite of his limited technical means and 'awkward writing' his original scores always show infinitely more true musical interest and genuine intuition than the 'perfection' of Rimsky's arrangements. My parents often told me that Mussorgsky was a connoisseur of Italian operatic music and that he accompanied concert singers in it extremely well. They also said that Mussorgsky's manners were always ceremonious and that he was the most fastidious of men in his personal relations. He was a frequent guest in our house at St Petersburg.

R.C. You often conduct Glinka's overtures. Have you always been fond of his music?

I.S. Glinka was the Russian musical hero of my childhood. He was always *sans reproche* and this is the way I still think of him. His music is minor, of course, but he is not; all music in Russia stems from him. In 1906, shortly after my marriage, I went with my wife and Nikolsky, my civics professor at the University of St Petersburg, to pay a visit of respect to Glinka's sister, Ludmilla Shestakova. An old lady of ninety-two or ninety-three, she was surrounded by servants almost as old as herself and she did not attempt to get up from her chair. She had been the wife of an admiral and one addressed her as 'Your Excellency'. I was thrilled to meet her because she had been very close to Glinka. She talked to me about Glinka, about my late father, whom she had known very well, about the Cui-Dargomizhsky circle and its rabid anti-Wagnerism. Afterwards as a memento of my visit she sent me a silver leaf of edelweiss.

R.C. Did you ever meet Balakirev?

I.S. I saw him once, standing with his pupil, Liapunov, at a concert in the St Petersburg Conservatory. He was a large man, bald, with a Kalmuck head and the shrewd, sharp-eyed look of Lenin. He was not greatly admired musically at this time – it was 1904 or 1905 – and, politically, because of his orthodoxy, the liberals considered him a hypocrite. His reputation as a pianist was firmly established by numerous pupils, however, all of them, like Balakirev himself, ardent Lisztians; whereas Rimsky-Korsakov kept a portrait of Wagner over his desk, Balakirev had one of Liszt. I pitied Balakirev because he suffered from cruel fits of depression.

R.C. You do not mention in your autobiography whether you attended Rimsky-Korsakov's funeral?

I.S. I did not mention it because it was one of the unhappiest days of my life. But I was there and I will remember Rimsky in his coffin as long as memory is. He looked so very beautiful I could not help crying. His widow, seeing me, came up to me and said: 'Why so unhappy? We still have Glazunov.' It was the cruellest remark I have ever heard and I have never hated again as I did in that moment.

DIAGHILEV

R.C. What were Diaghilev's powers of musical judgement? What, for example, was his response to *Le Sacre du printemps* when he first heard it?

I.S. Diaghilev did not have so much a good musical judgement as an immense flair for recognizing the potentiality of success in a piece of music or work of art in general. In spite of his surprise when I played him the beginning of the *Sacre* (*Les Augures printanières*) at the piano, in spite of his at first ironic attitude to the long line of repeated chords, he quickly realized that the reason was something other than my inability to compose more diversified music; he realized at once the seriousness of my new musical speech, its importance and the advantage of capitalizing on it. That, it seems to me, is what he thought on first hearing the *Sacre*.

R.C. Was the musical performance of the first *Sacre du printemps* reasonably correct? Do you recall anything more about that night of 29 May 1913, beyond what you have already written?

I.S. I was sitting in the fourth or fifth row on the right and the image of Monteux's back is more vivid in my mind today than the picture of the stage. He stood there apparently impervious and as nerveless as a crocodile. It is still almost incredible to me that he actually brought the orchestra through to the end. I left my seat when the heavy noises began – light noise had started from the very beginning – and went backstage behind Nijinsky in the right wing. Nijinsky stood on a chair, just out of view of the audience, shouting numbers to the dancers. I wondered what on earth these numbers had to do with the music for there are no 'thirteens' and 'seventeens' in the metrical scheme of the score.

From what I heard of the musical performance it was not bad. Sixteen full rehearsals had given the orchestra at least some security. After the 'performance' we were excited, angry, disgusted, and . . . happy. I went with Diaghilev and Nijinsky to a restaurant. So far from weeping and reciting Pushkin in the Bois de Boulogne as the legend is, Diaghilev's only comment was: 'Exactly what I wanted.' He certainly looked contented. No one could have been quicker to understand the publicity value and he immediately understood the good thing that had happened in that respect. Quite probably he had already thought about the possibility of such a scandal when I first played him the score, months before, in the east corner ground room of the Grand Hotel in Venice.

R.C. Had you ever planned a Russian 'liturgical ballet'? If so, did any of it become *Les Noces*?

I.S. No, that 'liturgical ballet' was entirely Diaghilev's idea. He knew that a Russian church spectacle in a Paris theatre would be enormously successful. He had wonderful ikons and costumes he wished to show and he kept pestering me to give him music. Diaghilev was not really religious, not really a believer, but only a deeply superstitious man. He wasn't at all shocked by the idea of the church in the theatre. I began to conceive *Les Noces*, and its form was already clear in my mind, from about the beginning of 1914. At the time of Sarajevo I was in Clarens. I needed Kireievsky's book of Russian folk poetry, from which I had made my libretto, and I determined to go to Kiev which was the only place where I knew I could get it. I took the train to Oustiloug, our summer home in Volhynia, in July 1914. After a few days there I went on to Warsaw and Kiev, where I found the book. I regret that on this last trip, my last view of Russia, I did not see the Vydubitsky Monastery which I knew and loved. On the return trip the border police were already very tense. I arrived in Switzerland only a few days before the war – thanking my stars. Incidentally, Kireievsky had asked Pushkin to send him his collection of folk verse and Pushkin sent him some verses with a note reading: 'Some of these are my own verses; can you tell the difference?' Kireievsky could not, and took them all for his book, so perhaps a line of Pushkin's is in *Les Noces*.

DEBUSSY

R.C. Of your early contemporaries, to whom do you owe the most? Debussy? Do you think Debussy changed from his contact with you?

I.S. I was handicapped in my earliest years by influences that restrained the growth of my composer's technique. I refer to the St Petersburg Conservatory's formalism, from which, however – and fortunately – I was soon free. But the musicians of my generation and I myself owe the most to Debussy.

I don't think there was a change in Debussy as a result of our contact. After reading his friendly and commendatory letters to me (he liked *Petroushka* very much) I was puzzled to find quite a different feeling concerning my music in some of his letters to his musical friends of the same period. Was it duplicity, or was he annoyed at his incapacity to digest the music of the *Sacre* when the younger generation enthusiastically voted for it? This is difficult to judge now at a distance of more than forty years.

LETTERS FROM DEBUSSY

I   *Saturday, 10 April 1913*
                   80 avenue de Bois de Boulogne
(Letter sent to me in Oustiloug.)
Dear Friend,

Thanks to you I have passed an enjoyable Easter vacation in the company of Petroushka, the terrible Moor, and the delicious Ballerina. I can imagine that you spent incomparable moments with the three puppets ... and I don't know many things more valuable than the section you call 'Tour de passe-passe'. .... There is in it a kind of sonorous magic, a mysterious transformation of mechanical souls which become human by a spell of which, until now, you seem to be the unique inventor.

Finally, there is an orchestral infallibility that I have found only in *Parsifal*. You will understand what I mean, of course. You will go much further than *Petroushka*, it is certain, but you can be proud already of the achievement of this work.

I am sorry, please accept my belated thanks in acknowledging your kind gift. But the dedication gives me much too high a place in the mastery of that music which we both serve with the same disinterested zeal. ... Unhappily, at this time, I was surrounded with sick people! especially my wife who has been suffering for many long days. ... I even had to be the 'man about the house' and I will admit to you at once that I have no talent for it.

Since the good idea of performing you again is talked about, I look forward with pleasure to see you soon here.

Please don't forget the way to my house where everyone is anxious to see you.

Very affectionately your

CLAUDE DEBUSSY

2

Paris, 8 November 1913

Don't fall to the ground, Dear Friend, it is only me!!! Of course, if we begin, you wishing to understand and I to explain why I haven't written yet, our hair will fall out.

And then, something marvellous is happening here: at least once a day everyone talks about you. Your friend Chouchou* has composed a fantasy on *Petroushka* which would make tigers roar. ... I have threatened her with torture, but she goes on, insisting that you will 'find it very beautiful'. So, how could you suppose that we are not thinking of you?

Our reading at the piano of *Le Sacre du printemps*, at Laloy's† house, is always present in my mind. It haunts me

* Debussy's daughter Emma-Claude, who died one year after her father.

† Which Louis Laloy, the critic, incorrectly attributes to the spring of 1913. What most impressed me at the time and what is still most memorable from the occasion of the sight-reading of *Le Sacre* was Debussy's brilliant piano playing. Recently, while listening to his *En blanc et noir* (one of which pieces is dedicated to me) I was struck by the way in which the extraordinary quality of this pianism had directed the thought of Debussy the composer.

like a beautiful nightmare and I try, in vain, to reinvoke the terrific impression.

That is why I wait for the stage performance like a greedy child impatient for promised sweets.

As soon as I have a good proof copy of *Jeux* I will send it to you. ... I would love to have your opinion on this 'badinage in three parts'. While speaking of *Jeux*, you were surprised that I chose this title to which you preferred *The Park*. I beg you to believe that *Jeux* is better, first because it is more appropriate, and then because it more nearly invokes the 'horrors' that occur among these three characters.*

When are you coming to Paris so one may at last play good music?

Very affectionately from us three to you and your wife.

Your very old friend,

CLAUDE DEBUSSY

3   *15 May 1913*

Dear Friend,

My telephone doesn't work and I fear you have tried to call without success. If you have seen Nijinsky and if he signed the papers please give them to the chauffeur. It is urgent that they are at the Société des Auteurs before five o'clock. Thank you, your old Debussy.

(*This note brought by Debussy's chauffeur refers to forms from the Société des Auteurs Debussy had given me to give Nijinsky the co-stage author of* Jeux. *I was seeing Nijinsky every day at this time and Debussy was only sure of reaching him through me.*)

* Debussy was in close contact with me during the composition of *Jeux* and he frequently consulted me about problems of orchestration. I still consider *Jeux* as an *orchestral* masterpiece, though I think some of the music is '*trop Lalique*'.

4   *Paris, 18 August 1913*

Dear Old Stravinsky,

Excuse me for being late in thanking you for a work whose dedication is priceless to me.* I have been taken with an attack of 'expulsive gingivitis'. It is ugly and dangerous and one could wake up in the morning to discover one's teeth falling out. Then, of course, they could be strung into a necklace. Perhaps this is not much consolation?

The music from the *Roi des étoiles* is still extraordinary. It is probably Plato's 'harmony of the eternal spheres' (but don't ask me which page of his). And, except on Sirius or Aldebaran, I do not foresee performances of this 'cantata for planets'. As for our more modest Earth, a performance would be lost in the abyss.

I hope that you have recovered. Take care, music needs you. Kindly convey my respects to your charming mother and best wishes to your wife.

Your old faithful

CLAUDE DEBUSSY

5   *Paris, 9 November 1913*

Dear Stravinsky,

Because one still belongs to certain traditions, one wonders why one's letter is not answered ... ! But the value of the music I have received† is more important because it contains something affirmative and victorious. Naturally, people who are a little bit embarrassed by your

---

*I had dedicated my short cantata *Le Roi des étoiles* (1911) to Debussy. He was obviously puzzled by the music, and nearly right in predicting it to be unperformable – it has had only a few performances in very recent years and remains in one sense my most 'radical' and difficult composition.

† I had sent him the score of *Le Sacre du printemps.*

growing mastery have not neglected to spread very discordant rumours – and if you are not already dead it is not their fault. I have never believed in a rumour – is it necessary to tell you this? – No! Also, it is not necessary to tell you of the joy I had to see my name associated with a very beautiful thing that with the passage of time will be more beautiful still.

For me, who descend the other slope of the hill but keep, however, an intense passion for music, for me it is a special satisfaction to tell you how much you have enlarged the boundaries of the permissible in the empire of sound.

Forgive me for using these pompous words, but they exactly express my thought.

You have probably heard about the melancholy end of the Théâtre des Champs Élysées? It is really a pity that the only place in Paris where one had started to play music honestly could not be successful. May I ask you dear friend, what you propose to do about it? I saw Diaghilev at *Boris Godunov*, the only performance it had, and he said nothing. . . . If you can give me some news without being indiscreet, do not hesitate. In any case are you coming to Paris? 'How many questions' I hear you saying. . . . If you are annoyed to answer. . . .

This very moment I received your postcard – and I see by it, dear friend, that you never received my letter. It is very regrettable for me – you are probably very angry with me. Perhaps I wrote the address incorrectly. And also, Oustiloug is so far away. I will not go to Lausanne – for some complicated reasons which are of no interest to you. This is one more reason for you to come to Paris – to have the joy of seeing each other.

Know that I am going to Moscow the first of December. I gather you will not be there? Believe me that for this reason my journey will be a little more painful. I wrote to

Kussevitsky asking him for some necessary information – he does not answer.

As for the Société de la Musique Actuelle, I want to do my best to be agreeable and to thank them for the honour they want to bestow on me. Only I don't know if I will have enough time to stay for the concert.

My wife and Chouchou send you their affectionate thoughts and ask you not to forget to give the same to your wife.

Always your old devoted

CLAUDE DEBUSSY

(postcard)

6

Paris, 17 November 1913

Dear Stravinsky, You have acquired the habit since childhood to play with the calendar and I confess that your last card confused me. At the same time I received a telegram from Kussevitsky telling me that I am expected in Moscow 3 December (new style). As the concert in St Petersburg is the 10th you can see that I will not have time to do anything. Are you recovered from your cold? I heartily hope so. If you have nothing better to do I advise you to go to Moscow. It is a marvellous city and you probably don't know it very well. You will meet there Claude Debussy, French musician, who loves you very much.

Affectionately, CLAUDE DEBUSSY

7

Paris, 24 October 1915

First of all, dearest friend, it is a joy to hear from you at last. .... I had some news from your friends, who, I don't know why, kept the state of your health and your residence a mystery.

We are all doing somewhat better, or in other words we are like the majority of the French people. We have our share of sorrows, of spiritual and domestic difficulties. But this is natural now that Europe and the rest of the world think it necessary to participate in this tragic 'concert'. Why don't the inhabitants of Mars join the fray?

As you wrote to me: 'They will be unable to make us join their madness.' All the same there is something higher than brute force; to 'close the windows' on beauty is against reason and destroys the true meaning of life.

But one must open one's eyes and ears to other sounds when the noise of the cannon has subsided! The world must be rid of this bad seed. We have all to kill the microbes of false grandeur, of organized ugliness, which we did not always realize was simply weakness.

You will be needed in the war against those other, and just as mortal, gases for which there are no masks.

Dear Stravinsky, you are a great artist. Be with all your strength a great Russian artist. It is so wonderful to be of one's country, to be attached to one's soil like the humblest of peasants! And when the foreigner treads upon it how bitter all the nonsense about internationalism seems.

In these last years, when I smelled 'austro-boches' miasma in art, I wished for more authority to shout my worries, warn of the dangers we so credulously approached. Did no one suspect these people of plotting the destruction of our art as they had prepared the destruction of our countries? And this ancient national hate that will end only with the last German! But will there ever be a 'last German'? For I am convinced that German soldiers beget German soldiers.

As for *Nocturnes*, Doret (the Swiss composer) is right, I made many modifications. Unhappily, they are published by a publisher, Fromont, Colysée Street, with whom I am no more associated. Another trouble is that there are no more copyists, at this moment, capable of doing this delicate work. I shall search further and try to find a way to satisfy M. Ansermet.

It must be confessed that music is in a bad situation here. ... It only serves charitable purposes, and we must not blame it for that. I remained here for more than a year without being able to write any music. Only during these last three months spent at the seaside with friends have I recovered the faculty of musical thinking. Unless one is personally involved in it, war is a state of mind contradictory to thought. That olympian egotist Goethe is the only one who could work, it is said, the day the French army came into Weimar. ... Then there was Pythagoras killed by a soldier at the moment when he was going to solve God knows what problem?

Recently I have written nothing but pure music, twelve piano *études* and two sonatas for different instruments, in our old form which, very graciously, did not impose any tetralogical auditory efforts.

And you, dear friend, what have you been doing? Don't for heaven's sake think you have to answer that question. I ask not out of vulgar curiosity but in pure affection.

And your wife and children? Have you worries about them?

My wife suffered badly from her eyes and from an unbearable neuralgia-rheumatism. Chouchou has a cold; she makes it into something very serious by the attention she pays to her little person.

It is very difficult to know when we will see each other and so we have only the weak resource of 'words'. ... Well, believe me your always devoted old

CLAUDE DEBUSSY

All our affectionate thoughts to your dear family. I have received news from the Société des Auteurs saying that you had chosen me as godfather for your entry in that society. I thank you.

JACQUES RIVIÈRE

R.C. You have said that Jacques Rivière, as editor of the *Nouvelle Revue française*, was the first critic to have had an intuition about your music. What were his musical capabilities?

I.S. At this distance I am not really able to answer that, for though I knew Rivière well before the 1914 war I never saw him again after it and in forty-five years memories change colour. However, I can say that at the time I considered his criticism of my ballets to be literary, inspired more by the whole spectacle than by my music. He *was* musical, certainly, and his musical tastes were genuine and cultivated, but whether he was capable of following the musical argument of *Le Sacre du printemps* I can no longer judge.

I remember Jacques Rivière as a tall, blond, intellectually energetic youth, a passionate balletomane and at the same time a man with a deep religious vocation. He came to Geneva from time to time when I lived there and these meetings with him always afforded me much pleasure. He lived in semi-retirement after the war, his health ruined by his years as a prisoner of the Germans, and he died still young, a broken man.

Re-reading his letters I am struck (*a*) by the malady of the French about theatre tickets; they will do absolutely anything to get tickets except *buy* them; if Rivière was so '*vivement*' interested in the *Nightingale* why didn't he go to the *guichet* and exchange a few francs for them?; and (*b*) by the evidence in the fourth letter of how quickly fashion had turned against Debussy in the year after his death.

LETTERS FROM JACQUES RIVIÈRE

I

> *Editions de la Nouvelle Revue française*
> *35 and 37 rue Madame, Paris*
> *4 February 1914*

My dear Stravinsky,

I am rather late in telling you how grateful I am. But I have been near you in my thoughts all these days as I have started to put on paper some ideas about the *Nightingale*.*

You were very kind to have sent these two cards to Gallimard and to me. They gave us great pleasure.

I intend to come to your concert† Saturday and perhaps I will be able to shake your hand.

Believe me, my dear Stravinsky . . .

JACQUES RIVIÈRE

---

* I was in Leysin in January 1914 completing the *Nightingale*. Cocteau came there in the hope of persuading me to collaborate with him on a work to be called *David*, and Diaghilev followed him a few days later with the express intention of discouraging this same project. Diaghilev-Cocteau relations were not ideal at the time, anyway, as Diaghilev could not stand Cocteau's fondness for Nijinsky, but Diaghilev's excuse for the trip was the *Nightingale*. Until then he had ignored the existence of this opera (out of jealousy, it had been commissioned by a Moscow theatre) but recently the people who were to produce it had declared bankruptcy and he was now very interested: I had been paid by them (10,000 roubles, a huge sum of money for 1909) and he could have the opera for nothing. We returned to Paris where I played the *Nightingale* for Ravel and a group of friends. Among these was Jacques Rivière.

† I have no recollection of this concert.

2   *Paris, 25 May 1914*

Dear Sir,

Is it extremely indiscreet of me to ask you for two or three tickets to the *première* of the *Nightingale?* I take this liberty only because yesterday evening I heard that a large number of complimentary tickets are available. You may well imagine how much I want my wife to hear this work from which I myself anticipate so much pleasure.* But if it is impossible please do not hesitate to refuse me.† If you are able to get tickets only for the second performance I certainly will not refuse them though of course I would prefer to attend the *première*. Yesterday I again heard the music of *Petroushka*, and with profound emotion. I beg you, dear sir, to excuse my importunity and to believe in my friendship and sympathy.

JACQUES RIVIÈRE
15 rue Froidevaux, Paris XIV

3   *Paris, May 1914*

Dear Sir,

You are exceedingly kind to have thought of me and I thank you with all my heart. Unfortunately, I had gone away the moment your telegram arrived and this is the reason why I did not use the place you offered me in your *loge*. I succeeded in entering the Opera, however, but the conditions under which I heard the *Nightingale* were so unfavourable that I am not yet able to judge it well. But already I see that it promises me beautiful discoveries for the next performances.

Again thank you, dear sir, and please believe in my admiration and my sympathy.

JACQUES RIVIÈRE

* He had attended some of the rehearsals.
† *Sic.*

4   *La Nouvelle Revue française*
35 and 37 rue Madame, Paris
6 April 1919

My dear Stravinsky,

I asked Auberjonois* to tell you how much pleasure your letter gave me. Probably he has done so, but I thank you most sincerely again.

It is another matter I want to talk to you about today, however. Perhaps you already know that my friends have decided to entrust me with the direction of the *Nouvelle Revue française*, which will reappear 1 June. It is an honour of which I am very proud, but it is also a heavy burden and a source of grave preoccupations.

I intend to direct the attention of the magazine to the anti-impressionist, anti-symbolist, and anti-Debussy movements that are becoming more and more precise and threatening to take the form and force of a vast new current. I would be extremely happy if you think you could show us in an article (you may decide the dimensions of it yourself) your present ideas on music and the meaning of the work you are devoting yourself to at the moment.

But do not think you have been forgotten here. Everyone I see talks about you constantly. The influence of *Petroushka* and *Sacre* and even of your recent works on the younger musicians is obvious. An article by you will be read with curiosity and sympathy everywhere in the world. To make it easier for you, you could write it in Russian. If you have no one around to translate it, I think I can take charge of that, with the condition that the manuscript you send me is very legibly written. Of course, I will submit my translation to you for rectification.

*René Auberjonois, the late Swiss painter, who designed the first production of my *L'Histoire du soldat*.

I do not need to tell you that, without promising mountains of gold, I will assure you of our best possible fee for your work.

Please forgive me for having fulfilled only one part of the requests you charged me with when we last saw each other in Geneva. Most of the people you asked me to see were not in Paris when I arrived there, however, and I myself was so long absent that by the time I finally returned some of the requests were out of date.

I will confidently await your answer hoping that it will not be otherwise than favourable, and with this conviction I beg you my dear Stravinsky to believe in my deepest friendship.

JACQUES RIVIÈRE

PS. Do not forget to give my best wishes to Ramuz* and Auberjonois. If it will be difficult for you to send me your manuscript because of the Russian, please inform me and I will ask someone I know at the Foreign Affairs Office to facilitate the sending, and obtain the necessary authorization for you.

5   *Paris, 21 April 1919*

My dear Stravinsky,

Of course your letter was disappointing as it deprives me of your collaboration; but it delighted me also because I think as you do, that a real creator should not lose his time discoursing about the tendencies and consequences of his art. His work must be self-explanatory. However, if one day the desire overtakes you to write not about yourself, but about others, about Debussy for instance, or Russian contemporary music, or some other subject, then think

*C. F. Ramuz, the late Swiss novelist and co-librettist with me of *L'Histoire du soldat*.

74

about me and do not forget that our pages are always open to you.

With friendship, your
JACQUES RIVIÈRE

PS. What is this new 'Suite from the *Firebird*', a ballet?*

RAVEL

R.C. Have you any notion where the manuscript of yours and Ravel's instrumentation of *Khovanshchina* might be?

I.S. I left it in Oustiloug on my last trip to Russia and therefore assume it to be lost or destroyed. (I wish someone travelling in Volhynia and passing through Oustiloug would investigate whether my house still stands; not long ago some kind person sent me a photograph of it but did not mention whether it had survived the Nazi invasion and I could not tell if the photo was pre- or post-war.) However, I feel certain that Bessel had already engraved it in Russia just before the [1914] war. The plates should exist, therefore, with the inheritors of Bessel's Russian firm. I remember a money struggle with Bessel who said we were demanding too much and argued that 'Mussorgsky received only a fraction of what you are asking'.

I replied that because they had given Mussorgsky precisely nothing, because they had succeeded in starving the poor man, was the greater reason to give us more.

The idea of asking Ravel to collaborate with me on an instrumentation of *Khovanshchina* was mine. I was afraid not to be ready for the spring season of 1913 and I needed help. Unfortunately, however, Diaghilev cared less about establishing a good instrumentation of the opera and rescuing it from Rimsky-Korsakov than about our version as a new

* My 1919 version of the *Firebird* suite, which I think he might have guessed.

75

vehicle for Chaliapin. That idiot from every non-vocal point of view, and from some of these, could not realize the value of such an instrumentation. He declined to sing and the project was abandoned, though we had already done considerable work. I orchestrated Shaklovity's famous and banal aria, the final chorus and some other music I no longer remember. Mussorgsky had only sketched, really only projected, the final chorus; I began with Mussorgsky's original and composed it from Mussorgsky ignoring Rimsky-Korsakov.

Ravel came to Clarens to live with me and we worked together there in March–April 1913. At that same time also, I composed my *Three Japanese Lyrics* and Ravel his *Trois Poèmes de Mallarmé* which I still prefer to any music of his. I remember an excursion I made with Ravel from Clarens to Varese, near Lago Maggiore, to buy Varese paper. The town was very crowded and we could not find two hotel rooms or even two beds, so we slept together in one.

Ravel? When I think of him, for example in relation to Satie, he appears quite ordinary. His musical judgement was very acute, however, and I would say that he was the only musician who immediately understood *Le Sacre du printemps*. He was dry and reserved and sometimes little darts were hidden in his remarks, but he was always a very good friend to me. He drove a truck or ambulance in the war, as you know, and I admired him for it because at his age and with his name he could have had an easier place – or done nothing. He looked rather pathetic in his uniform; so small, he was two or three inches smaller than I am.

I think Ravel knew when he went into the hospital for his last operation that he would go to sleep for the last time. He said to me: 'They can do what they want with my cranium as long as the ether works.' It didn't work, however, and the poor man felt the incision. I did not visit him in this hospital and my last view of him was in a funeral home. The top part of his skull was still bandaged. His final years were cruel, for he was gradually losing his memory and some of his co-ordinating powers, and, he was, of course, quite aware of it. Gogol died screaming and Diaghilev died laughing (and singing *La Bohème* which he loved genuinely and as much as any music), but Ravel died gradually. That is the worst.

LETTERS FROM RAVEL

1   *Comarques, Thorpe-Le-Soken*
13 December 1913

Vieux – it's a long time since I've had any sensational news about your health. Three weeks ago I heard about your sudden death, but was not stricken by it as the same morning we received a postcard from you.

Delage* surely told you that your 'Japanese' will be performed January 14th together with his 'Hindus' and my 'Mallarméans'. ... We count on your presence.

I will be in London in three days and hope to hear talk about the *Sacre*.

And the *Nightingale*, will he soon sing?

My respectful compliments to Mme Stravinsky, kiss the children, and believe in the affection of your devoted

MAURICE RAVEL

---

*Maurice Delage, the composer, a good friend to me at this time. My *Three Japanese Lyrics* are dedicated to Maurice Delage, Florent Schmitt, and Maurice Ravel respectively.

2   *St Jean de Luz*
                                                     14 February 1914

Dear Igor,

I hear from Casella* that Madame Stravinsky went to Leysin. I hope it is only a precaution. I beg you, reassure me by a word.

I have taken refuge here in the country of my birthplace to work, as work was becoming quite impossible in Paris. Kiss the children for me, and present to Mme Stravinsky my respectful compliments. Believe in the affection of your devoted

MAURICE RAVEL

3   *St Jean de Luz*
                                                     26 September 1914

Give me news of yourself, *mon vieux*. What becomes of you in all this?

Edouard† enlisted as a driver. I was not so lucky. They did not need me. I hope when they have re-examined all the discharged soldiers, and after all the measures I shall take, to be back in Paris, if I have the means.

The thought that I would go away forced me to do five months' work in five weeks. I have *finished* my Trio. But I was obliged to abandon the works I hoped to finish this winter; *La Cloche Engloutie*! ! and a symphonic poem: *Wein*! ! !‡ But, of course, that is now an untimely subject.

How is your wife? and the little ones? Write me quickly, *mon vieux*. If you only knew how painful it is to be far from everything!

*The composer, Alfredo Casella, and his wife were living in Paris at this time.
† His brother.
‡ Which became *La Valse*.

Affectionate souvenirs to all. No news from the Benois. What has become of them?

MAURICE RAVEL

4

Paris, 14 November 1914

Cher vieux, I am back in Paris ... and it does not suit me at all. I want to go away more than ever. I cannot work any more. When we arrived Maman had to stay in bed. Now she is up, but she has to keep to an albumin-free diet. Her age and her anxieties are of course the cause of this condition. No news from Edouard since the 28th October; a whole month and we do not know what has happened to him.

Delage is now in Fontainebleau. From time to time he is sent on a commission somewhere. Schmitt,* who was bored to death in Toul, finally obtained permission to go to the front. The Godebskis† are still at Carantec. I still haven't seen Misia.

Remember me to your family, *cher vieux*. Write to me very soon I beg you. Believe in my brotherly friendship.

MAURICE RAVEL

5

19 December 1914

Vieux, it's settled: you come and sleep (uncomfortably) in the lumber room, which was the bedroom of my brother, and which was transformed into a Persian room for you. But come quickly, otherwise you will not find me here any more. I will be working as a driver. It was the only means

*Florent Schmitt.

† Cipa Godebski, with his wife and children, Jean and Mimi. The Godebskis (especially Misia Godebski Sert) were good friends to Ravel and to me. The issue of *L'Oeil* for Christmas 1956 contains a history of this extraordinary family.

for me to get to the city where I had to see *Daphnis et Chloé*. You don't give me news from your brother. I hope he is completely recovered. Try to hasten your arrival.

Our affectionate thoughts to you.

MAURICE RAVEL

6   *2 January 1915*

Ainsi, vieux. Everything was prepared to give you, our ally, a proper welcome. The Persian room with voiles from Genoa, prints from Japan, toys from China, in short a synthesis of the 'Russian Season'. Yes, there was even a mechanical Nightingale – and you are not coming. ... Ah, the caprice of the Slav! Is it thanks to this caprice that I received a note from Szánto* who is delighted to know that I will be in Switzerland at the end of January? I wrote you that I will soon be away, but I doubt that they will send me in your direction.

I wait for news from your brother and from you and all your family. Meanwhile, accept all our affectionate wishes for the New Year (New Style).

Devotedly,

MAURICE RAVEL

7   *16 September 1919*

Dear Igor,

I am heartbroken that I did not see you. Why didn't you phone Durand?† They would have given you my address and my telephone number (Saint-Cloud 2.33). Well, I hope to meet you soon, perhaps even in Morges because I will try to

---

* Pianist and composer, acquaintance of all of us, he made a piano transcription of the 'Chinese March' in my *Nightingale*.

† The publishers.

go there to see my uncle before the end of the fall. I continue to do nothing. I am probably empty. Give me your news soon and if you go through Paris again try to be a little bit cleverer and do a little better.

To everybody my affectionate greetings,

MAURICE RAVEL

8 *26 June 1923*

Dear Igor,

Your *Noces* are marvellous! And I regret that I couldn't hear and see more performances of them. But it seemed already unwise to come the other evening; my foot was again very swollen and I now have to go back and rest again until next Sunday at least. Thank you, *mon vieux*,

Affectionately,

MAURICE RAVEL

SATIE

R.C. What do you recall of Erik Satie?

I.S. He was certainly the oddest person I have ever known, but the most rare and consistently witty person, too. I had a great liking for him and he appreciated my friendliness, I think, and liked me in return. With his pince-nez, umbrella, and galoshes he looked a perfect schoolmaster, but he looked just as much like one without these accoutrements. He spoke very softly, hardly opening his mouth, but he delivered each word in an inimitable, precise way. His handwriting recalls his speech to me: it is exact, drawn. His manuscripts were like him also, which is to say as the French say '*fin*'. No one ever saw him wash – he had a horror of soap. Instead he was forever rubbing his fingers with pumice. He was always very poor, poor by conviction, I think. He lived in a poor section and his neighbours seemed to appreciate his coming among them: he was greatly respected by them. His apartment was also very poor. It did not have a bed but only a hammock. In winter Satie would fill bottles with hot water and put them flat in a row underneath his hammock. It looked like some strange kind of marimba. I remember once when someone had promised him some money he replied: 'Monsieur, what you have said did not fall on a deaf ear.'

His sarcasm depended on French classic usages. The first time I heard *Socrate*, at a séance where he played it for a few of us, he turned around at the end and said in perfect bourgeoisie: '*Voila, messieurs, dames.*'

I met him in 1913, I believe, at any rate I photographed him with Debussy in that year. Debussy introduced him to me and Debussy 'protected' and remained a good friend to him. In those early years he played many of his compositions for me at the piano. (I don't think he knew much about instruments and I prefer *Socrate* as he played it to the clumsy orchestra score.) I always thought them literarily limited. The titles are literary, and whereas Klee's titles are literary they do not limit the painting; Satie's do, I think, and they are very much less amusing the second time. But the trouble with *Socrate* is that it is metrically boring. Who can stand that much regularity? All the same, the music of Socrates's death is touching and dignifying in a unique way. Satie's own sudden and mysterious death – shortly after *Socrate* – touched me too. He had been turned towards religion near the end of his life and he started going to Communion. I saw him after church one morning and he said in that extraordinary manner of his: '*Alors, j'ai un peu communiqué ce matin.*' He became ill very suddenly and died quickly and quietly.

SCHOENBERG, BERG, WEBERN

R.C. Will you describe your meeting with Schoenberg in Berlin in 1912? Did you speak German with him? Was he cordial or aloof? Was he an able conductor of *Pierrot*? Webern was present at the Berlin rehearsals of *Pierrot*; do you have any recollection of him? You wrote about the instrumentation of *Pierrot* but not about its use of strict contrapuntal devices or its polyphony; how did you feel about these innovations at the time?

I.S. Diaghilev invited Schoenberg to hear my ballets, *Firebird* and *Petroushka*, and Schoenberg invited us to hear his *Pierrot lunaire*. I do not remember whether Schoenberg or Scherchen or Webern conducted the rehearsals I heard. Diaghilev and I spoke German with Schoenberg and he was friendly and warm and I had the feeling that he was interested in my music, especially in *Petroushka*. It is difficult to recollect one's impressions at a distance of forty-five years; but this I remember very clearly: the instrumental substance of *Pierrot lunaire* impressed me immensely. And by saying 'instrumental' I mean not simply the instrumentation of this music but the whole contrapuntal and polyphonic structure of this brilliant instrumental masterpiece. Unfortunately I do not remember Webern – though I am sure I did at least meet him, in Schoenberg's house in Zehlendorf. Immediately after the war I received some very cordial letters from Schoenberg inquiring about various small pieces of mine that he and Webern were preparing for performance in his famous Vienna concert series, the Society for Private Performances. Then in 1925, he wrote a very nasty verse about me (though I almost forgive him, for setting it to such a remarkable mirror canon). I do not know what had happened in between.

R.C. And Berg, did you know him?

I.S. I met him only once, in Venice, in September 1934. He came to see me in the green room at La Fenice, where I conducted my *Capriccio* in a Biennale concert with my son, Soulima, at the piano. Although it was my first sight of him and I saw him for only a few minutes, I remember I was quite taken by his famous charm and subtlety.

R.C. Has your estimate of Schoenberg and his position been affected by the recent publication of his unfinished works?

I.S. His scope is greatly enlarged by them, but I think his position remains the same. However, any newly revealed work by a master will challenge judgement of him in some particular – as Eliot says that Dante's minor works are of interest because they are by Dante, so anything by Schoenberg, a piece of incunabula like the 1897 string Quartet, an arrangement like his 1900 reduction for two pianos of *The Barber of Seville*, is of interest to us because it is by Schoenberg. The most interesting of the unfinished works are the three pieces for an ensemble of solo instruments composed in 1910. They force us to reconsider the extent of Webern's indebtedness respecting instrumental style and the dimension of the short piece.* The last composed of the unfinished works, the *Modern Psalms* of 1950–1 show that Schoenberg continued to explore new ways and to search for new laws of serial music right up to his death. Of these posthumous publications *Moses und Aron* is in a category by itself: whereas the other works are unfinished, it is unfinished but complete – like Kafka stories in which the nature of the subject makes an ending in the ordinary sense impossible. *Moses und Aron* is the largest work of Schoenberg's maturity and the last he was to write in Europe. It does not affect our view of his historical role, however. *Jacob's Ladder*, or

---

* No. I have heard these pieces several times since. They are not much like Webern, and the most memorable of them, the third one, is very unlike Webern indeed.

the hundred bars of it that are in a performable state might still do that:*it dates from Schoenberg's period of greatest transition, is actually the only composition to represent the years 1915–22. Schoenberg's work has too many inequalities for us to embrace it as a whole. For example, nearly all of his texts are appallingly bad, some of them so bad as to discourage performance of the music. Then too, his orchestrations of Bach, Handel, Monn, Loewe, Brahms differ from the type of commercial orchestration only in the superiority of craftsmanship: his intentions are no better. Indeed, it is evident from his Handel arrangement that he was unable to appreciate music of 'limited' harmonic range, and I have been told that he considered the English virginalists, and in fact any music that did not show a 'developing harmony', primitive. His expressionism is of the naïvest sort, as, for example, in the directions for lighting the *Glückliche Hand*; his late tonal works are as dull as the Reger they resemble, or the César Franck, for the four-note motive in the *Ode to Napoleon* is like César Franck; and, his distinction between 'inspired melody' and mere 'technique' ('heart' *v.* 'brain') would be factitious if it weren't simply naïve, while the example he offers of the former, the unison *Adagio* in his fourth Quartet makes me squirm. We – and I mean the generation who are now saying 'Webern and me' – must remember only the perfect works, the *Five Pieces for Orchestra* (except for which I could bear the loss of the first nineteen opus numbers), *Herzgewächse*, *Pierrot*, the *Serenade*, the *Variations* for orchestra, and, for its orchestra, the *Seraphita* song from op. 22. By these works Schoenberg is among the great composers. Musicians will

* I now find *Jacob's Ladder* disappointing, and its *Sprechstimme* choruses less good than the beginning of *Die glückliche Hand*. The latter work is, in fact, so striking that it robs not only *Jacob's Ladder* but even a work like Boulez's *Le Visage nuptial* of originality.

take their bearings from them for a great while to come. They constitute together with a few works of not so many other composers, the true tradition.

R.C. How do you now esteem Berg's music?

I.S. If I were able to penetrate the barrier of style (Berg's radically alien emotional climate) I suspect he would appear to me as the most gifted constructor in form of the composers of this century. He transcends even his own most overt modelling. In fact, he is the only one to have achieved large-scale development-type forms without a suggestion of 'neo-classic' dissimulation. His legacy contains very little on which to build, however. He is at the end of a development (and form and style are not such independent growths that we can pretend to use the one and discard the other) whereas Webern, the Sphinx, has bequeathed a whole foundation, as well as a contemporary sensibility and style. Berg's forms are thematic (in which respect, as in most others, he is Webern's opposite); the essence of his work is thematic structure, and the thematic structure is responsible for the immediacy of the form. However complex, however 'mathematical' the latter are, they are always 'free' thematic forms born of 'pure feeling' and 'expression'. The perfect work in which to study this, and, I think, the essential work, with *Wozzeck*, for the study of all of his music, is the *Three Pieces for Orchestra*, op. 6. Berg's personality is mature in these pieces, and they seem to me a richer and freer expression of his talent than the twelve-note serial pieces. When one considers their early date – 1914, Berg was twenty-nine – they are something of a miracle. I wonder how many musicians have discovered them even now, forty years later. In many places they suggest the later Berg. The music at bar 54 in *Reigen* is very like the 'death' motive first heard in Marie's aria in *Wozzeck* for example. So is the drowning music in the opera like the music from bar 162 in the *Marsch*. The waltz and the music at bar 50 in *Reigen*, is Wozzeckian in the manner of the second act's Tavern Scene, and the trill music with which *Reigen* ends is like the famous orchestra trill at the end of the first act of *Wozzeck*. The violin solo at bar 168 in the *Marsch* is an adumbration of the music of the last pages of *Wozzeck*, and the rhythmic polyphony of the motive at bar 75 in the same piece is like a quotation from the opera. There are forecasts of the *Kammerkonzert*, too, for instance, in the *Nebenstimme* figure at bar 55 in *Reigen* and in the solo violin and wind music thereafter. And, each of *Lulu*'s three acts concludes with the same rhythm of chords employed near the end of *Reigen*.

Mahler dominates rather too much of the *Marsch* but even that piece is saved by a superb (un-Mahler-like) ending, that is – I hope I may be forgiven for pointing out – dramatically not unlike the ending of *Petroushka*: climax followed by quiet, then a few broken phrases in solo instruments, then the final protest of trumpets; the last bar in the trumpets is one of the finest things Berg ever did. *The Three Pieces for Orchestra* must be considered as a whole. They are a dramatic whole and all three of them are related thematically (the superb return of the theme of the *Preludium* at bar 160 in the *Marsch*). The form of each individual piece is dramatic also. In my judgement the most perfect of these in conception and realization is the *Preludium*. The form rises and falls, and it is round and unrepeating. It begins and ends in percussion, and the first notes of the timpani are already thematic. Then flute and bassoon state the principal rhythmic motive in preparation for the alto trombone solo, one of the noblest sounds Berg or anyone else ever caused to be heard in an orchestra. Berg's orchestral imagination and orchestral skill is phenomenal, especially in creating orchestral blocks, by which I mean balancing the whole orchestra in several polyphonic planes. One of the most remarkable noises he ever imagined is at bar 89 in *Reigen*, but there are many other striking sonorous inventions, the tuba entrance at bar 110 in *Reigen*, for instance, and bar 49 of the *Preludium*, and bar 144 of the *Marsch*.

I have a photograph on my wall of Berg and Webern together dating from about the time of the composition of the *Three Pieces for Orchestra*. Berg is tall, loose-set, almost too beautiful; his look is outward. Webern is short, hard-set, myopic, down-looking. Berg reveals an image of himself in his flowing 'artist's' cravat; Webern wears peasant-type shoes, and they are muddy – which to me reveals something profound. As I look at this photograph I cannot help remembering that so few years after it was taken both men died premature and tragic deaths after years of poverty, musical neglect, and, finally, musical banishment in their own country. I see Webern who in his last months frequented the churchyard at Mittersill where he was later buried, standing there in the quiet looking to the mountains – according to his daughter; and Berg in his last months suspecting that his illness might be fatal. I compare the fate of these men who heeded no claim of the world and who made music by which our half-century will be remembered, compare it with the 'careers' of conductors, pianists, violinists, vain excrescences all. Then this photograph of two great musicians, two pure-in-spirit, *herrliche Menschen*, restores my sense of justice at the deepest level.

*

R.C. Did you know Bartók personally?

I.S. I met him at least twice in my life, once in London, in the nineteen-twenties and later in New York in the early forties, but I had no opportunity to approach him closer either time. I knew the most important musician he was, I had heard wonders about the sensitivity of his ear, and I bowed deeply to his religiosity. However, I never could share his lifelong gusto for his native folklore. This devotion was certainly real and touching, but I couldn't help regretting it in the great musician. His death in circumstances of actual need has always impressed me as one of the tragedies of our society.

R.C. Do you still feel as you once did about the late Verdi (in the *Poetics of Music*)?

I.S. No. In fact, I am struck by the force, especially in *Falstaff*, with which he resisted Wagnerism, resisted or kept away from what had seized the advanced musical world. The presentation of musical monologues seems to me more original in *Falstaff* than in *Otello*. Original also are the instrumentation, harmony, and part-writing, yet none of these has left any element of the sort that could create a school — so different is Verdi's originality from Wagner's. Verdi's gift is pure; but even more remarkable than the gift itself is the strength with which he developed it from *Rigoletto* to *Falstaff*, to name the two operas I love best.

R.C. Do you now admit any of the operas of Richard Strauss?

I.S. I would like to admit all Strauss operas to whichever purgatory punishes triumphant banality. Their musical substance is cheap and poor; it cannot interest a musician today. That now so ascendant *Ariadne*? I cannot bear Strauss's six-four chords: *Ariadne* makes me want to scream. Strauss himself? I had the opportunity to observe him closely during Diaghilev's production of his *Legend of Joseph*, more closely than at any other time. He conducted the *première* of that work and spent some time in Paris during the preparation. He never wanted to speak German with me, though my German was better than his French. He was very tall, bald, energetic, a picture of the *bourgeois allemand*. I watched him at rehearsals and I admired the way he conducted. His manner to the orchestra was not admirable, however, and the musicians heartily detested him; but every corrective remark he made was exact: his ears and his musicianship were impregnable. At that time his music reminded me of Böcklin and Stuck, and the other painters of what we then called the German Green Horrors. I am glad that young musicians today have come to appreciate the lyric gift in the songs of the composer Strauss despised, and who is more significant in our music than he is: Gustav Mahler. My low esteem for Strauss's operas is somewhat compensated by my admiration for von Hofmannsthal. I knew this fine poet and librettist well, saw him often in Paris, and, I believe, for the last time at the Berlin *première* of my *Oedipus Rex* (where Albert Einstein also came to greet me). Hofmannsthal was a man of enormous culture and very elegant charm. I have read him recently, last year before travelling to Hosios Loukas, his essay on that extraordinary place, and was pleased to think him still good. His *Notebooks* (1922) are one of my most treasured books.

R.C. Are you interested in the current revival of eighteenth-century Italian masters?

I.S. Not very. Vivaldi is greatly over-rated – a dull fellow who could compose the same form so many times over. And, in spite of my predisposition in favour of Galuppi and Marcello (created more by Vernon Lee's *Studies of the Eighteenth Century in Italy* than by their music), they are poor composers. As for Cimarosa, I always expect him to abandon his four-times-four and turn into Mozart, and when he doesn't I am more exasperated than I should be if there had never been a Mozart. Caldara I respect largely because Mozart copied seven of his canons; I do not know much of his music. Pergolesi? *Pulcinella* is the only work of 'his' I like. Scarlatti is a different matter but even he varied the form so little. Living part of the last two years in Venice I have been exposed to an amount of this music. The Goldoni anniversary was an occasion to perform many Goldoni-libretto operas. I always regret I cannot fully appreciate Goldoni, with or without music – I do not understand his language – but Goldoni interests me more than his musicians. In the Teatro La Fenice or the Chiostro Verde of S. Giorgio, however, one likes everything a little bit more than one might elsewhere.

The 'Venetian' music I would like to revive is by Monteverdi and the Gabrielis, by Cipriano and Willaert, and so many others – why even the great Obrecht was 'Venetian' at one time – of that so much richer and so much closer-to-us period. True, I heard a Giovanni Gabrieli-Giovanni Croce concert there last year but almost nothing of the sense of their music remained. The tempi were wrong, the ornamentation didn't exist or was wrong when it did, the style and sentiment were ahead of the period by three and a half centuries, and the orchestra was eighteenth-century. When will musicians learn that the performance point of Gabrieli's music is rhythmic not harmonic? When will they stop trying to make mass choral effects out of simple harmonic changes and bring out, articulate, those marvellous rhythmic inventions? Gabrieli is rhythmic polyphony.

DYLAN THOMAS

R.C. What was the subject of the 'opera' you had planned to write with Dylan Thomas?

I.S. I don't think you can say that the project ever got as far as having a subject, but Dylan had a very beautiful idea.

I first heard of Dylan Thomas from Auden, in New York, in February or March of 1950. Coming late to an appointment one day Auden excused himself saying he had been busy helping to extricate an English poet from some sort of difficulty. He told me about Dylan Thomas. I read him after that, and in Urbana in the winter of 1950 my wife went to hear him read. Two years later, in January 1952, the

English film producer, Michael Powell, came to see me in Hollywood with a project that I found very attractive. Powell proposed to make a short film, a kind of masque, of a scene from the Odyssey; it would require two or three arias as well as pieces of pure instrumental music and recitations of pure poetry. Powell said that Thomas had agreed to write the verse; he asked me to compose the music. Alas, there was no money. Where were the angels, even the Broadway kind, and why are the world's commissions, grants, funds, foundations never available to Dylan Thomases? I regret that this project was not realized. *The Doctor and the Devils* proves, I think, that Dylan's talent could have created the new medium.

Then in May 1953 Boston University proposed to commission me to write an opera with Dylan. I was in Boston at the time and Dylan who was in New York or New Haven came to see me. As soon as I saw him I knew that the only thing to do was to love him. He was nervous, however, chain smoking the whole time, and he complained of severe gout pains . . . 'but I prefer the gout to the cure; I'm not going to let a doctor shove a bayonet into me twice a week'.

His face and skin had the colour and swelling of too much drinking. He was a shorter man than I expected from his portraits, not more than five feet five or six, with a large protuberant behind and belly. His nose was a red bulb and his eyes were glazed. He drank a glass of whisky with me which made him more at ease, though he kept worrying about his wife, saying he had to hurry home to Wales 'or it would be too late'. He talked to me about the *Rake's Progress*. He had heard the first broadcast of it from Venice. He knew the libretto well, and he admired it: 'Auden is the most skilful of us all.' I don't know how much he knew about music, but he talked about the operas he knew and liked, and about what he wanted to do. 'His' opera was to be about the rediscovery of our planet following an atomic misadventure. There would be a re-creation of language, only the new one would have no abstractions; there would be only people, objects, and words. He promised to avoid poetic indulgences: 'No conceits, I'll knock them all on the head.' He talked to me about Yeats who he said was almost the greatest lyric poet since Shakespeare, and quoted from memory the poem with the refrain 'Daybreak and a candle-end'. He agreed to come to me in Hollywood as soon as he could. Returning there I had a room built for him, an extension from our dining-room, as we have no guest room. I received two letters from him. I wrote him October 25th in New York and asked him for word of his arrival plans in Hollywood. I expected a telegram from him announcing the hour of his aeroplane. On November 9th the telegram came. It said he was dead. All I could do was cry.

LETTERS FROM DYLAN THOMAS

I   *The Boat House, Laugharne,*
Carmarthenshire, Wales.
16 June 1953

Dear Mr Stravinsky,

I was so very glad to meet you for a little time, in Boston; and you and Mrs Stravinsky couldn't have been kinder to me. I hope you get well very soon.

I haven't heard anything yet from Sarah Caldwell,* but I've been thinking a lot about the opera and have a number of ideas – good, bad, and chaotic. As soon as I can get something down on paper, I should, if I may, love to send it to you. I broke my arm just before leaving New York the week before last, and can't write properly yet. It was only a little break, they tell me, but it cracked like a gun.

* Of Boston University.

I should very much like – if you think you would still like me to work with you; and I'd be enormously honoured and excited to do that – to come to California in late September or early October. Would that be convenient? I hope so. And by that time, I hope too, to have some clearer ideas about a libretto.

Thank you again. And please give my regards to your wife and to Mr Craft.

Yours sincerely,

DYLAN THOMAS

2

The Boat House, Laugharne,
Carmarthenshire, Wales
22 September 1953

Dear Igor Stravinsky,

Thank you very very much for your two extremely nice letters, and for showing me the letter you had written to Mr Choate of Boston University. I would have written again long before this, but I kept on waiting until I knew for certain when I would be able to come to the States; and the lecture agent there in New York, who makes my coming across possible, has been terribly slow in arranging things. I heard from him only this week. Now it is certain that I shall be in New York on the 16th of October; and I'll have to stay there, giving some poetry-readings and taking part in a couple of performances of a small play of mine, until the end of October. I should like then, if I may, to come straight to California to be with you and to get down together, to the first stage of our work. (I'm sure I needn't tell you how excited I am to be able to write down that word 'our'. It's wonderful to think of.)

One of my chief troubles is, of course, money. I haven't any of my own, and most of the little I make seems to go to schools for my children, who will persist in getting older all the time. The man who's arranged my readings in October, at a few Eastern Universities and at the Poetry Center, New York, is paying my expenses to and from New York. But from there to California I will have to pay my own way on what I can make out of these readings. I do hope it will work out all right. Maybe I'll be able to give a few other readings or rantings, in California to help pay expenses. (I'd relied on drawing my travelling expenses, etc., from the original Boston University Commission.) I want to bring my wife, Caitlin, with me, and she thinks she can stay with a friend in San Francisco while I am working with you in Hollywood. Anyway, I'll have to work these things out the best I can, and I mustn't bother you with them now. Money for California will come somehow, I'll pray for ravens to drop some in the desert. The *main* thing, I know, is for me to get to you as soon as possible, so that we can begin – well, so that we can *begin*, whatever it will turn out to be. I've been thinking an awful lot about it.

I was so sorry to hear that you had been laid up for so long; I hope you're really well again by this time. My arm's fine now and quite as weak as the other one.

If you don't write to me at Wales before I leave, about October 7th, then my American address will be: c/o J. M. Brinnin, Poetry Center, YM-YWHA, 1395 Lexington Avenue, New York, 28. But anyway I'll write again as soon as I reach there.

I'm looking forward enormously to meeting you again, and to working with you. And I *promise* not to tell anyone about it – (though it's very hard not to).

Most sincerely,

DYLAN THOMAS

About My Life and Times
And Other Arts

R.C. I once heard you describe your childhood glimpses of the Tsar Alexander III.

I.S. I saw the Tsar many times while walking with my brothers and governess along the quays of St Petersburg's Moyka River or by the adjacent canals. The Tsar was a very large man. He occupied the entire seat of a droshky driven by a troika coachman as big and obese as himself. The coachman wore a dark blue uniform, the chest of which was covered with medals. He was seated in front of the Tsar, but elevated on the driver's seat where his enormous behind, like a gigantic pumpkin, was only a few inches from the Tsar's face. The Tsar had to answer greetings from people in the street by raising his right hand towards his temple. As he was recognized by everybody he was obliged to do this almost without interruption. His appearances gave me great pleasure and I eagerly anticipated them. We removed our hats and received the Tsar's acknowledging gesture, feeling very important indeed.

I also saw the same Tsar in an unforgettable pageant, a parade that passed our street on its way to the Imperial Mariinsky Theatre. It honoured the Shah of Persia and was the climax of an important state visit. We were given places in the first-floor window of our hairdresser's. The most brilliant procession of all kinds of cavalry passed by, imperial guards, coaches with grand dukes, ministers, generals. I remember a long, forest-like noise, the 'hurrah' of the crowds in the streets, coming in crescendo waves closer and closer with the approaching isolated car of the Tsar and the Shah.

R.C. Your Father and Dostoyevsky were friends. I suppose you as a child heard a great deal about Dostoyevsky?

I.S. Dostoyevsky became in my mind the symbol of the artist continually in need of money. My mother talked about him in this way; she said he was always grubbing. He gave readings from his own works and these were supported by my parents, who complained, however, that they were intolerably boring. Dostoyevsky liked music and often went to concerts with my father.

Incidently, I still consider Dostoyevsky to be the greatest Russian after Pushkin. Now, when one is supposed to reveal so much of oneself by one's choice of Freud or Jung, Stravinsky or Schoenberg, Dostoyevsky or Tolstoy, I am a Dostoyevskyan.

R.C. I have heard you say you saw Ibsen 'plain'.

I.S. In May 1905, shortly after the separation of Norway and Sweden, I and my younger brother, Goury, went on a holiday to Scandinavia where we stayed for about a month. We sailed from St Petersburg to Kronstadt and Helsingfors, staying in the latter city for a few days with my uncle, who was the civil governor of Finland. We then sailed to Stockholm, stopping long enough to hear a performance of the *Marriage of Figaro*, and through the beautiful Swedish lake canals to Göteborg, where we changed boats for Copenhagen and Oslo. It was delicious spring weather in Oslo, cold but pleasant. One day it seemed as if the whole population was in the streets. We were riding in a droshky and the friend who was with us told me to look at a smallish man on the sidewalk to our right. It was Henrik Ibsen. He wore a top hat and his hair was white. He was walking with his hands folded behind his back. Some things one sees never leave the eyes, never move into the back part of the mind. So Ibsen is in my eyes.

R.C. You were a friend of d'Annunzio's at one time, weren't you?

I.S. I saw rather a lot of him just before the 1914 war, but Diaghilev had known him before me; he was a great enthusiast of our Russian Ballet. I met him for the first time in Paris at Mme Golubev's, a Russian lady of the Mme Récamier school – throughout one's entire audience she would remain on a divan with her elbow raised and her head propped on her hand. One day, d'Annunzio entered her *salon*, a small man, brisk and natty, very perfumed and very bald (Harold Nicolson's likening his head to an egg, in *Some People*, is an exact comparison). He was a brilliant, fast, and very amusing talker, so unlike the 'talk' in his books. I remember that he was very excited about my opera *The Nightingale*; when after its *première* the French press had generally attacked it he wrote an article in its defence, an article I wish I still had. I saw him many times after that. He came to my apartment in Paris, he came to performances of the Ballet and to concerts of mine in France and Italy. Then, suddenly, it was discovered that his execrable taste in literature went together with Mussolini's execrable taste in everything else. He was no longer a 'character' and no longer amusing. But whether or not he survives as a readable author, his influence does still survive: the interiors of many Italian homes still follow descriptions in his novels.

On a recent visit to Asolo, to see the composer Malipiero, I was strongly reminded of d'Annunzio. Malipiero has a most extraordinary and not entirely un-d'Annunzian house, a fine Venetian building on a hillside. One enters under a Latin inscription and plunges into darkest night. The dark is in deference to pairs of owls who, from covered cages in obscure corners, hoot the two notes, in tune with Malipiero's piano after he plays them. There is evidence in the garden of affection for other of God's feathered creatures: chickens have been buried in marked graves; Malipiero's chickens die of old age.

R.C. You knew Rodin, didn't you?

I.S. I made his acquaintance in the Grand Hotel in Rome shortly after the beginning of the First World War. Diaghilev had organized a benefit concert there in which I conducted the Suite from *Petroushka*. I confess I was more interested in him because of his fame than because of his art for I did not share the enthusiasm of his numerous and serious admirers. I met him again, some time later, at one of our ballet perform-ances in Paris. He greeted me kindly, as though I were an old acquaintance, and at that moment I remembered the impression his fingers had made on me at our first hand-shaking. They were soft, quite the contrary of what I had expected, and they did not seem to belong to a male hand, especially not to a sculptor's hand. He had a long white beard that reached down to the navel of his long, buttoned-up surtout, and white hair covered his entire face. He sat reading a Ballet Russe programme through a pince-nez while people waited impatiently for the great old artist to stand up as they passed in his row – not knowing it was he. It has been said that Rodin drew a sketch of me. To the best of my knowledge that is not so. Perhaps the author of that information was confusing him with Bonnard who did in fact make a fine ink portrait of me in 1913 – lost, unfor-tunately, with all of my belongings, in our estate in Russia.

R.C. Wasn't there also a question of Modigliani doing a portrait of you?

I.S. Yes. I don't remember the circumstances very clearly, but I visited him in company with Leon Bakst in 1912 or 1913 because either he or I or Diaghilev had conceived the project of his doing a portrait. I don't know why it wasn't realized, whether Modigliani was ill, as he so often was, or whether I was called away with the Ballet. At that time I had an immense admiration for him.*

R.C. One more 'painter' question. I once heard you describe your meeting Claude Monet.

I.S. I don't know where Diaghilev found the old man or how he managed to get him into a *loge* at one of our Ballet Russe spectacles, but I saw him there and came to *serrer la main*. It was after the war, in 1922 or 1923, I think, and of course no one would believe it *was* Claude Monet. He wore a white beard and was nearly blind. I know now what I wouldn't have believed then, that he was painting his greatest pictures at the time, those huge, almost abstract canvases of pure colour and light (ignored until recently; I believe they are in the Orangeries, but a very beautiful *Water Lilies*, which now looks as good as any art of the period, I go to see in the Museum of Modern Art every time I am in New York†). Old Monet, hoary and near blind, couldn't have impressed me more if he had been Homer himself.

R.C. You were with Mayakovsky very often on his famous Paris trip in 1922?

I.S. Yes, but he was a closer friend to Prokofiev than to me. I remember him as a somewhat burly youth – he was twenty-

---

*A portrait of me by Modigliani has been discovered since these remarks were written. It is a large picture in grey, black, and ivory oils, undated but similar in period style to the Max Jacob and Cocteau portraits. It has been certified by such experts as Zborovsky, Schoeller, and Georges Guillaume and by a statement from Picasso: '*Je pense que ce tableau est un portrait de Stravinsky. Cannes, le 18.9.57 (signé) Picasso.*' Modigliani must have done it from memory. I regret to admit that it does resemble me.

† Alas, since I wrote this, the *Water Lilies* has been destroyed by fire.

eight or twenty-nine at the time – who drank more than he should have and who was deplorably dirty, like many of the poets I have known. Sometimes I am reminded of him when I see a photograph of Gromyko, though I don't know just where the resemblance is. I considered him a good poet and I admired and still do admire his verses. However, he insisted on talking to me about music, and his understanding of that art was wholly imaginary. He spoke no French, and therefore with him I was always obliged to be a translator. I remember one such occasion when I was between him and Cocteau. Curiously, I found the French for everything Mayakovsky said very easily, but not the Russian for Cocteau's remarks. His suicide a few years later was the first of the shocks that were to come regularly from Russia thereafter.

R.C. Raymond Radiguet was often in your company the year before his death. How do you remember him?

I.S. I saw him almost every day of 1922 that I spent in Paris. He was a silent youth with a serene, rather childlike look, but with something of the young bull in him, too. He was of medium build, handsome, rather pederastically so but without pederastic manners. The first time I saw him he was with Cocteau. I was sitting with Diaghilev in a café when they appeared.

    S.D. *'Qu'est ce que c'est, ce nouveau truc?'*

    I.S. *'Tu l'envies?'*

He immediately struck me as a gifted individual and he also had the other intelligence, the *machine à penser* kind. His opinions were immediate and they were his, whereas the opinions of those around him were too often 'composed'. I still think his poems very good indeed, and the two novels hardly less good. The latter were autobiographical, of course, and everyone in Paris knew who was who. But I remember that when Radiguet died (at twenty) even the man effigied as the Comte d'Orgel in the book was greatly grieved.

R.C. While you are reminiscing, would you describe your last meeting with Proust?

I.S. After the *premières* of *Mavra* and *Renard* in June 1922, I went to a party given by a friend of mine, Princess Violette Murat. Marcel Proust was there also. Most of the people came to that party from my *première* at the Grand Opera, but Proust came directly from his bed, getting up as usual very late in the evening. He was a pale man, elegantly and Frenchly dressed, wearing gloves and carrying a cane. I talked to him about music and he expressed much enthusiasm for the late Beethoven quartets — enthusiasm I would have shared were it not a commonplace among the intellectuals of that time and not a musical judgement but a literary pose.

R.C. Klee, Kandinsky, and Busoni attended the 1923 Weimar performance of *L'Histoire du soldat*. Do you remember anything about these gentlemen at the time?

I.S. I was only a very short time at Weimar — just long enough for the rehearsals and the performance of *L'Histoire*, conducted by Hermann Scherchen. Of the three artists you mention, I met only Ferruccio Busoni, who was sitting at this performance in the same box as I was. He had the noblest, most beautiful head I have ever seen and I watched him as much as the stage. He seemed to be very much touched by the work. But whether it was the play of Ramuz, my music, or the whole thing, was not easy to determine, especially since I knew that I was his *bête noire* in music. Now, thirty-five years later, I have a great admiration for his vision, for his literary talent, and for at least one of his works, *Doktor Faust*. Unfortunately, I did not meet Paul Klee there or later in my life.* I did have the good fortune to know Kandinsky in Paris in the nineteen-thirties,

*Klee's portrait drawing of me must have been done from memory.

and I will always remember him as an aristocrat, *un homme de choix*.

R.C. I often hear you speak of your admiration for Ortega y Gasset. Did you know him well?

I.S. I saw him only once, in Madrid, in March 1955, but I felt I knew him from his work long before that. That night in Madrid he came to my hotel with Mme La Marquise de Slauzol, and we drank a bottle of whisky together and were very gay. He was charming and very kind. I have often thought since that he must have been aware that he had cancer; a few months later he was dead. He was not tall, but I remember him as a large man because of his great head. His bust reminded me of a Roman statesman or philosopher and I tried all evening to recall just which Roman he really was. He spoke vivid r-rolling French in a strong, slightly husky voice. Everything he said was vivid. The Tagus at Toledo was 'arteriosclerotic'; Cordoba was 'a rose bush but with the flowers in the ground and the roots in the air'. The art of the Portuguese 'is their memory of China, of pagodas'. Of his philosopher contemporaries, he spoke reverently of Scheler, of Husserl, of his master Cohen, of Heidegger. As for the Wittgenstein school: 'Philosophy calling itself Logical Positivism now claims to be a science, but this is only a brief attack of modesty.' He talked about Spain (I regret his *Castles in Castile* does not exist in English) and laughed at tourists' sentiments 'for the poor people living in caves' which he said they do not do out of poverty but because it is a very ancient tradition. He was sympathetic and intelligent about the United States when we talked of them – the unique European 'intellectual' I encountered that trip who knew something about them beyond what he had read in Melville and the magazines. He proudly showed me a photograph, which he took from his wallet, of himself and Gary Cooper taken in Aspen in 1949. He said that Thornton

103

Wilder had translated for him there but that his audiences had understood before the translations came, 'because of my extravagant gestures'.

R.C. How did Giacometti come to make his drawings of you?

I.S. He had done five or six designs from photographs before he saw me, and he didn't like them. Then, sitting a few feet from me, he did a whole series, working very fast with only a few minutes of actual drawing for each one. He says that in sculpture also he accomplishes the final product very quickly but does the sometimes hundreds of discarded preparatory ones slowly over long periods of time. He drew with a very hard lead, smudging the lines with erasers from time to time. He was forever mumbling: '*Non . . . impossible . . . je ne peux pas . . . une tête violente . . . je n'ai pas de talent . . . je ne peux pas. . . .*' He surprised me the first time he came for I expected a 'Giacometti' tall and thin. He said he had just escaped from an automobile manufacturer who had been offering him a considerable sum to say that automobiles and sculptures are the same things, i.e., beautiful objects. In fact, Giacometti's almost favourite topic was the difference between a sculpture and an object. 'Men in the street walking in different directions are not objects in space.' 'Sculpture,' he said, 'is a *matière* transformed into expression, expression in which nature counts for less than style.' 'Sculpture is expression in space, which means that it can never be complete; to be complete is to be static.' 'All busts are ridiculous; the whole body is the only subject for sculpture.'

His conversation about sculptors was sometimes surprising. He liked Pigalle, thought him the greatest sculptor of the *dix-huitième*, especially in the memorial of the Maréchal de Saxe at Strasbourg. He much preferred Pigalle's rejected 'nude Voltaire' to Houdon's famous official Voltaire 'because of its greater nervousness'. For him Canova was not really a sculptor, while Rodin was 'the last great sculptor and in the same line as Donatello (not the Rodin of the Balzac or the Burghers, of course)'. Brancusi wasn't a sculptor at all, he said, but a 'maker of objects'. I like Giacometti's work – I have one of those full-of-sculptural-space paintings of his on my dining-room wall – and I have an affection for himself, for his own 'nervousness'. I like the character of him in a story he told me. He had a great admiration for Klee and one time in the late nineteen-thirties, when both artists were living in Switzerland, he at last determined to go and call on him. He walked from the station to what he thought was Klee's house – it was on a mountainside some distance from the town – but when he arrived there he discovered that Klee actually lived farther up the mountain. 'I lost all courage and didn't go – I had just enough courage to get that far.'

PAINTERS OF THE RUSSIAN BALLET

R.C. Do you remember Balla's set for your *Fireworks*?

I.S. Vaguely, but I couldn't have described it even at the time (Rome, 1917) as anything more than a few splashes of paint on an otherwise empty backcloth. I do remember that it baffled the audience, however, and that when Balla came out to bow there was no applause: the public didn't know who he was, what he had done, why he should be bowing. Balla then reached in his pocket and squeezed a device that made his papillon necktie do tricks. This sent Diaghilev and me – we were in a box – into uncontrollable laughter, but the audience remained dumb.

Balla was always amusing and always likeable and some of the drollest hours of my life were spent in his and his fellow Futurists' company. The idea of doing a Futurist ballet was Diaghilev's but we decided together on my *Fireworks* music: it was 'Modern' enough and only four minutes long. Balla had impressed us as a gifted painter and we asked him to design a set. I made fast friends with him after that, visiting him often in his apartment in Rome. He lived near the zoo, so near in fact that his balcony overhung a large cage. One heard animal noises in his rooms as one hears street noises in a New York hotel room.

Futurism's headquarters were in Milan, however, and it was there that my meetings with Balla, and also Boccioni, Russolo the noise-maker, Carra and Marinetti took place. Milan was to Switzerland as Hollywood is to these hills except that it was easier then to take the train and descend to the Italian city for an evening performance than it is now to drive to downtown Los Angeles. And in wartime Milan my few Swiss francs made me feel agreeably rich.

On one of my Milanese visits Marinetti and Russolo, a genial, quiet man but with wild hair and beard, and Pratella, another noisemaker, put me through a demonstration of their 'Futurist Music'. Five phonographs standing on five tables in a large and otherwise empty room emitted digestive noises, static, etc., remarkably like the *musique concrète* of seven or eight years ago (so perhaps they were futurist after all; or perhaps Futurisms aren't progressive enough). I pretended to be enthusiastic and told them that sets of five phonographs with such music, mass produced, would surely sell like Steinway Grand Pianos.

Some years after this demonstration Marinetti invented what he called 'discreet noises', noises to be associated with objects. I remember one such sound (to be truthful, it wasn't at all discreet) and the object it accompanied, a substance that looked like velvet but had the roughest surface I have ever touched. Balla must have participated in the 'noise' movement, too, for he once gave me an Easter present, a papiermâché Pascha cake that sighed very peculiarly when opened.

The most memorable event in all my years of friendship with the Futurists was a performance we saw together at the Milan puppet theatre of *The Chinese Pirates*, a 'drama in three acts'. It was in fact one of the most impressive theatrical experiences of my life. The theatre itself was puppet-sized. An invisible orchestra, clarinet, piano, violin, bass, played an overture and bits of incidental music. There were tiny windows on either side of the tiny stage. In the last act we heard singing and were terrified to see that it came from giants standing behind these windows; they were normal-statured human singers, of course, but we were accustomed to the puppet scale.

The Futurists were absurd, but sympathetically so, and they were infinitely less pretentious than some of the later movements that borrowed from them – than Surrealism, for instance, which had more substance; unlike the Surrealists they were able to laugh at their own pose of artist-contra-Gentiles. Marinetti himself was a balalaika – a chatterbox – but he was also the kindest of men, I regret that he seemed to me the least gifted of the whole group – compared to Boccioni, Balla, and Carra, who were all able painters. The Futurists were not the aeroplanes they wanted to be but they were at any rate a pack of very nice, noisy Vespas.

R.C. Did you choose Nicolas Roerich to do the *Sacre du printemps* décors?

I.S. Yes. I had admired his sets for *Prince Igor* and imagined he might do something similar for the *Sacre*; above all, I knew he would not overload. Diaghilev agreed with me and accordingly, in the summer of 1912, I met Roerich in Smolensk and worked with him there in the country house of the Princess Tenischev, a patroness and liberal who had helped Diaghilev.

I still have a good opinion of Roerich's *Le Sacre*. He had

designed a backdrop of steppes and sky, the *Hic Sunt Leones* country of old mapmakers' imaginations. The row of twelve blonde, square-shouldered girls against this landscape made a very striking tableau. And Roerich's costumes were said to have been historically exact as well as scenically satisfying.

I met Roerich, a blond-bearded, Kalmuck-eyed, pug-nosed man, in 1904. His wife was a relative of Mitusov's, my friend and co-librettist of the *Nightingale*, and I often saw the Roerichs at Mitusov's St Petersburg house. Roerich claimed descent from Rurik, the Russo-Scandinavian Ur-Prince. Whether or not this was true (he looked Scandinavian, but one can't say such things any more), he was certainly a *seigneur*. I became quite fond of him in those early years, though not of his painting, which was a kind of advanced Puvis de Chavannes. I was not surprised during the last war to hear of his secret activities and of his curious connexion with Vice-President Wallace in Tibet; he looked as though he ought to have been either a mystic or a spy. Roerich came to Paris for *Le Sacre*, but he received very little attention and, after the *première*, disappeared, slighted I think, back to Russia. I never saw him again.

R.C. Was Henri Matisse your choice of painter for the *Chant du rossignol* sets?

I.S. No, his collaboration was Diaghilev's idea entirely. In fact, I opposed it, but too directly (Amiel says: 'Every direct resistance ends in disaster'). The production, and especially Matisse's part in it, were failures. Diaghilev hoped Matisse would do something very Chinese and charming. All he did do, however, was to copy the China of the shops in the rue de la Boëtie. Matisse designed not merely the sets, as you say, but also the costumes and curtain.

Matisse's art has never attracted me, but at the time of the *Chant du rossignol* I saw him often and liked him personally.

I remember an afternoon together with him in the Louvre. He was never a rousing conversationalist, but he stopped in front of a Rembrandt and started to talk excitedly about it. At one point he took a white handkerchief from his pocket: 'Which is white, this handkerchief or the white in that picture? Even the absence of colour does not exist, but only "white" or each and every white.'

Our Matisse collaboration made Picasso very angry: 'Matisse! What is a Matisse? A balcony with a big red flower-pot falling all over it.'

R.C. Do you remember Golovine's décors for the first *Firebird*?

I.S. All I remember about them is that the costumes pleased me at the time. The curtain was the curtain of the Opéra. I do not remember how many sets Golovine did, but I am certain that if I were transported back to that *Firebird* of 1910 I would find them very opulent indeed.

Golovine was several years my senior, and he was not our first choice. Diaghilev wanted Vroubel, the most talented of all the Russian painters of that epoch, but Vroubel was dying or going mad. We also considered Benois but Diaghilev preferred Golovine for his realization of the fantastic scenes in *Russlan*; and Golovine's orientalism conformed to the ideals of Diaghilev's own magazine, *Mir Isskustva*, rather than to the academic orientalism then so popular. As an easel painter Golovine was a kind of Russian pointillist.

I do not remember Golovine at the first *Firebird* performance. Diaghilev probably did not have money enough to pay his trip (I myself received 1,000 roubles, £100, for the commission and the expenses of all the travel and stay in Paris). The first *Firebird*! I stood in the dark of the Opéra through eight orchestra rehearsals conducted by Pierné. The stage and the whole theatre glittered at the *première* and that is all I remember.

R.C. How do you regard Leon Bakst?

I.S. No one could describe him as concisely as Cocteau has done in his caricature. We were friends from our first meeting in St Petersburg, in 1909, though our conversation was largely Bakst's accounts of his exploits in the conquest of women, and my incredulity: 'Now Lev ... you couldn't have done all that.' Bakst wore elegant hats, canes, spats, etc., but I think these were meant to detract from his Venetian comedy-mask nose. Like other dandies, Bakst was sensitive – and privately mysterious. Roerich told me that 'Bakst' was a Jewish word meaning 'little umbrella'. Roerich said he discovered this one day in Minsk, when he was caught in a thunder-shower and heard people sending their children home for 'Baksts', which then turned out to be what he said they were.

There was a question of Bakst designing *Mavra* for me, but a money quarrel resulted with Diaghilev. None of us was ever reconciled and I regretted it, especially when only three years later, aboard the *Paris* on my first trip to the United States, I saw the notice of his death in the ship's newspaper.

Bakst loved Greece and all things Greek. He travelled there with Serov (Serov was the conscience of our whole circle and a very important friend to me in my youth; even Diaghilev feared him) and published a book of travel diaries called *With Serov in Greece* (1922) that ought to have been put into English long ago.

I had seen Bakst's easel painting before I knew any of his theatrical work, but I could not admire it. In fact, it represented everything in Russia against which *Le Sacre du printemps* is the revolt. I consider Bakst's *Sheherazade* to be a masterpiece, however, perhaps the perfect achievement of the Russian Ballet from the scenic point of view. Costumes, sets, the curtain, were colourful in an indescribable way – we are so much poorer in these things now. I remember, too, that Picasso considered *Sheherazade* a masterpiece. In fact, it was the one production of the ballet he really did admire: '*Vous savez, c'est très spécialiste, mais admirablement fait.*'

R.C. And Benois?

I.S. I knew him before I knew Bakst. He was at that time the most cultivated Italophile I had ever met, and except for Eugene Berman he would be still: and Benois and Berman are very like in the fact of their Russian background, their Romantic theatre, their Italophilia. Benois knew more about music than any of the other painters, though of course the music he knew was nineteenth-century Italian opera. I think he liked my *Petroushka*, however, or at any rate, he wasn't calling it *Petroushka-ka* as many others of his generation were. But Benois was the conservative of the company and *Petroushka* was his exceptional work.

I collaborated with him in a small way before *Petroushka* with two orchestrations contributed to *Les Sylphides* (I doubt if I would like these arrangements today – I no longer care for that 'clarinet solo' kind of music). But though I was delighted with his work in *Les Sylphides* I wouldn't have chosen him to do *Petroushka* on the strength of it. My real friendship with him began in Rome in 1911 when I was finishing *Petroushka*. We stayed in the Albergo Italia near the Quattro Fontane and for two months were with each other every day.

Benois was very quickly up on his *amour propre*. The ballet's greatest success at that time was the *Spectre de la rose* with Nijinsky, and Benois was plainly jealous of Bakst's role in that success. Jealousy accounts for an incident that occurred the following year. Benois was painting the backdrop of Petroushka's cell when Bakst happened on the set, picked up a brush, and started to help. Benois fairly flew at him.

R.C. And was Michel Larionov your choice of painter for *Renard*?

I.S. Diaghilev suggested him first, but he became my choice also. As you know, I composed *Renard* for the Princess Edmonde de Polignac. In 1914 I was cut off from my Russian estate money and lived in Switzerland on a very small income. Diaghilev could pay me nothing in those war years so I accepted a commission of 2,500 Swiss francs from the Princess de Polignac. Diaghilev was furious with jealousy (but Diaghilev was always jealous; I think I am fair in saying that about him and I certainly knew him well enough to be able to say it now). For two years he would not mention *Renard* to me (which didn't prevent him from talking about it to others: 'Our Igor, always money, money, money, and for what? This *Renard* is some old scraps he found in his dresser drawer').

Diaghilev visited me in Ouchy in January or Feburary 1917 and I played *Les Noces* for him. He wept (it was very surprising to see this huge man weep), saying it had touched him more than anything he had ever heard, but he would not inquire about *Renard*, even though he knew I had completed it. And he knew also that the Princess Polignac had no theatre, that she had commissioned me only to help me, that she would give *Renard* to him to perform. (Some years later the Princess de Polignac gave an *avant-propos* piano performance of *Oedipus Rex* at her house and paid me 12,000 francs which I gave to Diaghilev to help finance the public performance.)

Larionov was a huge blond mujik of a man, even bigger than Diaghilev (Larionov, who had an uncontrollable temper, once knocked Diaghilev down). He made a vocation of laziness, like Oblomov, and we always believed that his wife, Goncharova, did his work for him. He was a talented painter, nevertheless, and I still like his *Renard* set and costumes. *Renard* was performed together with *Mavra*, as you know, and both works were preceded by a big orchestral ballet which made my small-scale pieces seem even smaller.

Renard was no huge success, but compared to it *Mavra* was even less of a 'hit'. *Mavra* was very ably designed by Survage, an unknown artist who had been commissioned after Diaghilev had quarrelled with Bakst. The *Mavra* failure annoyed Diaghilev. He was anxious to impress Otto Kahn, who attended the *première* in Diaghilev's box and who was to have brought the company to America. Otto Khan's only comment was: 'I liked it all, then "poop" it ends too quickly.' Diaghilev asked me to change the ending. I refused, of course, and he never forgave me.

Another 'ballet' painter I saw a lot of at this time was Derain. I liked his *parigot* talk, liked him more than his pictures, in fact, though there are charming small Derains. He was a man of large build – Balthus's portrait of him is a good resemblance – and a copious drinker. During the latter activity furniture was sometimes smashed, but I always found Derain very agreeable. I mediated for him in a quarrel with Diaghilev, who wanted to change something in *La Boutique fantasque*. In his later years Derain was a solitary figure and we no longer saw him at concerts or spectacles. My last meeting with him was an extraordinary coincidence. I was driving near Toulon and stopped to walk in a pine wood. I came upon someone standing before an easel, painting, and it turned out to be Derain.

*

Now that I have mentioned Derain I would also like to record my associations with some other artists, most of them associated with Diaghilev or the Ballet. I think, for example, of Alexis Jawlensky. Diaghilev had described him to me in St Petersburg days as a strong follower of the new Munich school. In spite of this he was a contributor to *Mir Isskustva*; I say 'in spite' because Diaghilev considered the Munich school to be the ultimate in 'Boche' bad taste. I did not meet Jawlensky in Russia but in Switzerland. At the beginning of the war I was living in Morges and he in St Prex, which is nearby. I sometimes walked with my children from our Morges house to his in St Prex. He was always hospitable, and his studio was a little island of Russian colour that delighted my children.

Max Liebermann was another friend, especially during the first period of our Ballet in Berlin. I made his acquaintance, together with Gerhardt Hauptmann's, after a performance of *Petroushka* and I saw him quite often thereafter. He was a celebrated wit. In a story then circulating, a portrait painter commissioned to do von Hindenburg complains to Liebermann of his inability to draw von Hindenburg's features, whereupon Liebermann exclaims: '*Ich kann den Alten in den Schnee pissen.*' As you know, it was Liebermann who nominated me to the Prussian Academy.

Jacques-Émile Blanche was another friend of my early Diaghilev years. He painted two portraits of me that are now in the Luxembourg. I remember sitting for him, and how he drew my head and features only after a great amount of modelling, while everything else, the body and the background, was added *in absentia*. This meant that one's legs might turn out too long and one's middle too capacious, or that one might find oneself promenading on the beach at Deauville, as I am made to do in one of my portraits. However, Blanche's faces were usually accurately characterized and that was the important thing. Blanche was a *fine mouche* for celebrities; he came to make my portrait almost the morning after the *première* of the *Firebird*.

Robert Delauney was another painter I saw very often at one time. He talked too much and too enthusiastically about 'modern art', but was otherwise quite likeable. He did a portrait of me too. I don't know what has become of it but it was certainly better than Albert Gleizes's cubist one, which is my moustache plus what-have-you. Delauney never did design a ballet for Diaghilev but he was often with him, and in Madrid, in 1921, we were all three constantly together.

Fernand Léger I knew throughout the Diaghilev period, but we were closer friends in the United States during the second war. I remember a French dinner we had prepared for him in our house in Hollywood in the dark early days of the war. It concluded with French Caporal cigarettes and Léger was so touched upon seeing these, he burst out crying. The Léger drawing of a parrot on our living-room wall was given to us by him at this time.

Pavel Tchelichev I met in 1922 in Berlin where I was awaiting my mother's arrival from the Soviet Union (she had been petitioning since the Revolution for permission to emigrate, had at last obtained it, but her boat was several times delayed). Tchelichev was talented and handsome and he was quick to understand the value of that combination in Diaghilev *ambience*. I was not attracted by his earliest 'Russian style' paintings but his sets for Nabokov's ballet *Ode* convinced me of his abilities. Later he made my *Balustrade* one of the most visually satisfying of all my ballets.

Marc Chagall I had heard of in Diaghilev days from Larionov who belonged to Chagall's circle of Russian painters, but I first met him in New York. My wife, Vera de Bosset, had arranged with him for a show of his *Aleko* designs and sketches in her Hollywood gallery, *La Boutique*. Accordingly, we called on him one day in his Riverside Drive apartment. He was in mourning for his wife and he hardly spoke without mentioning her. (I now remember that Lipnitsky the photographer was there and made several photographs of us together, but I have never seen them.) Two or three years later Chagall was asked to do stage settings and costumes for my *Renard*. I regret very much that he refused (saying, as I was told, that he wanted to do only 'a major work of Stravinsky's'). I still hope he will one day do *Renard* and *Les Noces*; no one could be more perfect for them.

Chagall's *Firebird* was a very flamboyant exhibition, though perhaps more successful in the painting than in the costumes. He made an ink portrait of me and presented it to me as a memento of our collaboration.

There were others too, like Marie Laurencin (though I couldn't like her *couleur de rose* painting; I like *rose*, of course, but not when I am *emmerdé* with it; and I had the same trouble with her *gris* after Cocteau said: '*Marie, tu as inventé les nuances de gris*'); Constantine Brancusi; Braque (who gave valuable advice to my painter son, Theodore); André Bauchant (a kind man; the idea that he should decorate my *Apollo* was entirely Diaghilev's, however, and his set for that ballet was very far from what I had in mind); Christian Bérard; and Georges Rouault (with whom my wife, Vera de Bosset, worked designing the ballet *Fils prodigue*).

R.C. You must have seen a great deal of José Maria Sert in the Diaghilev days.

I.S. Yes, but his wife Misia was much more a friend to me and, in truth, I could not help finding Sert slightly ridiculous. The Serts were among the first people I met in Paris when I arrived there in 1910 (though they were not yet legally 'Serts'). He knew a great lot of 'interesting people', especially 'interesting *rich* people', and he was very good at getting commissions from them. I believe that he became a 'painter of the Russian Ballet' chiefly because he knew Fürstner, Richard Strauss's publisher. Diaghilev wanted Strauss to compose a ballet, and the only way he could get at him was through Fürstner. Sert became the ambassador of the project and therefore its painter. The ballet was the *Legend of Joseph*, as you know. Sert's sets for it were overcrowded and the result was not one of Diaghilev's greatest successes.

Sert might have figured more permanently in the history of painting as a subject. A big, black-bearded man, *démodé*-distinguished, he would have made an excellent portrait subject for Manet. His manner was very grand and he played at being Spanish, but he had a sense of humour that somewhat redeemed these affectations. I remember asking him once how he intended to move one of his huge murals, and his answer: 'You turn a little valve and it deflates to one-hundredth the size.' We came to the U.S. on the *Normandie* together in the nineteen-thirties and the last time I saw him was in the U.S. Poor Sert, he wanted to be a painter but his painting, alas, is *quelconque*.

R.C. Have you any notion where Picasso's backdrop for *Pulcinella* might be?

I.S. It was in the dome of the Paris Opéra when I last heard, and completely faded save for the moon, whose yellow had been renewed, in part, by a cat. Diaghilev, I suppose, was in debt to the Director of the Opéra, and when our company withdrew after the *Pulcinella* performances the Picasso was kept there.

I have a vague recollection of meeting Picasso with Vollard at my friend Prince Argutinsky's about 1910, but I did not know him until 1917, when we were together in Rome. I immediately liked his flat, unenthusiastic manner of speaking, and his Spanish way of accenting each syllable; '*He ne suis pas musicien, he comprends rien dans la musique*,' all said as though he couldn't care less. It was the moment of the Russian Revolution, and we could no longer precede our ballet programmes with the Imperial Anthem. I orchestrated the 'Song of the Volga Boatmen' to replace it, and on the title page of my manuscript Picasso painted a red circle as a symbol of the Revolution.

Picasso drew my portrait at this same time (the first one; the arm-chair portrait was done in his rue de la Boëtie apartment, and the third one was conceived as a mutual gift from Picasso and myself to our friend Eugenia Errazuriz). It was in the Hotel de la Russie, near the Piazza del Popolo, where many of the ballet dancers were staying, including Picasso's future wife Olga (Olga, who had changed his social life; she had many new robes from Chanel to show, besides Picasso, and suddenly the great painter was to be seen at every cocktail party, theatre, and dinner). Picasso was always very generous in making gifts of his art. I have a dozen paintings or drawings given to me by him at various times including some beautiful ink designs of horses drawn on letter envelopes and a fine phallic circle-drawing for a cover of my *Ragtime*.

We journeyed to Naples together (Picasso's portrait of Massine was drawn in the train) and spent some weeks in close company there. We were both much impressed with the Commedia dell'Arte, which we saw in a crowded little room reeking of garlic. The Pulcinella was a great drunken lout whose every gesture, and probably every word if I had understood, was obscene. The only other incident of our Neapolitan holiday I can remember is that we were both arrested one night for urinating against a wall of the *Galleria*. I asked the policeman to take us across the street to the San Carlo Opera to find someone to vouch for us. The policeman granted our request. Then, as the three of us marched backstage he heard us being addressed as *maestri* and let us go.

Picasso's original *Pulcinella* was very different from the pure Commedia dell'Arte Diaghilev wanted. His first designs were for Offenbach-period costumes with side-whiskered faces instead of masks. When he showed them, Diaghilev was very brusque: 'Oh, this isn't it at all', and proceeded to tell Picasso how to do it. The evening concluded with Diaghilev actually throwing the drawings on the floor, stamping on them, and slamming the door as he left. The next day all of Diaghilev's charm was needed to reconcile the deeply insulted Picasso, but Diaghilev did succeed in getting him to do a Commedia dell'Arte *Pulcinella*. I might add that Diaghilev was equally against my *Pulcinella* music at first. He had expected a strict, mannered orchestration of something very sweet.

About Music Today

R.C. What do you mean when you say that critics are incompetent?

I.S. I mean that they are not even equipped to judge one's grammar. They do not see how a musical phrase is constructed, do not know how music is written; they are incompetent in the technique of the contemporary musical language. Critics misinform the public and delay comprehension. Because of critics many valuable things come too late. Also, how often we read criticisms of first performances of new music – in which the critic praises or blames (but usually praises) performance. Performances are of something; they do not exist in the abstract, apart from the music they purport to perform. How can the critic know whether a piece of music he does not know is well or ill performed?

R.C. What does 'genius' mean to you?

I.S. A 'pathetic' term strictly; or, in literature, a propaganda word used by people who do not deserve rational opposition. I detest it literarily and cannot read it in descriptive works without pain. If it doesn't already appear in the *Dictionnaire des idées reçues*, it should be put there with, as its automatic responses, 'Michelangelo' and 'Beethoven'.

R.C. What does 'sincerity' mean to you?

I.S. It is a *sine qua non* that at the same time guarantees nothing. Most artists are sincere anyway and most art is bad – though of course, some insincere art (sincerely insincere) is quite good. One's belief that one is sincere is not so dangerous, however, as one's conviction that one is right. We all feel we are right; but we felt the same way twenty years ago and to-day we know we weren't always right then.

R.C. Would you 'draw' your recent music? For example:

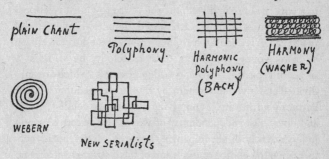

I.S. This is *my* music:

HARMONY, MELODY, RHYTHM

R.C. You have often remarked that the period of harmonic discovery is over, that harmony is no longer open to exploration and exploitation. Would you explain?

I.S. Harmony, considered as a doctrine dealing with chords and chord relations, has had a brilliant but short history. This history shows that chords gradually abandoned their direct function of harmonic guidance and began to seduce with the individual splendours of their harmonic effects. Today harmonic novelty is at an end. As a medium of musical construction, harmony offers no further resources in which to inquire and from which to seek profit. The contemporary ear requires a completely different approach to music. It is one of nature's ways that we often feel closer to distant generations than to the generation immediately preceding us. Therefore, the present generation's interests are directed towards music before the 'harmonic age'. Rhythm, rhythmic polyphony, melodic, or intervallic construction are the elements of musical building to be explored today. When I say that I still compose 'harmonically' I mean to use the word in a special sense and without reference to chord relations.

R.C. Isn't Busoni's famous 'attempted definition of melody' (1922) a fairly accurate prophecy of the melodic conception of many young composers today? Melody, he said, is 'a series of repeated rising and falling intervals, which are subdivided and given movement by rhythm; containing a latent harmony within itself and giving out a mood-feeling; it can and does exist independently of words as an expression and independently of accompanying parts as a form; in its performance the choice of pitch and of the instrument makes no difference to its essence'.

I.S. The last two points are the most remarkable coming from Busoni. The idea that the actual pitch of the note is not so important in an absolute sense has been supplanted, to my mind, by the idea that pitch matters only because of the interval. Today the composer does not think of notes in isolation but of notes in their intervallic position in the series, in their dynamic, their octave, and their timbre. Apart from the series notes are nothing; but in the series their recurrence, their pitch, their dynamic, their timbre, and their rhythmic relation determine form. The note functions only in the series. The form is serial, not only some or all of the musical elements that compose it. The individual note determines the form only as part of its group or order.

R.C. Has any new development in the domain of rhythm caught your attention?

I.S. The tempo controls – if tempo comes under the heading of rhythm – in the central movement of *Le Marteau sans maître* are an important innovation. In this movement the beat is accelerated or retarded to basic fast or slow metronome speeds with indications *en route* of exactly the speed one should be travelling. This amounts to controlled ritard- and accelerando. Used systematically, as in the Marteau, where you are never in a tempo but always going to one, these controls are able to effect a new and wonderfully supple kind of music.

The free-but-coordinated cadenzas in Stockhausen's *Zeitmasse* (I have not yet heard his *Gruppen* for three orchestras) are also a rhythmic innovation of great value.

In exploring the possibilities of variable metres young composers have contributed but little. In fact, I have seen no advance on the *Sacre du printemps*, if I may mention that work, in all the half-century since it was written.

R.C. Do you know that a whole school of *Klangfarbenmelodie* composers is flourishing at present?

I.S. Most of that is the merest stylistic imitation, of course, and nothing could be more ephemeral. But the German word needs definition; it has come to mean too many things. For example, I don't think the *melodie* part of it is good or useful applied to a work such as Webern's *Concerto*, and I am sure that in the same piece *farben* is less important than *klang*-design which isn't the same thing.

If by *Klangfarbenmelodie* you mean no more than a line of music which is divided among two or more instruments, that habit has already reached a *reductio ad absurdum*. Looking at a ridiculously difficult score recently – it was really the map of an idea that had begun not in musical composition but before it – I was reminded of a Russian band I knew in my childhood. This band was made up of twelve open, that is, valveless horns. Each horn had one note to play and together they could produce the chromatic scale. They would practise hours and hours in order to surmount the rhythmic problems presented by simple melodies. I do not see the difference between the idea of this band of hunting horns and the idea of some of the *Klangfarben* scores I have seen.

If a serious composer intends the lines of two or more instruments to produce one melodic line, I advise him to follow Elliott Carter's practice in his string Quartet, and write out the one line reduction as a guide.

ELECTRONIC MUSIC

R.C. Do you have an opinion about *electronic music*?

I.S. I think that the *matière* is limited; more exactly, the composers have demonstrated but a very limited *matière* in all the examples of 'electronic music' I have heard. This is surprising because the possibilities as we know are astronomical. Another criticism I have is that the shortest pieces of 'electronic music' seem endless and within those pieces we feel no time control.

Therefore the amount of repetition, imaginary or real, is excessive.

Electronic composers are making a mistake, in my opinion, when they continue to employ significative noises in the manner of *musique concrète*. In Stockhausen's *Gesang der Jünglinge*, a work manifesting a strong personality and an indigenous feeling for the medium, I like the way the sound descends as though from auras, but the burbling fade-out noises and especially the organ are, I find, incongruous elements. Noises can be music of course, but they ought not to be significative; music itself does not signify anything.

What interests me most in 'electronic music' so far is the notation, the 'score'.

R.C. In the music of Stockhausen and others of his generation the elements of pitch, density, dynamics, duration, frequency (register), rhythm, timbre have been subjected to the serial variation principle. How will the non-serial element of 'surprise' be introduced in the rigid planning of this music?

I.S. The problem that now besets the totalitarian serialist is how to compose 'surprise' since by electronic computer it doesn't exist (though in fact it does, even if every case is computable; even at its worst, we listen to music as music and not as a computing game). Some composers are inclined to turn the problem over to the performer – as Stockhausen does in his *Piano Piece No. XI*. I myself am inclined to leave very little to the performers. I would not give them margin to play only half or selected fragments of my pieces. Also, I think it inconsistent to have controlled everything so minutely and then leave the ultimate shape of the piece to a performer (while pretending that all possible shapes have been allowed for).

R.C. Do you think there is a danger at present of novelty for its own sake?

I.S. Not really. Nevertheless, certain festivals of contemporary music by their very nature cannot help but encourage mere novelty. And, by a curious reversal of tradition, some critics encourage it too. The classic situation in which conservative and academic critics deride the composer's innovations is no more. Now composers can hardly keep up with the demands of some critics to 'make it new'. Novelties sometimes result that could not interest anyone twice. I am more cautious of the power of the acclaimers than of the disclaimers, of those critics who hail on principle what they cannot possibly contact directly with their own ears or understanding. This is musical politics, not music. Critics, like composers, must know what they love. Anything else is pose and propaganda, or what D. H. Lawrence called 'would-be'.

CONTEMPORARY MUSIC
AND THE GENERAL PUBLIC

R.C. Isn't the general public everywhere just as isolated from contemporary music since about 1909 as the Soviet Union?

I.S. Not everywhere, not in Germany where, for example, my

own later music is performed almost as frequently for the general public as are Strauss and Sibelius in the U.S. But the year 1909 means 'atonality' and 'atonality' did create a hiatus which Marxists attempt to explain as a problem of social pressures when in fact it was an irresistible pull within the art.

R.C. Do you wish to say anything about patronage?

I.S. Haphazard patronage, whether or not it is better than systematic patronage, is extremely inadequate. It called into being all of the music of Schoenberg, Berg, Webern, Bartók, and myself, though most of our music was not called into being at all, but only written and left to compete against more conventional types of music in the commercial market. This is part of the reason why four of those composers died in mid twentieth century in humiliating circumstances, or at least in circumstances that were far from affluent. This kind of patronage has not changed in a hundred and fifty years except that today there seems to be less of it.

R.C. Do you know the present status of your music east of N.A.T.O.?

I.S. Friends who attended the Warsaw conference of contemporary music in October 1956 say that my music was officially boycotted there but enthusiastically received nevertheless by composers from the Soviet sphere. My music is unobtainable, all of it and in any form, disc or printed score, east of N.A.T.O.; not only my music but Webern's, Schoenberg's, Berg's, as well. Russia's musical isolation – she will call it our isolation – is at least thirty years old. We hear much about Russian virtuoso violinists, pianists, orchestras. The point is, of what are they virtuosi? Instruments are nothing in themselves; the literature they play creates them. The mandolin and guitar, for instance, did not exist until Schoenberg imagined them in an entirely new way in his *Serenade*. A new musical masterpiece of that kind is a demand that musicians be created to play it. The Soviet virtuoso has no literature beyond the nineteenth century.

I am often asked if I would consent to conduct in the Soviet Union. For purely musical reasons I could not. Their orchestras do not perform the music of the three Viennese and myself, and they would be, I am sure, unable to cope with the simplest problems of rhythmic execution that we introduced to music fifty years ago. The style of my music would also be alien to them. These difficulties are not to be overcome in a few rehearsals; they require a twenty- or thirty-year tradition. I discovered something of the same situation in Germany at the end of the war. After so many years of Hitler in which my *L'Histoire du soldat*, Schoenberg's *Pierrot lunaire*, Berg's and Webern's music were banned, the musicians were unable for a long time to play the new music, though they have certainly more than made up for it since.

It is the same thing with ballet. A ballet exists in its repertoire as much as, or more than, in the technical perfection of its dancers. The repertoire is a few nineteenth-century ballets. These and sentimental, realist, Technicolor *Kitsch* are all the Soviets do. Ballet in this century means the Diaghilev repertoire and the creations of the very few good choreographers since.

R.C. You have known American musical life since 1925; would you comment on any aspect of its development since then.

I.S. I hope I am wrong, but I fear that in some ways the American composer is more isolated today than he was in 1925. He has at present a strong tendency to say: 'We'll leave all of that *avant-garde* stuff to Europe and develop our own musical style, an American style.' The result of having already done that is now clear in the way the 'Intellectual advanced stuff' (some of it, that is, for at least ninety-nine per cent of all *avant-garde* products are transparent puerilities) is embarrassing everybody; compared to Webern, for example, most of our simple homespun 'American style' is fatuous in expression and in technique the vilest cliché. In the phrase 'American Music', 'American' not only robs emphasis from 'music' but it asks for lower standards. Of course, good music that has grown up here will be American.

We have no capital for new music as New York was a capital in 1925. Look at the League of Composers' programmes of the nineteen-twenties and see if anything comparable is taking place in New York at the present. Of course, more contemporary music is played there now, and more American music, but the really consequential, controversial, new music is not played, and it was then. True we have those wonderful orchestras, but they are growing flabby on their diet of repertoire and second-rate new music – too much sugar. Recently I was asked to conduct two programmes with one of the glamorous American orchestras. But my programmes were rejected and the engagement cancelled because I refused to play Tchaikovsky instead of a programme entirely of my own music. This could not happen in Europe and at this date it shouldn't happen here. Boards of Directors and managers must stop assuming that their limited educations and tastes are reliable gauges for an audience's. An audience is an abstraction; it has no taste. It must depend on the only person who has (pardon, should have), the conductor.

The United States as a whole have certainly a far richer musical life today, with first-rate orchestras everywhere and good opera production in places like San Francisco, Santa Fé, Chicago, and the universities. But the crux of a vital musical society is new music.

JAZZ

R.C. What is your attitude to jazz?

I.S. Jazz is a different fraternity altogether, a wholly different kind of music making. It has nothing to do with composed music and when it seeks to be influenced by contemporary music it isn't jazz and it isn't good. Improvisation has its own time world, necessarily a loose and large one since only in an imprecisely limited time could real improvisation be worked up to; the stage has to be set, and there must be heat. The percussion and bass (not the piano; that instrument is too hybrid and besides, most of the players have just discovered Debussy) function as a central-heating system. They must keep the temperature 'cool', not cool. It is a kind of masturbation that never arrives anywhere (of course) but which supplies the 'artificial' genesis the art requires. The point of interest is instrumental virtuosity, instrumental personality, not melody, not harmony, and certainly not rhythm. Rhythm doesn't exist really because no rhythmic proportion or relaxation exists. Instead of rhythm there is 'beat'. The players beat all the time merely to keep up and to know which side of the beat they are on. The ideas are instrumental, or, rather, they aren't ideas because they come after, come from the instruments. Shorty Rogers's* trumpet playing is an example of what I mean by instrumental derivation, though his trumpet is really a deep-bored bugle-sounding instrument which reminds me of the keyed bugles I liked so much and wrote for in the first version of *Les Noces*.† His patterns are instrumental: half-valve effects with lip glissandos, intervals and runs that derive from the fingers, 'trills' on one note, for example, G to G on a B-flat instrument (between open and first-and-third fingers), etc.

As an example of what I have said about timing, I can listen to Shorty Rogers's good style with its dotted-note

---

*West-coast jazz musician.

†Hearing Mr Rogers play this instrument in Los Angeles last year perhaps influenced me to use it in *Threni*.

tradition, for stretches of fifteen minutes and more and not feel the time at all, whereas the weight of every 'serious' virtuoso I know depresses me beyond the counter-action of equanil in about five. Has jazz influenced me? Jazz patterns and, especially, jazz instrumental combinations did influence me forty years ago, of course, but not the idea of jazz. As I say, that is another world. I don't follow it but I respect it. It can be an art of very touching dignity as it is in the New Orleans jazz funerals. And, at its rare best, it is certainly the best musical entertainment in the U.S.

THE PERFORMANCE OF MUSIC

R.C. Do you agree that in some cases the composer should indicate how he wishes the conductor to beat his music?

I.S. I think he should always indicate the unit of the beat and whether or not subdivision is to be felt. Also, he should show whether the conductor is to beat the beat or the rhythmic shape of the music if that shape is against the beat. For example, the triplets, three in the time of four, in Webern's *Das Augenlicht* and in my *Surge Aquilo*: I contend that to beat three here (in other words, to beat the music) is to lose the 'in the time of four' feeling, and instead of a triplet feeling you have merely a three-beat bar *in a new tempo*.

R.C. Do you agree with Schoenberg's premise that a good composition is playable in only one tempo? (Schoenberg's example of a piece of music of uncertain tempo was the Austrian hymn from Haydn's *Emperor* Quartet.)

I.S. I think that any musical composition must necessarily possess its unique tempo (pulsation): the variety of tempi comes from performers who often are not very familiar with the composition they perform or feel a personal interest in interpreting it. In the case of Haydn's famous melody, if there is any uncertainty in the tempo the fault is in the alarming behaviour of its numerous interpreters.

R.C. Have you ever considered whether a piece of 'classic' music is more difficult to kill by mis-performance than a 'romantic' piece?

I.S. It depends, of course, on what we decide to mean by those divisions, and also on the kinds and degrees of mis-performance. Let us take refuge in examples, contemporary ones, preferably. My *Agon* and Berg's *Kammerkonzert* divide, I should think, on most of the characteristic issues we imagine to determine those categories.

The *Kammerkonzert* depends strongly on mood or interpretation. Unless mood dominates the whole, the parts do not relate, the form is not achieved, detail is not suffused, and the music fails to say what it has to say – for 'romantic' pieces are presumed to have messages beyond the purely musical messages of their notes. The romantic piece is always in need of a 'perfect' performance. By perfect one means inspired – rather than strict or correct. In fact, considerable fluctuations in tempo are possible in a 'romantic' piece (metronomes are marked *circa* in the Berg, and performance times sometimes diverge as much as ten minutes). There are other freedoms as well, and 'freedom' itself must be conveyed by the performer of a 'romantic' piece.

It is interesting to note that conductors' careers are made for the most part with 'romantic' music. 'Classic' music eliminates the conductor; we do not remember him in it, and we think we need him for his *métier* alone, not for his mediumistic abilities – I am speaking of my music.

But does all of this turned around fit the contrary? Perhaps, though the question of degree is important for the characteristics of each category apply at some point to both. For example, when a conductor has ruined a piece of mine, having failed to convey a sense of 'freedom' and 'mood' let him not tell me that these things are joined exclusively to another kind of music.

R.C. What do you regard as the principal performance problems of your music?

I.S. Tempo is the principal item. A piece of mine can survive almost anything but wrong or uncertain tempo. (To anticipate your next question, yes, a tempo can be metronomically wrong but right in spirit, though obviously the metronomic margin cannot be very great.) And not only my music, of course. What does it matter if the trills, the ornamentation, and the instruments themselves are all correct in the performance of a Bach concerto if the tempo is absurd? I have often said that my music is to be 'read', to be 'executed', but not to be 'interpreted'. I will say it still because I see in it nothing that requires interpretation (I am trying to sound immodest, not modest). But you will protest, stylistic questions in my music are not conclusively indicated by the notation; my style requires interpretation. This is true and it is also why I regard my recordings as indispensable supplements to the printed music. But that isn't the kind of 'interpretation' my critics mean. What they would like to know is whether the bass clarinet repeated notes at the end of the first movement of my *Symphony in Three Movements* might be interpreted as 'laughter'. Let us suppose I agree that it is meant to be 'laughter'; what difference could this make to the performer? Notes are still intangible. They are not symbols but signs.

The stylistic performance problem in my music is one of articulation and rhythmic diction. Nuance depends on these. Articulation is mainly separation, and I can give no better example of what I mean by it than to refer the reader to W. B. Yeats's recording of three of his poems. Yeats pauses at the end of each line, he dwells a precise time on and in between each word – one could as easily notate his verses in musical rhythm as scan them in poetic metres.

For fifty years I have endeavoured to teach musicians to

play [musical notation] instead of [musical notation]

in certain cases, depending on the style. I have also laboured to teach them to accent syncopated notes and to phrase before them in order to do so. (German orchestras are as unable to do this, so far, as the Japanese are unable to pronounce 'L'.)

In the performance of my music, simple questions like this consume half of my rehearsals: when will musicians learn to abandon the tied-into note, to lift from it, and not to rush the semiquavers afterwards? These are elementary things, but solfeggio is still at an elementary level. And why should solfeggio be taught, when it is taught, as a thing apart from style? Isn't this why Mozart concertos are still played as though they were Tchaikovsky concertos?

The chief performance problem of new music is rhythmic. For example, a piece like Dallapiccola's *Cinque canti* contains no interval problems of instrumental technique (its Cross shapes in the manner of George Herbert are for the eye and present no aural problems; one does not hear musically-shaped Crosses). The difficulties are entirely rhythmic and the average musician has to learn such a piece bar by bar. He has not got beyond *Le Sacre du printemps*, if he has got that far. He cannot play simple triplets, much less subdivisions of them. Difficult new music must be studied in schools even if only as exercises in reading.

Myself as a conductor? Well, reviewers have certainly resisted me in that capacity for forty years, in spite of my recordings, in spite of my special qualifications for knowing what the composer wants, and my perhaps one thousand times greater experience conducting my music than anyone else. Last year, *Time* called my San Marco performance of my

Canticum Sacrum 'Murder in the Cathedral'. Now I don't mind my music going on trial, for if I'm to keep my position as a promising young composer I must accept that; but how could *Time* or anybody know whether I ably conducted a work I alone knew? (In London, shortly after the *Time* episode, I was at tea one day with Mr Eliot, being tweaked by a story of his, when my wife asked that kindest, wisest, and gentlest of men, did he know what he had in common with me. Mr Eliot examined his nose; he regarded me and then reflected on himself, tall, hunched, and with an American gait; he pondered the possible communalities of our arts. When my wife said 'Murder in the Cathedral', the great poet was so disconcerted he made me feel he would rather not have written this *opus theatricum* than have its title loaned to insult me.)

R.C. Do you agree that perhaps the composer should try to notate 'style' more precisely. For example, in the finale of your *Octuor*, the bassoons play quavers with dots; wouldn't it have been more exact to write semiquavers followed by rests?

I.S. I do not believe that it is possible to convey a complete or lasting conception of style purely by notation. Some elements must always be transmitted by the performer, bless him. In the case of the *Octuor*, for example, if I had written semiquavers, the problem of their length, whether they should be cut off on or before the rests would be substituted for the original problem, and imagine reading all those flags!

R.C. Have you noticed any influence of electronic technique on the compositions by the new serial composers?

I.S. Yes, in several ways; and the electronic technique of certain composers interests me far more in their 'live' compositions than in their electronic ones. To mention only one influence, electronic music has made composers more aware of range problems. But here again, Webern was ahead in realizing that the same material, if it is to be worked out on equal levels, must be limited to four or five octaves (Webern extended beyond that only for important outlines of the form). But electronic music has influenced rhythm (for example, that curious sound which trails off into slower and slower dots), articulation, and many items of texture, dynamics, etc.

R.C. Which of your recorded performances do you prefer, which do you consider definitive?

I.S. I cannot evaluate my records for the reason that I am always too busy with new works to have time to listen to them. However, a composer is not as easily satisfied with recordings of his works as a performer is satisfied for him, in his name, and this is true even when the composer and the performer are the same person. The composer fears that errors will become authentic copy, and that one possible performance, one set of variables will be accepted as the only one. First recordings are standard-setting and we are too quickly accustomed to them. But to the composer-conductor the advantage of being able to anticipate performances of his new works with his own recordings outweighs all complaints. For one thing, the danger of the middle musician is reduced. For another, the time-lag in disseminating new music has been cut from a generation or two to six months or a year. If a work like *Le Marteau sans maître* had been written before the present era of recording it would have reached young musicians outside of the principal cities only years later. As it is this same *Marteau*, considered so difficult to perform a few years ago, is now within the technique of many players, thanks to their being taught by record.

But the public is still too little aware that the word 'performance' applied to recording is often extremely euphemistic. Instead of 'performing' a piece, the recording artist 'breaks it down'. He records according to the size (cost) of the orchestra. Thus Haydn's *Farewell* Symphony would be recorded from the beginning to the end in order; but *Bolero* would be done backwards, so to speak, if it were sectionally divisible. Another problem is that the orchestra is seated according to the acoustical arrangement required by the engineering. This means that the orchestra does not always sound like an orchestra to the orchestra.

I still prefer productions to reproductions. (No photograph matches the colours of the original nor is any phonographed sound the same as live sound; and we know from experience that in five years new processes and equipment will make us despise what we now accept as good enough imitations.) But the reproduced repertoire is so much greater than the produced, concerts are no longer any competition at all.

MUSIC AND THE CHURCH

R.C. Your *Mass*, *Canticum Sacrum*, and *Threni* are the strongest challenges in two hundred years to the decline of the Church as a musical institution.

I.S. I wish they were effective challenges. I had hoped my *Mass* would be used liturgically, but I have no such aspiration for the *Threni*, which is why I call it not *Tenebrae Service*, but *Lamentations*.

Whether or not the Church was the wisest patron – though I think it was; we commit fewer musical sins in church – it was rich in musical forms. How much poorer we are without the sacred musical services, without the Masses, the Passions, the round-the-calendar cantatas of the Protestants, the motets and Sacred Concerts, and Vespers and so many others. These are not merely defunct forms but parts of the musical spirit in disuse.

The Church knew what the Psalmist knew: music praises God. Music is as well or better able to praise Him than the building of the church and all its decoration; it is the Church's greatest ornament. Glory, glory, glory; the music of Orlando Lassus's motet praises God, and this particular 'glory' does not exist in secular music. And not only glory, though I think of it first because the glory of the Laudate, the joy of the Doxology, are all but extinct, but prayer and penitence and many others cannot be secularized. The spirit disappears with the form. I am not comparing 'emotional range' or 'variety' in sacred and secular music. The music of the nineteenth and twentieth centuries – it is all secular – is 'expressively' and 'emotionally' beyond anything in the music of the earlier centuries: the *Angst* in *Lulu*, for instance (gory, gory, gory), or the tension, the perpetuation of the moment of epitasis, in Schoenberg's music. I say, simply, that without the Church, 'left to our own devices', we are poorer by many musical forms.

When I call the nineteenth century 'secular' I mean by it to distinguish between religious religious music and secular religious music. The latter is inspired by humanity in general, by art, by *Übermensch*, by goodness, and by goodness knows what. Religious music without religion is almost always vulgar. It can also be dull. There is dull church music from Hucbald to Haydn, but not vulgar church music. (Of course there is vulgar church music now, but it is not really of or for the church.) I hope, too, that my sacred music is a protest against the Platonic tradition, which has been the Church's tradition through Plotinus and Erigena, of music as anti-moral. Of course Lucifer had music. Ezekiel refers to his 'tabrets and pipes' and Isaiah to the 'noise of his viols'. But Lucifer took his music with him from Paradise, and even in Hell, as Bosch shows, music is able to represent Paradise and become the 'bride of the cosmos'.

'It has been corrupted by musicians,' is the Church's answer, the Church whose musical history is a series of attacks against polyphony, the true musical expression of Western Christendom, until music retires from it in the eighteenth century or confounds it with the theatre. The corrupting musicians Bosch means are probably Josquin and Ockeghem, the corrupting artifacts the polyphonic marvels of Josquin, Ockeghem, Compère, Brumel.

R.C. Must one be a believer to compose in these forms?

I.S. Certainly, and not merely a believer in 'symbolic figures', but in the Person of the Lord, the Person of the Devil, and the Miracles of the Church.

THE YOUNGER GENERATION

R.C. Of your works, the young *avant-garde* admire *Le Sacre du printemps*, the *Three Japanese Lyrics*, various of the Russian songs, *Renard*, and the *Symphonies of Wind Instruments*. They react strongly against your so-called neo-classic music, however (*Apollo*, the piano Concerto, *Jeu de cartes*, etc.), and though they affirm your more recent music they complain that triadic harmonies and tonic cadences are solecisms in the backward direction of the tonal system. What do you say to all this?

I.S. Let me answer the latter complaint first: my recent works *are* composed in the – my – tonal system. These composers are more concerned with direction than with realistic judgements of music. This is as it should be. But in any case they could not have followed the twenty years of their immediate forebears, they had to find new antecedents. A change in direction does not mean that the out-of-influence is worthless however. In science, where each new scientific truth corrects some prior truth, it does sometimes mean that. But in music advance is only in the sense of developing the instrument of the language – we are able to do new things in rhythm, in sound, in structure. We claim greater concentration in certain ways and therefore contend that we have evolved, in this one sense, progressively. But a step in this evolution does not cancel the one before. Mondrian's series of trees can be seen as a study of progress from the more *resemblant* to the more abstract; but no one would be so silly as to call any of the trees more or less beautiful than any other *for the reason that it is more or less abstract*. If my music from *Apollo* and *Oedipus* to the *Rake's Progress* did not continue to explore in the direction that interests the younger generation today, these pieces will none the less continue to exist.

Every age is a historical unity. It may never appear as anything but either/or to its partisan contemporaries, of course, but semblance is gradual, and in time either and or come to be components of the same thing. For instance, 'neo-classic' now begins to apply to all of the between-the-war composers (not that notion of the neo-classic composer as someone who rifles his predecessors and each other and then arranges the theft in a new 'style'). The music of Schoenberg, Berg, and Webern in the twenties was considered extremely iconoclastic at that time but these composers now appear to have used musical form as I did, 'historically'. My use of it was overt, however, and theirs elaborately disguised. (Take, for example, the Rondo of Webern's *Trio*; the music is wonderfully interesting but no one hears it as a rondo.) We all explored and discovered new music in the twenties, of course, but we attached it to the very tradition we were so busily outgrowing a decade before.

R.C. What music delights you most today?

I.S. I play the English virginalists with never-failing delight. I also play Couperin, Bach cantatas too numerous to distinguish, Italian madrigals even more numerous, Schütz *sinfoniae sacrae* pieces, and masses by Josquin, Ockeghem, Obrecht, and others. Haydn quartets and symphonies,

Beethoven quartets, sonatas, and especially symphonies like the Second, Fourth, and Eighth, are sometimes wholly fresh and delightful to me. Of the music of this century I am still most attracted by two periods of Webern: the later instrumental works and the songs he wrote after the first twelve opus numbers and before the Trio – music which escaped the danger of the too great preciosity of the earlier pieces, and which is perhaps the richest Webern ever wrote. I do not say that the late cantatas are a decline – quite the contrary – but their sentiment is alien to me and I prefer the instrumental works. People who do not share my feeling for this music will wonder at my attitude. So I explain: Webern is for me the *juste de la musique* and I do not hesitate to shelter myself by the beneficent protection of his not yet canonized art.

R.C. What piece of music has most attracted you from a composer of the younger generation?

I.S. *Le Marteau sans maître* by Pierre Boulez. The ordinary musician's trouble in judging composers like Boulez and the young German, Stockhausen, is that he doesn't see their roots. These composers have sprung full-grown. With Webern, for example, we trace his origins back to the musical traditions of the nineteenth and earlier centuries. But the ordinary musician is not aware of Webern. He asks questions like: 'What sort of music would Boulez and Stockhausen write if they were asked to write tonal music?' It will be a considerable time before the value of *Le Marteau sans maître* is recognized. Meanwhile I shall not explain my admiration for it but adapt Gertrude Stein's answer when asked why she liked Picasso's paintings: 'I like to look at them' – I like to listen to Boulez.

R.C. What do you actually 'hear' vertically in music such as Boulez's *Deux Improvisations sur Mallarmé* or *Le Marteau sans maître*?

I.S. 'Hear' is a very complicated word. In a purely acoustical sense I hear everything played or sounded. In another sense, too, I am aware of everything played. But you mean, really, what tonal relationships am I conscious of, what does my ear analyse, and does it filter the pitches of all the individual notes? Your question implies that you still seek to relate the notes tonally; that you are looking for a 'key' that will enable you to do so (like Hardy's Jude, who imagined that Greek was only a different pronunciation of English). However, all that the ear can be aware of in this sense is density (nobody under thirty, and only rare antediluvians like myself over thirty, uses the word 'harmony' any more, but only 'density'). And density has become a strict serial matter, an element for variation and permutation like any other; according to one's system one gets from two to twelve notes in the vertical aggregation. (Is this mathematical? Of course it is, but the composer composes the mathematics.) All of this goes back to Webern who understood the whole problem of variable densities (a fact so remarkable that I wonder if even Webern knew who Webern was). But the question of harmonic hearing is an older one, of course. Every ordinary listener (if there is any such extraordinary creature) has been troubled by harmonic hearing in the music of the Vienna school from *circa* 1909 – in *Erwartung*, for example. He hears all of the notes acoustically but cannot analyse their harmonic structure. The reason is, of course, that this music isn't harmonic in the same way. (In the case of the *Erwartung* recording there is another reason, too; the vocal part is sung off pitch most of the time.)

Do I hear the chord structure of these non-harmonic-bass chords? It is difficult to say exactly what I do hear. For one thing it is a question of practice (while perhaps not entirely a question of practice). But whatever the limits of hearing and awareness are, I shouldn't like to have to define them. We already hear a great deal more in the harmony of these non-tonal-system harmonic pieces. For example, I now hear the whole first movement of Webern's *Symphony* tonally (not just the famous C minor place), and melodically I think everyone hears it more nearly tonally now than twenty years ago. Also, young people born to this music are able to hear more of it than we are.

The Boulez music? Parts of the *Marteau* are not difficult to hear *in toto*; the '*bourreaux de solitude*', for instance, which resembles the first movement of the Webern *Symphony*. With a piece like '*après l'artisanat furieux*', however, one follows the line of only a single instrument and is content to be 'aware of' the others. Perhaps later the second line and the third will be familiar, but one mustn't try to hear them in the tonal-harmonic sense. What is 'aware of'? Instrumentalists often ask that question: 'If we leave out such and such bits, who will know?' The answer is that one does know. Many people today are too ready to condemn a composer for 'not being able to hear what he has written'. In fact, if he is a real composer, he always does hear, at least by calculation, everything he writes. Tallis calculated the forty parts of his *Spem in alium nunquam habui*, he did not hear them; and even in twelve-part polyphony such as Orlando's, vertically we hear only four-part music. I even wonder if in complicated Renaissance polyphony the singers knew where they were in relation to each other – which shows how good their rhythmic training must have been (to maintain such independence).

R.C. How do you understand Anton Webern's remark: 'Don't write music entirely by ear. Your ears will always guide you all right, but you must know why'?

I.S. Webern was not satisfied with the, from one point of view, passive act of hearing: his music requires that the hearer, whether composer or listener, make cognizant relations of what he hears: 'you must know why'. It obliges the *hearer* to become a *listener*, summons him to active relations with music.

THE FUTURE OF MUSIC

R.C. Young composers are exploring dynamics; what kind of new use of them may we expect?

I.S. An example of the kind of dynamic use we might anticipate is in Stockhausen's *Zeitmasse*. In that piece, at bar 187, a chord is sustained in all five instruments, but the intensities of the individual instruments continue to change throughout the duration of the chord: the oboe begins *ppp* and makes a short crescendo to *p* at the end: the flute diminuendos slowly from *p*, then crescendos a little more quickly to *p* where it remains through the last third of the bar; the English horn crescendos slowly, then more quickly, from *ppp* to *mp*, and diminuendos symmetrically; the clarinet sustains *p*, then slowly diminuendos from it.

Such dynamic exploitation is not new, of course – a serial use of dynamics as well as of articulation, a related subject and just as important, is already clearly indicated in Webern's *Concerto for Nine Instruments* – but I think electronic instruments, and especially electronic control might carry it much further. I myself employ dynamics for various purposes and in various ways, but always to emphasize and articulate musical ideas: I have never regarded them as exploitable in themselves. In places such as the tenor ricercare in my *Cantata* I ignore volume almost altogether. Perhaps my experience as a performer has persuaded me that circumstances are so different as to require every score to be re-marked for every performance. However, a general scale of dynamic relationships – there are no absolute dynamics – must be clear in the performer's mind.

The inflexions of a constantly changing dynamic register are alien to my music. I do not breathe in ritardandos or accelerandos, diminuendos or crescendos, in every phrase. And infinitely subtle graduations – pianissimi at the limits of audibility and beyond – are suspect to me. My musical structure does not depend on dynamics – though my 'expression' employs them. I stand on this point in contrast to Webern.

R.C. Will you make any prediction about the 'music of the future'?

I.S. There may be add-a-part electronic sonatas, of course, and pre-composed symphonies ('Symphonies for the Imagination' – you buy a tone row complete with slide rules for duration, pitch, timbre, rhythm, and calculus tables to chart what happens in bar 12 or 73 or 200), and certainly all music will be mood-classified (kaleidoscopic montages for contortuplicate personalities, simultaneous concerts binaurally disaligned to soothe both men in the schizophrenic, etc.), but mostly it will very much resemble 'the music of the present' – for the man in the satellite, super Hi-fi Rachmaninov.

R.C. Do you think it likely that the masterpiece of the next decade will be composed in serial technique?

I.S. Nothing is likely about masterpieces, least of all whether there will be any. Nevertheless, a masterpiece is more likely to happen to the composer with the most highly developed language. This language is serial at present and though our contemporary development of it could be tangential to an evolution we do not yet see, for us this doesn't matter. Its resources have enlarged the present language and changed our perspective in it. Developments in language are not easily abandoned, and the composer who fails to take account of them may lose the mainstream. Masterpieces aside, it seems to me the new music will be serial.

ADVICE TO YOUNG COMPOSERS

R.C. Will you offer any cautions to young composers?

I.S. A composer is or isn't; he cannot learn to acquire the gift that makes him one, and whether he has it or not, in either case, he will not need anything I can tell him. The composer will know that he is one if composition creates exact appetites in him, and if in satisfying them he is aware of their exact limits. Similarly, he will know he is not one if he has only a 'desire to compose' or 'wish to express himself in music'. These appetites determine weight and size. They are more than manifestations of personality, are in fact indispensable human measurements. In much new music, however, we do not feel these dimensions, which is why it seems to 'flee music', to touch it and rush away, like the mujik who when asked what he would do if he was made Tsar said: 'I would steal 100 roubles and run as fast as I can.'

I would warn young composers, too, Americans especially, against university teaching. However pleasant and profitable to teach counterpoint at a rich American gynaeceum like Smith or Vassar, I am not sure that that is the right background for a composer. The numerous young people on university faculties who write music and who fail to develop into composers cannot blame their university careers, of course, and there is no pattern for the real composer anyway. The point is, however, that teaching is academic (Webster: 'Literary rather than technical or professional; conforming to rules, conventional; theoretical and not expected to produce a practical result') which means that it may not be the right contrast for a composer's non-composing time. The real composer thinks about his work the whole time; he is not always conscious of this, but he is aware of it later when he suddenly knows what he will do.

R.C. Do you allow that some of the new 'experimental' composers might be going 'too far'?

I.S. 'Experiment' means something in the sciences; it means nothing at all in musical composition. No good musical composition could be merely 'experimental'; it is music or it isn't; it must be heard and judged as any other. A successful 'experiment' in musical composition would be as great a failure as an unsuccessful one, if it were no more than an experiment. But in your question the question that interests me is the one which implies the drawing of lines: 'thus far and no farther; beyond this point music cannot go'. I suppose psychology has studied the effects of various types of challenges on various groups, and I suppose it knows what are normal responses and when they occur – in this case, when one begins to seek defence from new ideas and to rationalize them away. I have no information about this. But I have all around me the spectacle of composers who, after their generation has had its decade of influence and fashion, seal themselves off from further development and from the next generation (as I say this, exceptions come to mind, Krenek, for instance). Of course, it requires greater effort to learn from one's juniors, and their manners are not invariably good. But when you are seventy-five and your generation has overlapped with four younger ones, it behoves you not to decide in advance 'how far composers can go', but to try to discover whatever new thing it is makes the new generation new.

The very people who have done the breaking through are themselves often the first to try to put a scab on their achievement. What fear tells them to cry halt? What security do they seek, and how can it be secure if it is limited? How can they forget that they once fought against what they have become?

September–December 1957

IGOR STRAVINSKY:
MEMORIES AND COMMENTARIES

Socrates, to the Eleatic Stranger: ' . . . I shall only beg of you to say whether you like and are accustomed to make a long oration on a subject which you want to explain to another . . . or to proceed by the method of question and answer. I remember hearing a very noble discussion in which Parmenides employed the latter of the two methods, when I was a young man, and he was far advanced in years.'

SOPHIST 217

TO

NADIA BOULANGER

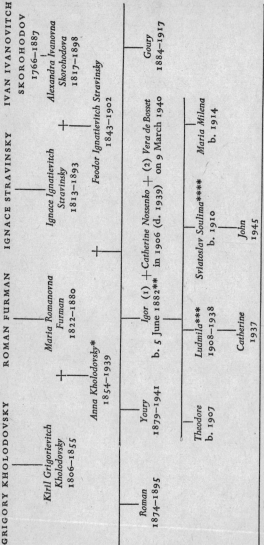

GRIGORY KHOLODOVSKY   ROMAN FURMAN   IGNACE STRAVINSKY   IVAN IVANOVITCH SKOROHODOV 1766–1887

Kiril Grigorievitch Kholodovsky 1806–1855   Maria Romanovna Furman 1822–1880   Ignace Ignatievitch Stravinsky 1813–1893   Alexandra Ivanovna Skorohodova 1817–1898

Anna Kholodovsky* 1854–1939 + Feodor Ignatievitch Stravinsky 1843–1902

Roman 1874–1895   Youry 1879–1941   Igor (1) + Catherine Nossenko + (2) Vera de Bosset on 9 March 1940
in 1906 (d. 1939)
b. 5 June 1882**

Theodore b. 1907   Ludmila*** 1908–1938   Sviatoslav Soulima**** b. 1910   Maria Milena b. 1914

Catherine 1937   John 1945

Goury 1884–1917

* Her eldest sister, Maria, was the mother of my first wife, Catherine Nossenko.
** Old Style. My birthday is 17 June 1882, New Style, but because the difference between the Gregorian and Julian calendars increases by one day each century, it has been 18 June since 1900. In only 23,360 centuries I shall have been born later than my grandson.
*** Married Youry Mandelstam who was killed by the Germans in Poland sometime between 1941 and 1945.
**** Married Françoise Blondlat.

Autobiographical

A RUSSIAN EDUCATION

FAMILY

R.C. Do you know the origin of your name?

I.S. 'Stravinsky' comes from 'Strava', the name of a small river, tributary to the Vistula, in eastern Poland. We were originally called Soulima-Stravinsky – Soulima being the name of another Vistula branch – but when Russia annexed this part of Poland the Soulima was for some reason dropped. The Soulima-Stravinskys were landowners in eastern Poland, as far back as they can be traced. In the reign of Catherine the Great they moved from Poland to Russia.

R.C. Would you draw your family tree?

I.S. (See Genealogical Table opposite).

R.C. What do you know about your grandparents and great-grandparents?

I.S. The only great-grandparent about whom I had heard anything at all was Roman Furman, and about him I know only that he was a high 'Excellency', that he came from the Baltic provinces, and that he was also an ancestor of Diaghilev's – which made Diaghilev my distant cousin. Of my grandfathers, too, I know very little. Ignace Stravinsky was more famous for his escapades with women than for anything else, and stories of his Don Juan-like behaviour reached me in my childhood. His amorous propensities continued until his very old age and were an embarrassment to my very staid father. He was a Pole, and therefore a Catholic, but Alexandra Skorohodova was Orthodox; according to Russian law the children of a mixed marriage had to be Orthodox, so my father was baptized in the Russian Church. Rimsky used to tease me, saying: 'So your grandfather's name was Ignace? I smell a Catholic there.' Kiril Kholodovsky was born in Kiev, a 'little Russian', as the Kievlani are called. He was a minister of agriculture and served on the Tsar's famous 'Council of Thirty'. He died of tuberculosis, a disease that has attacked our family ever since: my wife, Catherine Nossenko, her mother (who was my aunt), and our elder daughter died of it; my younger daughter and granddaughter have spent years in sanatoriums with it, and I myself have suffered from it at various times, but most severely in 1939 when I was five months in the sanatorium at Sancellemoz.

R.C. And about your parents?

I.S. I only know that they met in my mother's city of Kiev, where my father was the first basso of the Opera, and that they were married there. My father had been a law student in the Niéjinsky Lyceum when he discovered his good bass voice and good musical ear. He went from the Lyceum to the St Petersburg Conservatory and became a pupil of Professor Everardi, whose school for the voice was as celebrated as Auer's school for the violin. At graduation he accepted a position in the Kiev Opera which he held for a few years until he was ready for the Opera in St Petersburg.

R.C. Did anyone in your family beside your father possess musical ability?

I.S. I think not. At least I never heard my father or mother claim any musical talent for their parents or grandparents, and I know that my father considered his own musical ear and memory as a kind of supra-Mendelian phenomenon. I should add, however, that my mother was a competent pianist and a good sight-reader, and that she was at least mildly interested in music all her life.

R.C. How did it happen that you were born in Oranienbaum –

New York, 1954, listening to recording playbacks.

Near Oustiloug (Volynski Government), 1900. Stravinsky (wearing cap, beardless) with his brothers Goury (1884–1917, holding cap in hand), Youry (1879–1941, whose two daughters are still living in Leningrad), and his Nossenko cousins, Catherine Nossenko (in hood, who became Stravinsky's wife in 1906) Ludmilla (extreme right), her sister, and Vera Nossenko (extreme left, a cousin of Catherine's, and an M.D. still living in Switzerland). The remaining woman is another Nossenko, Vera's sister.

St Petersburg, 1908. Stravinsky and his wife (extremes of picture) with Rimsky-Korsakov, and Nadejda Rimsky-Korsakov with her fiancé Maximilian Steinberg.

3

(a) Clarens, 1913, the Hôtel du Chatelard. The paintings to the left are Japanese (this is the period of Stravinsky's *Three Japanese Lyrics*). The large picture, extreme right just over the couch, is a Gauguin, given Stravinsky by 'an admirer of Petroushka' in Paris in 1912, but lost with all of Stravinsky's possessions in Oustiloug.

(b) With Ravel, Clarens, 1913.

Morges (Switzerland), 1915. Stravinsky with his sons Soulima (b. 1910, on his back), and Theodore (1907–   ), and his daughter (Ludmilla, 1909-38).

(a) With Diaghilev at the Alfonso XIII Hotel, Seville, 1921.

(b) With Madame Stravinsky at the opening of an exhibition of her paintings, New York, January 1957.

With Robert Craft (standing) and Pierre Boulez, Hollywood, 1957.

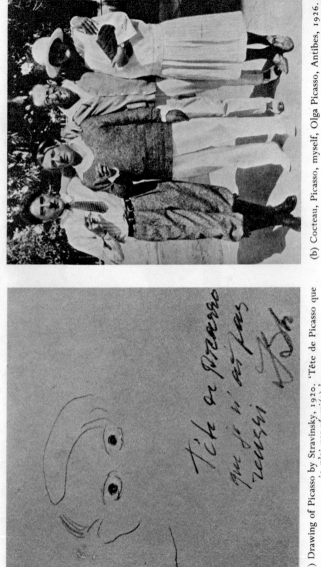

(b) Cocteau, Picasso, myself, Olga Picasso, Antibes, 1926.

(a) Drawing of Picasso by Stravinsky, 1920. 'Tête de Picasso que je n'ai pas réussi(e).'

8

that is, why did your family move there from St Petersburg?

I.S. Oranienbaum was a pleasant seaside village built round an eighteenth-century palace. It faced Kronstadt, and my parents had gone there a month before I was born to enjoy the early summer air. We never returned to Oranienbaum after my birth, however, and I have never seen it since – if I saw it then. My friend Charles-Albert Cingria – a critic of 'the Stravinsky of the international style' – used to call me '*le maître d'Oranienbaum*'.

R.C. Can you describe your father's character?

I.S. Oh, oh, he was not very *commode*. In fact, I was constantly frightened of him, which, I suppose, has deeply harmed my own character. He had an uncontrollable temper, and life with him was very difficult. He would lose himself in his anger, suddenly and unexpectedly, and without regard to where he might happen to be. I remember being terribly humiliated in a street in Bad Homburg when he suddenly ordered me to return to our hotel room – I was in my eleventh or twelfth year – and when I sulked instead of immediately obeying him, he caused a major scandal in the street. He was affectionate to me only when I was ill – which seems to me an excellent excuse for any hypochondriac tendencies I might have. Whether or not to gain his affection, I caught pleurisy when I was thirteen and was left with tuberculosis for a time afterwards. During this period of illness he was a different man to me and I forgave him everything that had happened before. He was a distant parent, however – distant not only to his children but also, or so he seemed to me, to his surroundings. He impressed me in his death more than he had ever done in his life. He had once fallen on the stage of the Opera and, some time later, he suddenly complained of great pain in his back in the place that had been struck by the fall. He went to Berlin for Röntgen treatment, but the cancer, which is what it was, had developed beyond hope of cure. He died a year and a half later, on the couch in his study, saying, 'I feel so good, so very good.' His death brought us close together.

R.C. And the character of your mother and brothers?

I.S. I was close to no one in my family except my brother Goury. For my mother I felt only 'duties'. My feelings were all fixed upon Bertha, my nurse. Bertha was an East Prussian who knew almost no Russian; German was the language of my nursery. Perhaps I should blame Bertha for corrupting me (somewhat as Byron must have been corrupted in Aberdeen by May Gray), but I do not. She lived on to nurse my own children and was forty years in our family when she died, in Morges, in 1917. I mourned her more than I did, later, my mother. When I remember my older brothers at all, it is to remind myself how exceedingly they used to annoy me. Roman was a law student. At eleven he caught diphtheria which weakened his heart and killed him ten years later. I thought him a very handsome brother and I was proud of him, but I could not confide in him for he was absolutely untouched by music.

Youry – George – was an architectural engineer and he continued to work as one in Leningrad until his death there in 1941. He was not close to me as a child, nor later, for he never wrote to me when I left Russia, and I last saw him in 1908. His wife did write to me once in Paris, however, and in 1925 their elder daughter Tatiana visited me there. Youry died shortly before the German invasion, as I learned from a Mr Borodin, a friend of Rimsky's eldest son Michael, who used to send me letters from somewhere on Long Island with news of friends of mine in Russia; I heard of Andrei Rimsky-Korsakov's death from him (but I also had this news from Rachmaninov), of Maximilian Steinberg's, and finally of Youry's.

Goury began his career, like Roman and myself, as a law

student. He had inherited my father's voice and musical ear, however, and he was determined to be a singer. Rather than enter the Conservatory he studied with Tartakov, a famous St Petersburg singer, and sang professionally in a private St Petersburg theatre from 1912–14. To my great regret I did not hear him there, but Diaghilev did, and reported to me that Goury was very good. He had a baritone voice, like my father's in quality, but not so low. I composed my Verlaine songs for him and I was always grieved that he did not live to sing them professionally. He was conscripted early in the 1914 war and sent to the southern front in a Red Cross unit. He died of scarlet fever in Romania, in April 1917, and was buried next to my father in St Petersburg's Alexandro-Nevsky cemetery, which the Bolsheviks later turned into a national artists' cemetery. Goury and my father were both respected by the Bolsheviks – a glorification that seems very remote now. My father had been buried in the Novodevitchy (the New Maiden) cemetery, but was reburied in the Alexandro-Nevsky cemetery in 1917, with Tchaikovsky, Rimsky, Dostoyevsky, Gogol, and, I think, Leskov.

Though I have not seen Goury since 1910, his death made me very lonely. We had been together constantly as children, and we felt that as long as we *were* together, all was well with the world. We found in each other the love and understanding denied us by our parents, who specially favoured neither of us, though Goury was in some respects the Benjamin of the family.

R.C. Did your parents recognize your musical talent?

I.S. No. The only member of the family who believed I had any was my uncle Alexander Ielatchitch. I think that my father judged my possibilities as a musician from his own experience and decided that the musical life would be too difficult for me. I could hardly blame him, however, for before his death I had written nothing, and though I was progressing in my piano technique it was already clear that I would not become a virtuoso of that instrument.

Alexander Ielatchitch had married my mother's sister Sophie five years before my father's marriage. His five children were therefore just enough older than the four of us to ensure that we suffered an ample amount of taunting and misery. I still resent the way they despised us because of their superior age, and I am even now a little triumphant that I have outlived them all. But Uncle Ielatchitch himself was nice to me. He owned vast farms and forests in the Samara Government, east of the Volga, where he invited us to spend our summers with him. I composed my first large-scale work there, incidentally, the lost – fortunately lost – piano sonata.

The four-day trips on the Volga to Pavlovka, as the Ielatchitch Samara estate was called, were among the happiest days of my life. I first made the trip in 1885 (*sic*), but of that I remember only a portrait of the Tsar on the wall of our state-room (which was supposed to have made me cry 'conductor', for his cap and uniform were like those of a railway conductor). The second excursion came eighteen years later, and my companion this time was Vladimir Rimsky-Korsakov. We heralded his father with postcards from each of the boat's stopping places: Rybinsk (literally, 'fish-town'), a white and gold city with monasteries and glittering churches – it looked like a set of *Tsar Saltan*, as one came upon it round a sudden bend in the river; Jaroslav, with its blue and gold churches and its yellow, Italian-style office buildings (I saw coloured slides of Jaroslav recently in Manila, at Ambassador Bohlen's); and Nishni-Novgorod where, surrounded by mendicant monks, we would walk to little booths where we bought and drank kumiss (mare's milk).

Uncle Ielatchitch who, as I have said in our first book, introduced me to the music of Brahms, adored Beethoven and was, I think, a good guide in my early understanding of that composer. He had two portraits on the wall of his study, Renan – Uncle Ielatchitch was a liberal – and Beethoven. The latter was a copy of the Waldmüller portrait. It seemed to contradict the whole hero-worshipping notion of Beethoven then prevalent. (In fact, as a small child I did not know it was Beethoven until one day while playing in the sand-dunes of the Alexander Park I saw an old woman whose face was exactly the face on my uncle's wall, which led me to ask my uncle who the woman was.) In any case, I did not hero-worship Beethoven, nor have I ever done so, and the nature of Beethoven's talent and work are more 'human' and more comprehensible to me than are, say, the talents and works of more 'perfect' composers like Bach and Mozart; I think I know how Beethoven composed.* I have little enough Beethoven in me, alas, but some people have found I have some. Someone has even compared the first movement of the *Eroica*, bars 272-5, with the three chords following Fig. 173 in *Le Sacre*, with Fig. 22 in *Renard*, and with the same musical figure in the first movement of my *Symphony in Three Movements*, bars 69–71.

R.C. Would you describe your home in St Petersburg?

* Though I do not understand how a man of such powers could lapse so frequently into such banality. The octave passage for violins in the *Malinconia* (op. 18, no. 6) is an early and tiny example of what I mean. A late and terrible example is the first movement of the ninth symphony. How could Beethoven have been satisfied – if he was satisfied – with such quadrilateral phrasing and pedantic development (cf. bars 387–400), such poor rhythmic invention (how dull is

), and such patently false pathos.

The mere fact that I can talk about Beethoven in this fashion proves my point, however, for about Bach I can only say that he is so elegant, so wise, so 'indispensable'.

i.s. We occupied a flat in a large old house: apartment 66, Krukov Canal. The house no longer exists, thanks to a German bomb, but Ansermet could give a description of it more recent than my own, for he visited my brother there in 1938. It was a four-storey house. We lived on the third floor, and, at one time, Karsavina rented the floor above us. On the other side of the canal stood a very handsome empire-style building, yellow in colour like the Villa Medici in Rome – but a prison, unfortunately. The building next to us was an apartment house also, and the conductor Napravnik lived there.

Our flat was furnished in the usual Victorian manner – with the usual bad paintings, the usual mauve upholstery, etc., but with an unusual library and two grand pianos. To recall it gives me no pleasure, however. I do not like to remember my childhood, and the four walls of my and Goury's room represent my most abiding impression of home. Our room was like Petroushka's cell, and most of my time was spent there. I was allowed out of doors only after my parents had put me through a medical examination, and I was considered too frail to participate in any sports or games when I *was* out. I suspect even now that my hatred of sports is my jealousy at having been deprived of them.

A new life began for me after the death of my father, when I began to live more in accordance with my own wishes. I even left home altogether on one occasion, leaving my mother the traditional note to the effect that life at 66 Krukov Canal was impossible. I sought refuge with a recently married Ielatchitch cousin, a man devoted to any form of revolution or protestation, but after a few days my mother managed to fall ill enough to force me to come back. She did behave slightly less egotistically after that, however, and her delight in torturing me seemed slightly less intense. I continued to live at home during the first year of my marriage, then moved to another apartment on the English Prospect, my last residence in St Petersburg.

TEACHERS

R.C. Would you describe your piano lessons with Mlle Kashperova?

I.S. She was an excellent pianist and a blockhead – a not unusual combination. By which I mean that her aesthetics and her bad taste were impregnable but her pianism of a high order. She was well known in St Petersburg, and though her name would not appear in Grove or Riemann, I think she might have been listed in a Russian dictionary of the time. She talked endlessly about her teacher, Anton Rubinstein, and I was attentive to this because I had seen Rubinstein in his coffin. (It was a sight I shall never forget. I was somewhat prepared for it because at an even earlier age I had seen the dead Emperor Alexander III – a yellow, waxen, uniformed doll – lying in State in the S.S. Peter and Paul Cathedral. Rubinstein was white, but with a thick black mane; he was in full dress, as though for a concert, and his hands were folded over a Cross; I did not see Tchaikovsky in his coffin, incidentally, because my parents thought the weather too dangerously bad for me to risk going out.) I learned to play the Mendelssohn G minor concerto with Mlle Kashperova, and many sonatas by Clementi and Mozart, as well as sonatas and other pieces by Haydn, Beethoven, Schubert, and Schumann. Chopin was forbidden, and she tried to discourage my interest in Wagner. Nevertheless, I knew all Wagner's works from the piano scores, and when I was sixteen or seventeen, and at last had the money to buy them, from the orchestral scores. We played Rimsky's operas together four-hands, and I remember deriving much pleasure from *Christmas Eve* this way. Mlle Kashperova's only idiosyncrasy as a teacher was in forbidding me all use of pedals; I had to sustain with my fingers, like an organist – an omen, perhaps, as I have never been a pedal composer. I am most in Kashperova's debt, however, for something she would not have appreciated. Her narrowness and her formulae greatly encouraged the supply of bitterness that accumulated in my soul until, in my mid-twenties, I broke loose and revolted from her and from every stultification in my studies, my schools, and my family. The real answer to your questions about my childhood is that it was a period of waiting for the moment when I could send everyone and everything connected with it to hell.

R.C. What schools did you attend in St Petersburg?

I.S. I attended a government school, the Second St Petersburg Gymnasium, until I was fourteen or fifteen. From there I went to the Gourévitch Gymnasium, a private school where Youry had been before me. The Gourévitch Gymnasium was about eight miles from our house, in a neighbourhood called '*peski*', 'the sands', and these eight miles kept me in constant debt. Always too late in the mornings for the tram, I would have to take a fiacre and pay forty or fifty kopecks. But the fiacre rides were the only thing about school I liked, especially in winter. On the way home, what a pleasure it was to drive through the Nevsky Prospect in a sleigh, protected by a net from the dirty snow kicked up by the horse, and then, at home, to warm myself in front of our big white porcelain stove.

The Gourévitch Gymnasium was divided into a 'classical' and a *Realschule*. My own curriculum belonged to the former: history, Latin, Greek, Russian and French literatures, mathematics. I was of course a very bad pupil, and I hated this school as I did all my schools, profoundly and forever.

R.C. Did you have any sympathetic teachers?

I.S. My mathematics professor in this same Gourévitch

Gymnasium – a man called Woolf – did understand me, I think. He was an ex-Hussar officer with a real talent for mathematics, but he had been, and still was, a drunkard. (Another of my professors was a drunkard too, a man in perpetual disgrace who would walk to the window, turn his back to us, and steal a nip from a little bottle in his coat pocket; the other boys mocked him cruelly.) Professor Woolf was also an amateur musician. He knew that I composed – I had already been reproached for it by the school director – and he helped, protected, and encouraged me.

UNIVERSITY

R.C. What are your memories of St Petersburg University?

I.S. As attendance at lectures was optional, I opted not to attend, and in all my four years there I probably did not hear more than fifty. I have only a vague and uninterested memory of the University. I read criminal law and legal philosophy, and I was interested in the theoretical and abstract questions of both, but by the time I entered the University so much of my time was spent with Rimsky-Korsakov I could hardly do justice to any other studies. I can now recall only two incidents connected with my life there. I was walking through the Kazansky Place one afternoon in the politically tense months following the Russo-Japanese war, when a group of students began to stage a protest. The police were prepared, however, and the protestants were arrested, myself with them. I was detained seven hours, but seventy years will not erase the memory of my fears. The other incident occurred during the last spring cramming season, when, realizing that I would never pass one of my examinations, I proposed to exchange names with Nicolai Yussupov, that he might take my examinination and I one of his: we were better in each other's subject. Our ruse was never detected because our faces were quite unknown to the professors, but poor

Nicolai – whose brother later killed Rasputin – died shortly after passing my paper, in a duel in Tashkent.

R.C. What did you read in your University years?

I.S. Russian literature mostly, and the literature of other countries in Russian translation. Dostoyevsky was always my hero. Of the new writers, I liked Gorky most and disliked most Andreyev. The Scandinavians then so popular – Lagerlöf and Hamsun – did not appeal to me at all, but I admired Strindberg and, of course, Ibsen. Ibsen's plays were as popular in Russia in those years as Tchaikovsky's music. Südermann and Hauptmann were also in great vogue then, and Dickens, and Mark Twain (whose daughter I later knew in Hollywood), and Scott, whose *Ivanhoe* (pronounced in Russian as a four-syllable paroxytone – *Ivanhoê*) was as popular a children's book as it ever was in the English-speaking countries.

CONCERTS IN ST PETERSBURG

R.C. You often mention the St Petersburg concert series 'Evenings of Contemporary Music'. What music did you hear there?

I.S. First of all, my own. Nicolas Richter played my early piano sonata there, and this was the first music of mine to be performed in public. It was, I suppose, an inept imitation of late Beethoven. I myself performed there, too, as accompanist to a singer, a certain Miss Petrenko, in my Gorodetsky songs. Works by young Russian composers were in the majority, of course, but French music – the quartets and songs of Debussy and Ravel, and various pieces by Dukas and d'Indy – was also promoted.* Brahms was played, too, and Reger. Like

---

* When I met d'Indy at a rehearsal of *Le Sacre* in 1921 I told him I had heard an amount of his music in St Petersburg in my youth, but he probably understood that it had been part of the background that had provoked me into writing *Le Sacre*, for he said nothing.

the 'Monday Evening Concerts' in Los Angeles, these St Petersburg concerts, in spite of their name, tried to match the new with the old. This was important, and rare, for so many organizations are dedicated to new music, and so few to the centuries before Bach. I heard Monteverdi there for the first time, in an arrangement by d'Indy, I think, and Couperin and Montéclair; and Bach was performed in quantity.

The people I met at these concerts were also a great part of the interest. All the composers, the poets, and the artists of St Petersburg were there, and also the intelligent amateurs – like my friends Ivan Pokrovsky and Stepan Mitusov, who were always aware of the newest art developments in Berlin and Paris.

R.C. Were there any 'advanced' orchestral concerts in St Petersburg?

I.S. No, the programmes of the Imperial Symphony were very much like the programmes of American orchestras today: standard repertory, and from time to time a piece of second-rate, locally-composed music. The symphonies of Bruckner and Brahms were considered new music still and therefore were rarely and very timidly played. Belayev's 'Russian Symphony Concerts' were more interesting, but they concentrated too much on the Russian 'Five'. Incidentally, I knew Belayev and I met him at concerts. He was the great music patron of his time – a kind of Russian Rockefeller who played the violin. His Éditions Belayev in Leipzig had published my *Faune et Bergère* – probably on Rimsky's advice, since Glazunov, his other adviser, would not have recommended it.* Once I saw him stand up in his box – he was a

* I am not being unfair to Glazunov; he was so consumed with animosity that when I saw him for the last time, backstage after a concert he conducted in Paris in 1935, and said 'Greetings to you, Alexander Konstantinovitch', all he could do was to look dour, half offer his hand, and say nothing.

tall man with very artistic hair – and stare with amazement at the stage where Kussevitsky had just come on carrying his double-bass to play a solo. Belayev turned to me and said: 'Until now such things have been seen only in circuses.'

*

R.C. What did you love most in Russia?

I.S. The violent Russian spring that seemed to begin in an hour and was like the whole earth cracking. That was the most wonderful event of every year of my childhood.

DIAGHILEV AND HIS DANCERS

R.C. Do you remember your first attendance at a ballet performance?

I.S. At the age of seven or eight I was taken to see *The Sleeping Beauty*. I realize now that I was older than this when I saw *A Life for the Tsar*, which contradicts what I said in our first series of conversations, that the latter was my first attendance at a theatrical-musical performance. I was enchanted by the ballet, but I had been prepared for what I saw, for ballet was an important part of our culture and a familiar subject to me from my earliest childhood. Therefore I was able to identify the dance positions and steps, and I knew the plot and the music long in advance. Moreover, Petipa, the choreographer, was a friend of my father's, and I had seen him several times myself. Of the performance itself, I remember only my musical impressions, however, and perhaps those are really my parents' impressions of my impressions, repeated to me afterwards. But I do know that I was excited by the dance and that I applauded it with all my strength. If I could transport myself back to that night seventy years ago I would do so only to satisfy my curiosity about the musical tempi, for I am always interested in the question of tempo in other periods.

As I grew up I became aware that the ballet was petrifying, that it was, in fact, already quite rigidly conventional. I could not regard it as an exploitable musical medium, of course, and I would have been quite incredulous had anyone suggested that a modern movement in the arts was to be born through it. But would that movement have taken place without Diaghilev? I do not think so.

PAVLOVA

R.C. What ballet dancer did you most admire in your student years?

I.S. Anna Pavlova. She was never a member of Diaghilev's company, however, though Diaghilev had very much wanted her to join. I met her in December 1909 at her home in St Petersburg. Diaghilev had asked her to invite me to a party, hoping that after she had met me she might agree to dance the part of the Firebird. I remember that Benois and Fokine were there that night, too, and that we drank much champagne. But whatever Pavlova thought of me personally, she did not dance in the *Firebird*. The reasons for her refusal were, I think, my *Scherzo fantastique* and *Fireworks*. She considered these pieces horribly decadent. ('Decadent' and 'modern' were interchangeable then, whereas 'decadent' now very often means 'not modern enough'.)

The lines of Pavlova's form and her mobile expression were ever beautiful to behold, but the dance itself was always the same and quite devoid of constructive interest. In fact, I remember no difference in her dance from the first time I saw it, in St Petersburg in 1905 or 1906, to the last time, which was in Paris in the 1930s. Pavlova was an *artiste*, but of an art far removed from the world of the Diaghilev Ballet.

R.C. Who taught you most about the technique of the dance?

I.S. Maestro Cecchetti, the elder of the Ballet and the final authority for every dance step in every ballet we did. Everyone in the company from Nijinsky to the apprentices venerated him. He was a very cosy man and I had become friends with him already in St Petersburg. His knowledge was limited to the classical dance, of course, and he therefore opposed the trend of our Ballet as a whole, but it was precisely his academicism, not his aesthetics, that Diaghilev required. He remained the Company's dance-conscience throughout its entire existence. There was a Signora Cecchetti too, also a dancer, and as like her husband as a twin. Diaghilev called her 'the Cecchetti in petticoats'. I once saw her dance in crinolines and with a great papiermâché boat on her head. Imagine how delighted I was when Cecchetti agreed to dance the Magician in *Petroushka*. We didn't have to paste a false beard on *him*!

FOKINE

R.C. Do you remember Fokine's choreography for the original *Firebird* and *Petroushka*?

I.S. I do, but I didn't really like the dance movement of either ballet. The female dancers in the *Firebird*, the Princesses, were insipidly sweet, while the male dancers were the *ne plus ultra* of brute masculinity: in the Kastchei scene, they sat on the floor kicking their legs in an incredibly stupid manner. I prefer Balanchine's choreography for the 1945 version of the *Firebird* suite to the whole Fokine ballet (and the music too: the music of the complete ballet is too long and patchy in quality).

Nor did Fokine realize my ideas for *Petroushka*, though I suspect that this time the fault was rather with Diaghilev than with Fokine. I conceived the Charlatan as a character out of Hoffman, a lackey in a tightly modelled blue *frac* with gold stars, and not at all as a Russian Metropolitan. The flute music, too, is Weber-like, or Hoffmann-like, not Russian 'Five'. Also, I had thought of the Moor as a kind of Wilhelm Busch caricature and not as the merely mechanical comic-relief character he is usually made out to be. Another of my ideas was that Petroushka should watch the dances of the fourth tableau (the Coachmen, the Nurses, etc.) from a hole in his cell and that we, the audience, should see them, too, from the perspective of his cell. I never did like the full-stage dance carrousel at this point of the drama. And Fokine's choreography was ambiguous at the most important moment. Petroushka's ghost, as I conceived the story, is the real Petroushka, and his appearance at the end makes the Petroushka of the preceding play a mere doll. His gesture is not one of triumph or protest, as is so often said, but a nose-thumbing addressed to the audience. The significance of this gesture is not and never was clear in Fokine's staging. One great invention of Fokine's, however, was the rigid arm movement that Nijinsky was to make such an unforgettable gesture.

Fokine was easily the most disagreeable man I have ever worked with. In fact, with Glazunov, he was the most disagreeable man I have ever met; but Glazunov was a time-to-time drunkard which redeemed him – from time to time; he would lock his door for two-week binges on Château Yquem! Imagine bingeing on Château Yquem! I was never a friend of Fokine's, not even in our first years together, for I was a partisan of Cecchetti's, and Cecchetti was for him the merest academician. Diaghilev agreed with me, however, that his dances for *Prince Igor* suggested that he was the best qualified of our choreographers to deal with the *Firebird*. Then, after the *Firebird* and *Petroushka*, I had little to do with him. He was spoiled by his success in America and ever after wore the 'I-have-made-an-American-kill' look. I saw him last with Ida Rubinstein. He was to have choreographed my *Baiser de la fée* for her but finally Bronislava Nijinska did it, and I was much relieved. After that and until the end of his life (1940) I received complaints from him about business or royalty matters connected with the *Firebird*, which he would actually refer to as *my* 'musical accompaniment' to *his* 'choreographic poem'.

NIJINSKY AND NIJINSKA

R.C. Have you any further recollections to add to what you have already written about Vaslav Nijinsky?

1.s. When Diaghilev introduced me to Nijinsky – it was in St Petersburg in 1909 – I was aware of him as an extraordinary physical being. I was aware, too, of curious absences in his personality. I liked his shy manner and his soft, Polish speech, and he was immediately very open and affectionate with me – but he was always that. Later, when I knew him better, I thought him childishly spoiled and impulsive. Later, too, I came to understand the absences as a kind of stigmata; I could not imagine that they would so soon and so tragically destroy him. I often think of Nijinsky in his final years, a captive in his own mind, his most perfect gift of expression in movement stricken, immobile.

*

Already a celebrity when I first knew him, Nijinsky was to become even more celebrated shortly afterwards because of a scandal. Diaghilev had taken charge of his costuming – they were living together – with the result that Nijinsky appeared at the Imperial Theatre in the tightest tights anyone had ever seen (in fact, an athletic support padded with handkerchiefs), and little else. The Tsar's mother had attended a performance and was shocked. Diaghilev and Prince Wolkonsky, the Director of the Theatre and a man of similar sensibilities, were thought to have conspired against public decency. The Tsar himself was shocked. He alluded to the matter in conversation with Diaghilev but was so curtly answered that Diaghilev was never thereafter in official good odour. I discovered this for myself when Diaghilev asked me to approach Ambassador Izvolsky in an attempt to secure a passport for a dancer of conscription age. When Izvolsky understood my request to be on Diaghilev's behalf he became quite coldly diplomatic. (But I was often Diaghilev's ambassador in later years, especially his 'financial' ambassador – or, as he called me, his tax-collector.)

To return to the Imperial Theatre scandal, the truth is that the exhibitionist was not Nijinsky but Diaghilev. Nijinsky was always very serious and high-minded and, in my judgement, never conscious of his performances from Diaghilev's point of view. I was even more certain of this later, in Paris, when he danced the *Afternoon of a Faun*. This ballet's famous representation of the act of love, and its exhibition of sexual organs, was entirely Diaghilev's idea. Even so, Nijinsky's performance was such marvellously concentrated art that only a fool could have been shocked by it – but then, I adored the ballet myself.

Nijinsky was wholly without guile. More than that, he was naïvely – appallingly – honest. He never understood that in Society one does not always say all that one thinks. At a party in London, some time before the *Sacre du printemps première*, Lady Ripon proposed a parlour game in which we were all to decide what sort of animal each of us most resembled – a dangerous game. Lady Ripon initiated it herself by saying that 'Diaghilev looks like a bulldog and Stravinsky like a *renard*. Now, M. Nijinsky, what do you think I look like?' Nijinsky thought a moment, then spoke the awful, exact truth: '*Vous, Madame – chameau*' – just the three words; Nijinsky did not speak much French. Lady Ripon did not expect that, of course, and in spite of her repeating: 'A camel? How amusing! I declare. Really? A camel?' – she was flustered all evening.

My own disappointment with Nijinsky was due to the fact that he did not know the musical alphabet. He never understood musical metres and he had no very certain sense of tempo. You may imagine from this the rhythmic chaos that was *Le Sacre du printemps*, and especially the chaos of the last dance where poor Mlle Piltz, the sacrificial maiden, was not even aware of the changing bars. Nor did Nijinsky make any attempt to understand my own choreographic ideas for

Le Sacre. In the *Danses des adolescents*, for example, I had imagined a row of almost motionless dancers. Nijinsky made of this piece a big jumping match.

I do not say that Nijinsky's creative imagination lacked abundance; on the contrary, it was almost too rich. The point is simply that he did not know music, and therefore his notion of the relation of dance to it was primitive. To some extent this might have been remedied by education, for of course he was musical. But at the time he was made chief choreographer of the Ballet he was hopelessly incompetent in musical technique. He believed that the choreography should re-emphasize the musical beat and pattern through constant coordination. In effect, this restricted the dance to rhythmic duplication of the music and made of it an imitation. Choreography, as I conceive it, must realize its own form, one independent of the musical form though measured to the musical unit. Its construction will be based on whatever correspondences the choreographer may invent, but it must not seek merely to duplicate the line and beat of the music. I do not see how one can be a choreographer unless, like Balanchine, one is a musician first.

If Nijinsky was the least capable musically of my choreographic collaborators, his talent was elsewhere – and one talent such as he had is enough. To call him a dancer is not enough, however, for he was an even greater dramatic actor. His beautiful, but certainly not handsome, face could become the most powerful actor's mask I have ever seen and, as Petroushka, he was the most exciting human being I have ever seen on a stage.

*

I recently discovered a Nijinsky letter – addressed to me in Russia but forwarded to Switzerland, where I was then staying. It is a document of such astounding innocence – if Nijinsky hadn't written it, I think only a character in

Dostoyevsky might have. It seems incredible to me even now that he was so unaware of the politics and sexual jealousies and motives within the Ballet. I never saw Nijinsky again after *Le Sacre du printemps*, so, in fact, I knew him for only four years. But those four years were the great age of the Ballet and I was with him then almost every day. I do not recall what I answered, but Diaghilev had already returned to Russia, and when I saw him on his next trip to Paris, Massine had 'replaced' poor Nijinsky.

> *Tuesday, 9 December 1913*
> *1 Hidegkuti ut 51 (Budapest)*

Dear Igor: I cannot hide from you what has happened to me these last months. You know that I went to South America and have not been in Europe for four months. These four months cost me dearly in money and health. My room with board cost 150 francs daily. I did not earn this money from Serge, however, but was obliged to take it from my own capital. What did Serge do all this time while we were in South America? I do not know. I wrote to him many times without receiving any answer. And I needed an answer, too, as I had worked on two new ballets – *Joseph and Potiphar*, by Strauss,* and another one, with Bach's music. All the preparatory work for these ballets was completed and I had only to put them in rehearsal. I could not rehearse in America because of the terrible heat, from which we almost died. How I managed to stay in good health up to the last evening there I do not know. But though I was lucky in America, here I have been ill for two months. Now I am all right.

I did not send you an invitation to my wedding as I knew you would not come, and I did not write you because I had so much to do. Please excuse me. I went with my wife to her

* Strauss's *Josephslegende*, first performed in Paris in 1914.

parents' home in Budapest and there I immediately sent a telegram to Serge asking him when we could see each other. The answer to my telegram was a letter from Grigoriev* informing me that I shall not be asked to stage any ballets this season, and that I am not needed as an artist.

Please write to me whether this is true. I do not believe that Serge can act so meanly to me. Serge owes me a lot of money. I have received nothing for two years, neither for my dancing nor for my staging *Faune*, *Jeux*, and *Sacre du printemps*. I worked for the Ballet without a contract. If it is true that Serge does not want to work with me – then I have lost everything. You understand the situation I am in. I cannot imagine what has happened, what is the reason for his behaviour. Please ask Serge what is the matter, and write to me about it. In all the newspapers of Germany, Paris, and London, etc., it is reported that I am not working any more with Diaghilev. But the whole press is against him (including the *feuilletons*). They also say that I am gathering a company of my own. In truth, I am receiving propositions from every side, and the biggest of these comes from a very rich businessman, who offers one million francs to organize a new Diaghilev† Russian Ballet – they wish me to have sole artistic direction and large sums of money to commission décors, music, etc. But I won't give them a definite answer before I have news from you.

My numerous friends send me letters of revolt and rage against Diaghilev – and propositions to help me and join me in my new enterprise. I hope you will not forget me and will answer my letter immediately.

Your loving

VASLAV

Regards to your wife and to all I know. V.

* Serge Grigoriev, the *régisseur* of the Ballet.
† *Sic.*

R.C. Who, then, was your most successful choreographer in the Diaghilev period?

I.S. Bronislava Nijinska, Nijinsky's sister. Her choreography for the original productions of *Renard* (1922) and *Noces* (1923) pleased me more than any other works of mine interpreted by the Diaghilev troupe. Her conception of *Noces* in blocks and masses, and her acrobatic *Renard*, coincided with my ideas, as well as with the real – not realistic – décors. The set of *Noces* was a bees-wax yellow and the costumes were brown peasant costumes, instead of the hideously un-Russian reds, greens, and blues one usually sees in foreign stagings of Russian plays. *Renard* was also a real Russian satire. The animals saluted very like the Russian Army (Orwell would have liked this), and there was always an underlying significance to their movements. Nijinska's *Renard* was superior in every way to the 1929 revival, though the latter was ruined chiefly by some jugglers Diaghilev had borrowed from a circus – an idea of his that did not succeed at all.

Poor Bronislava had no luck with Diaghilev. Because her face was bony and interesting, instead of doll-like, Diaghilev was opposed to her dancing the Ballerina in *Petroushka*. And as a dancer she was second to none. Indeed, the Nijinskys – brother and sister together – were the best dancing pair imaginable. Then, later, after Nijinsky's marriage, Diaghilev could not overcome his prejudice. She looked like Nijinsky, was even shaped like him – with the same big shoulders. She was a constant reminder to him of her brother. It pained Diaghilev doubly, too, that this person who dared look like Nijinsky was a woman. You can hardly imagine how indomitable was Diaghilev's sexual prejudice. He had argued for years to convince me that the exclusive love of women was morbid (though I don't know how he could have known very much about that), that I was an incomplete artist because ... 'morbid'. He would draw cartoons on restaurant tablecloths of steatopygous and gourd-geously mammiferous women – they looked like Dubuffet madonnas – argue about Socrates, Jesus, Leonardo da Vinci, Michelangelo (what a chaos of pederasty is Michelangelo's *Conversion of St Paul* – including even the horse – and how unnecessary, in any case, to Paul's conversion), and go on about 'all great artists', etc. He would describe his own latest *mignon* in the most gratifying terms and quote Verlaine: '*Démon femelle ...*' etc. At the same time, however, he was show-man enough to know how to emphasize the beauty of the female body in the ballet.

Poor Bronislava's sex, looks, and name were against her. I regretted this because, except for her and Fokine, the chor-eographers of my ballets were not so much dance composers as dance performers. They had been elevated to the position of choreographers not by education or experience but through being Diaghilev's *eromenoi*.*

MASSINE

R.C. Do you remember Massine's choreography for the first *Pulcinella*?

I.S. I do and, on the whole, I considered it very good. It was

---

*It is almost impossible to describe the perversity of Diaghilev's entourage – a kind of homosexual Swiss Guard – and the incidents and stories concerning it. I remember a rehearsal for the revival of *Renard*, in Monaco in 1929, at which our pianist – a handsome *fificus* of Diaghi-lev's – suddenly began looking very intently beyond the music rack. I followed his gaze to a Monegasque soldier in a tricorne, and then asked what the matter was. He answered: 'I long to surrender myself to him.'

Another of Diaghilev's protégés was discovered nude by the police beneath a bridge near Nice, and when one of the policemen said, 'Ou vous êtes un vicieux ou vous êtes fou,' he is supposed to have replied, 'Je suis sûrement vicieux.' And so on.

sometimes mechanical, but only the variation movement was contradictory to the music. Massine had already choreographed the variations before I had scored the music, and Diaghilev had told him I would use a large orchestra with harps. Instead of this, my orchestra, as you know, is a solo woodwind quartet. In 1914 – after Nijinsky's marriage – Diaghilev returned from Russia with Leonid Massine. Massine's first ballet was Strauss's *Legend of Joseph*. Of my music, besides *Pulcinella*, Massine did the choreography of the *Nightingale*. The performances of the latter were not good, however, because of insufficient orchestra rehearsals. There was a lack of coordination between pit and stage, and the result was unworthy of the best standards of the company.

Later, Massine did the choreography for the revival of *Le Sacre du printemps*. I thought this excellent – incomparably clearer than Nijinsky's.

THE DIAGHILEV BALLET
AND DIAGHILEV

R.C. Are there any other dancers and choreographers you would like to mention?

I.S. I should mention Idzikovsky, the great jumper and, after Nijinsky, the greatest Petroushka; Woizikovsky; Lopokova of the perfect technique; Karsavina, the lady of the ballet, the first ballerina in *Petroushka* and the first Firebird (though she should have been the Princess and Pavlova the Firebird); Tchernicheva, a beautiful *Firebird* Princess and a beautiful woman too – she had infatuated Alfonso XIII and was the only woman who had attracted Ravel; Piltz, the Russian with the German name who danced in the *Firebird* with Fokina and Tchernicheva and was the star of the first *Sacre du printemps*; Sokolova, who danced the revival of *Le Sacre*; Lifar, who was so beautiful as Apollo; Adolphe Bolm who choreographed the first *Apollo* and who became my close friend in America; George Balanchine who choreographed the first European *Apollo* (I had met him in 1925, in Nice, as he was preparing a revival of the *Chant du rossignol*).

*

I see that while attempting to remember the 'dancers of the Russian Ballet' I have actually said more about Diaghilev himself and his abnormal psychology (though I have not exaggerated the latter) than about the Terpsichorean arts and artists in his company. But this was inevitable since Diaghilev was more strong-willed than all his artists and since he controlled every detail of every ballet he produced.

Diaghilev was sometimes possessed by very odd and impractical ideas, and as he was a stubborn man, many hours of my (and his) life were spent in trying to argue him out of these eccentric notions. That I was not always successful, from my point of view, is illustrated by his use of jugglers in *Renard*. I did win in one important case though – *L'Histoire du soldat*. Diaghilev could not bear the name *L'Histoire du soldat* because his company had not produced it (as indeed it could not have done in 1918, temporarily dissolved as it was in the war). But in the early 1920s, he suddenly decided to stage it. His plan was eccentric. The dancers were to go about wearing advertisements, American sidewalk walking-advertisements, 'sandwich men', as they are called, or pickets. Massine would eventually have been blamed for the choreography of this undanceable ballet, but it was all Diaghilev's idea.

Diaghilev was in no sense an intellectual. He was much too sensual for that; besides, intellectuals never have any real taste – and has anyone ever had so much taste as Diaghilev? He was a deeply cultured man, however – a scholar in certain areas of art history, and an authority on

Russian painting.* He had been a bibliophile all his life, also, and his Russian library was one of the finest in the world. But his mind was so preyed upon by superstition that he was incapable of true intellectual examination. At times I thought him pathologically superstitious. He carried amulets, he pronounced talismanic formulas; like Dr Johnson he counted paving stones; he avoided thirteens, black cats, open ladders. Vassili, his domestic – who was always by his side holding Turkish towels, or hair brushes; but you know Cocteau's caricature – Vassili was made to perform what Diaghilev regarded as the more orthodox superstition of prayer, for while he was not a believer, he did not want to exclude the Christian possibility altogether. Vassili once told me that when they were *en route* to America in 1916, Diaghilev was so frightened by rough seas that he made him go down on his knees and pray, while he, Diaghilev, lay on his bed worrying for both – a real division of labour.

I remember a trip in the English Channel with him myself, and how he kept looking at a barometer, crossing himself, and saying 'Salvo, Salvo'.

*

Diaghilev feared the *iettatore* and would make the sign with the first two fingers of his right hand against its spell. Once when we were talking together in a theatre I was surprised to see his right hand occupied with the sign while he continued to talk to me, so to speak, with his left hand. 'Seriosha, what

* Diaghilev once told me about his visit to Tolstoy to see Tolstoy's old family portraits. The old man received him cordially and showed him round his gallery with a big lantern, but his only real interest in Diaghilev was as a draughts opponent. He asked Diaghilev if he played draughts and Diaghilev said he did, so terrified was he, though he had never played in his life. They played, and of course Diaghilev did everything wrong. Tolstoy said: 'Young man, you should have told the truth right away; now go upstairs and take tea.'

are you doing?' I asked. He pointed to three men behind
him and said that one of them had the *malocchio*. I looked and
saw that he was mistaken and told him so, but he would not
abandon the digital counter-influence until the three men
had gone.

Diaghilev was self-destructively vain. He starved himself
for the sake of his figure. I remember him – the next to last
time I saw him – opening his overcoat and proudly showing
me how slender he had become. This was for the benefit of
one of his last protégés – a modest, self-effacing, and utterly
ruthless careerist who was about as fond of Diaghilev as
Herod was of children. Diaghilev was a diabetic, but he was
not saved by insulin (he feared injections and preferred to
take his chances with the disease). I do not know the medical
explanation of his death, but I do know that this event was a
terrible shock to me, the more so because I had broken with
him over *Le Baiser de la fée* (which, as I have said, Ida
Rubinstein had staged, and which he had very bitterly
criticized), and because we were not reconciled when he
died.

I have recently uncovered a packet of letters and other
documents addressed to me at the time of Diaghilev's
death. One of the documents is a German newspaper describing Diaghilev as *ein berühmter Tanzer*. I quote two of the
letters.

> *Antequeruela Alta 11,*
> *Granada,*
> *22 August 1929*

Bien cher Igor, I am profoundly moved by the death of Diaghilev and it is my wish to write to you before I speak to
anyone else. What a terrible loss for you. Of all the admirable things he did, the first was his revelation of you. We
owe him that above all. And without you, besides, the

Ballet couldn't have existed. .... However, it is a consolation that our poor friend died without surviving his work. I always remember his fears during the war that someone might come and take his place. Later we understood how useless were such fears, for of course no one could ever take his place. And now I beg one favour of you: please give my most passionate condolences to the head of the Diaghilev Ballet, whoever that is now. I ask you to do this because I do not know anyone there now who could receive them.

    I embrace you with all my old and true affection,

MANUEL DE FALLA

PS. I hope you received my last letter which I sent registered, thinking you might be absent.

    The second letter is from Walter Nouvel, the secretary of the Ballet and Diaghilev's most intimate friend since they were students together in St Petersburg University. Nouvel's sensibilities were similar to Diaghilev's (indeed, he used to say: 'I like Italians; they recognize one right away; everyone in Italy always says "*grazie, tante*" to me'). His calm and intelligence saved the Ballet more than once. He was a good musician too, and to me personally the kindest of friends.

Paris,
30 August 1929

My dear Igor, I was touched to my soul by your deeply felt letter. We are sharing the same sorrow. I am bereft of a man to whom I was tied by a friendship of forty years. But I am happy today that I never failed to be faithful to this friendship. Many things united us and many things separated us. Often I suffered from him, often I was revolted by him, but now that he is in the grave all is forgotten and all forgiven. And I understand now that no ordinary measure of the conduct of human relations could be applied to so exceptional a man. He lived and died 'one of the favoured of God'. But he was a heathen, and a Dionysian heathen, not an Apollonian. He loved all earthly things: earthly love, earthly passions, earthly beauty. The sky was for him no more than a beautiful cupola above a beautiful earth.

This does not mean that he was without mysticism. No, but his mysticism was that of a pagan, not of a Christian, order. With him, Faith was replaced by a deep superstition; he had no fear of God but was terrified before the elements and their mysteries; he possessed no Christian humility but was instead a man of sensual, almost childlike emotions and feelings. His death, a pagan's death, was beautiful. He died in love and beauty and under the smiles of those two gods he swore by, and served his whole life, with such passion. Such a man must be loved by Christ.

I embrace you,

WALTER NOUVEL

These are four letters from Diaghilev to me:

I *Firenze,*
Quattro viale Torricelli,
1 November 1914

You awful pig. I wire you that I have signed the American contract, and that Mestrovic* answered that he expected me

*The ballet Diaghilev had planned with Mestrovic was *Liturgie*. I went to Rome for two weeks as his guest to discuss the project with him and with Mestrovic, but I refused to do the ballet, both because I disapproved of the idea of presenting the Mass as a ballet spectacle, and because Diaghilev wanted me to compose it and *Les Noces* for the same price.

in Rome in November. And you, not a word. You force me, an old man, to take to my pen. We stay here until 10 November, then go to Rome. We were in Ravenna and were overwhelmed by this magnificent cemetery. I have received a mad telegram from Misia saying she will not leave Paris because it is now the most beautiful city in the world. I have received a telegram from Nijinsky, too. He has no right to leave Budapest for the moment because of the war. Prokofiev is working with Gorodetsky and it seems he will finish his piano concerto. Kussevitsky is going to conduct in Rome and I shall see him. I received from your Mr Fokine an amiable inquiry about my affairs. The Fokines are at Biarritz. Well, and you, which tableau of *Noces* have you reached? Write, Dog.

Yours,

SERIOSHA

2   *Grand Hotel, Roma,*
25 November 1914

Dear Igor,

Our concert did not work out for some last-minute reason. When I originally proposed it to San Martino* he jumped up on his divan in transports and shouted 'but I will take Stravinsky with four hands'. Then when I saw him next time he told me how good it was to be an absolute Tsar and boasted that he could invite you without asking anybody. All details were settled and the concert arranged for the third of January when suddenly I received a letter with the following: ...' as to the fee, you can imagine in what an embarrassing condition the Academy finds itself in a season like this, when it has so few resources. On the other hand, Stravinsky is young and since he is not trying

* President of the Santa Cecilia.

to make a regular conductor's career I hope he will be satisfied with a very modest sum which could be between six and seven hundred francs.' I hastened to San Martino and explained to him that the train ticket costs 240 francs and your sojourn in Rome seven days at 50 francs a day, 350, *id est* 600 francs, the sum he proposed. All that I can do is to invite you to stay with me so you will have no expenses in Rome, and argue you into accepting 1,200 francs. He agreed with me and said that to get the money he will shrink his budget (!!) (he has also invited Strauss, Debussy, and Kussevitsky from Moscow, and others) so that the concert could take place. I even spoke with him and with their conductor about the order of the programme and I insisted that they give you twelve rehearsals. Then I received this note from him:

'My dear friend, as to Stravinsky's concert I regret very much to have to cancel it for reasons which I will explain to you with my own voice on my return.'

He went for three days to Turin and I shall see him at Sunday's concert. I will propose to him the following: to take on your travelling expenses myself and ask him to pay you 1,000 francs. If this also fails to work out, then to hell with him.

We absolutely must see each other. You must come here for two weeks – the best time would be from about the twentieth of December. If you pass the holidays here, you can have a little, quiet room in our apartment, and one eats not badly here. But you must come: our plan with Mestrovic is progressing. Mestrovic is a timid man with an exaggerated *amour propre* and a distrust of everything one does. He has genius in fulfilling his work, but his advice is mediocre. His intentions are always good, and he is inflamed by ideas. But we must take care ourselves about everything. Your being at such a distance makes this all impossibly difficult. I work together with him and Massine; bless us, I want Massine to stage this ballet!

Nijinsky behaves so stupidly.* He didn't even answer my detailed and, in my opinion, fair letter, and to my modest telegram requesting, 'reply paid', whether he had received it, he answered only: 'Letter received. Cannot come.'

I am sure that his wife is busy making him into the first ballet master of the Budapest Opera. As for *Noces*, do not worry. I will write him a second, less modest and less reasonable letter and this miserable person will understand that now is not the moment for joking. The invention of movement in *Noces* is definitely for Nijinsky, but I will not discuss the thing with him for several months yet. As for Massine, he is still too young, but each day he becomes more and more ours, and this is important. I am not going into any details now but let me tell you that what I have in mind is a performance of the MASS in six or seven short tableaux. The epoch will be Byzantine, which Mestrovic will arrange in his own way. The music should be a series of *a cappella* sacred choruses, inspired, perhaps, by Gregorian chant, but more of that later. When you come you will meet a great connoisseur of these matters – Mestrovic.

The frescos in the Roman underground churches of the first century are really astounding.

For the moment, that is all. I hope you approve. The main thing is that you come. Please answer me immediately at the Grand Hotel.

I embrace you,

SERGE

---

* Diaghilev's vengeance had begun. Almost every letter from him for the next few years contained a complaint about Nijinsky, and when Nijinsky wrote to him from N.Y. addressing him '*tu*', he was more offended than ever.

3   *Grand Hotel*
(we are in the Grand Hotel until 8 March)
3 March 1915

Dear, you are a little mad. San Martino buy something? His wife would choke to death first. They'll never do it. However, the American Russell was here; he found the price very high, though he said he would try to do something if you would send him a manuscript. He has gone to America, and his address is c/o Metropolitan Opera House, New York, Henry Russell, Esquire.

I am afraid to send him the manuscript, however, because someone could print it in America without paying you a penny. If you want to, however, do it yourself. I on my side will speak to Ricordi, although with little hope. As to the material of the *Nightingale*, you are not so much mad as ridiculous. If Teliatina* stages it at all he will not do so earlier than 1917, when everybody will have forgotten about the war. Why in hell should Prokofiev (who is coming today) drag the material with him so that it can stay two years in Petrogrrrrrad?† Tell me if we have to fulfil this foolish order.

Now about us. We are going to Naples and Palermo on 8 March for 10–12 days and afterwards coming to you to take *Les Noces*. It must be finished by that time. Then, with you, or without you, we are going for about three weeks to Spain. And afterwards? I don't know what and where, but we shall work, and not twiddle our thumbs as some people do. So, expect us about the twentieth of March, and have a big ballet ready – without that I shall be very angry.

* Teliakovsky, Director of the Opera in St Petersburg. Teliatina means veal.

† Diaghilev is making fun of the word as we all did when the 'St' was dropped and the 'burg' made 'grad'.

Before speaking with Dalcroze we must see what his material is.*

Everybody greets you. You left an 'indelible mark', as they say here.

SERGE D.

PS. Khvotschinsky leaves for the war, drafted in Russia.

PPS. It is as hot as summer here, and the sun beats down full force.

4   *Hotel de Paris,*
Monto Carlo,
7 April 1926

Mon cher Igor, I read your letter in tears. Not for a single minute have I ever stopped thinking of you except as a brother. Therefore, I feel joyful and full of light today because in your thoughts you have embraced me as one. I remember the letter you wrote me after the death of your brother Goury. I remember also the letter I wrote you not long ago telling you that when in moments of deep disturbance I remember that you are living almost next door in the world, I start to feel better. To forgive, it seems to me, is within the power of God alone; only He can judge. But we other little lecherous people, we ought in our moments of quarrelling or repentance to have enough strength to embrace each other like brothers and forget. This can evoke the thirst for forgiveness, and if you have this thirst, turn it towards me. I do not fast or go to confession or Communion (I am not a communicant). However, I ask you to forgive me my sins, voluntary and involuntary, and to keep in your heart only this feeling of brotherly love which I feel towards you.

SERIOSHA

*I don't remember what Dalcroze's project was, but I do remember having been to him and having seen demonstrations of his eurhythmic gymnastics.

SOME RUSSIAN COMPOSERS

RIMSKY-KORSAKOV

R.C. What are your present feelings, personal and otherwise, towards Rimsky-Korsakov, and do you remember the *Chant funèbre* you composed in his memory?

I.S. After fifty years it is quite impossible to discriminate between memories personal and impersonal; all memories are personal, yet mine are removed so far from the person that they cannot be told otherwise than impersonally. Few people can have been as close to Rimsky as I was, especially after the death of my father, when, for me, he was like an adopted parent. We try not to judge our parents, but we judge them, none the less, and often unjustly. I hope I am not unjust to Rimsky.

*

A great difference in character existed between the Rimsky of the Autobiography, which is the one most people knew, and the Rimsky who was my teacher. Readers of that well-written but matter-of-fact book think of him as someone not very easy with his sympathy and not abundantly generous or kind; moreover, the artist in the Autobiography was sometimes shockingly shallow in his artistic aims. My Rimsky was deeply sympathetic, however, deeply and unshowingly generous, and unkind only to admirers of Tchaikovsky. The shallow I cannot counter, for obviously there was nothing profound either in Rimsky's nature or in his music.

I adored Rimsky but did not like his 'mentality', by

which I mean his almost bourgeois atheism (he would call it his 'rationalism'). His mind was closed to any religious or metaphysical idea. If conversation happened to touch on some point of religion or philosophy he would simply refuse to allow that point to be considered in the light of 'revealed religion'. I was accustomed to dine with the Rimsky-Korsakov family after my lessons. We drank vodka and ate *zakousky* together, then started the dinner. I would sit next to Rimsky and often continue to discuss some problem from my previous lesson. Rimsky's sons and daughters occupied the rest of the table. His second son, Andrei, had studied philosophy at Heidelberg, and he often came to dinner with one Mironov, a university friend. But in spite of these young people's interest in philosophy, Rimsky would permit no discussion of it in his presence. I remember someone introducing 'Resurrection' as a table topic, and Rimsky drawing a zero on the tablecloth as he said, 'there is nothing after death, death is the end'. I then had the temerity to suggest that perhaps this was also merely one point of view, but was made to feel for some time thereafter that I should have held my peace.

I thought I had found friends in Rimsky's younger sons, two young gentlemen who, at least in provincial St Petersburg, were beacons of enlightenment. Andrei, a man three years my senior and a cellist of some ability, was especially kind to me, though this kindness lasted only while his father was alive; after the success of the *Firebird* in 1910 he, and in fact the entire Rimsky-Korsakov family, turned against me.* He even reviewed *Petroushka* for a Russian newspaper dismissing it as 'Russian vodka with French perfumes'. Vladimir, his brother, was a competent violinist and I owe to him my first knowledge of violin fingerings. I was not

---

* I think this was musical rather than personal. My music was too 'advanced' for them. Glazunov was their darling.

close to Sophie and Nadejda, Rimsky's daughters,* though my last contact with the Rimsky-Korsakov family was through Nadejda's husband, Maximilian Steinberg, who had come to Paris in 1924 and heard me play my piano concerto there. But you may imagine his response to that work when I tell you that the best he could do even for my *Fireworks* was to shrug his shoulders. After hearing the concerto he wanted to lecture me about the whole of my mistaken career. He returned to Russia thoroughly annoyed when I refused to see him.

*

Rimsky was a tall man, like Berg or Aldous Huxley, and like Huxley, too, he suffered from poor eyesight. He wore blue-tinted spectacles, sometimes keeping an extra pair on his forehead, a habit of his I have caught. When conducting an orchestra he would bend over the score, and, hardly ever looking up, wave the baton in the direction of his knees. His difficulty in seeing the score was so great, and he was so absorbed in listening, that he gave almost no directions to the orchestra at all. Like Berg, he suffered from asthma. In the last year of his life he began to fail very suddenly from the effects of this disease, and though he was only sixty-four years old we were aware that he would not last very long. He had a series of severe attacks in January 1908. Telephone calls came every morning from his house to ours, and I waited every morning not knowing whether he was still alive.

Rimsky was a strict man and a strict, though at the same time very patient, teacher (he would say '*ponimyete, ponimyete*', 'you understand', again and again throughout my lessons). His knowledge was precise, and he was able to

* My *Pastorale* was written with Nadejda's voice in mind, and dedicated to her. I later arranged this piece for violin and four woodwinds for the simple reason that songs as such were no longer performed.

impart whatever he knew with great clarity. His teaching was all 'technical'. But, whereas he knew valuable details about harmony and practical orchestral writing, what he knew about composition itself was not all it should have been. He was for me, when I first came to him, *sans reproche* musically, but before very long I began to wish for someone even less 'reproachable' and for music that would satisfy the ideals of my growing mind as Rimsky's was failing to do. The revival of polyphony and the renewal of form that had begun in Vienna in the very year of Rimsky's death were developments entirely unknown to the Rimsky school. I am grateful to Rimsky for many things, and I do not wish to blame him for what he did not know; nevertheless, the most important tools of my art I had to discover for myself. I should mention, too, that by the time I had become his pupil he was a reactionary who would oppose on principle anything new that came from France or Germany. I never ceased to be surprised by this attitude since outside the arts he was a radical, anti-Tsarist progressive.

*

Though Rimsky had wit and a lively sense of humour, though he had developed a literary style of his own, his literary taste was parochial, and in the worst sense. The librettos of his operas, except that of *The Snow Maiden* (Ostrovsky) and *Mozart and Salieri* (Pushkin), are, on the whole, embarrassingly bad. I once drew his attention to an anachronism in one of them: 'But, dear master, do you really think such an expression was in use in the fifteenth century?' 'It is in use now and that is all we need concern ourselves with.' Rimsky could not conceive of Tchaikovsky otherwise than as a 'rival'. Tchaikovsky had been more influential in Germany than Rimsky, and Rimsky was jealous (it seems to me that Tchaikovsky had a distinct influence on Mahler; listen to Figs. 16 to 21 in the fourth movement of Mahler's first symphony, and from Fig. 21 in the fifth movement of the second symphony). He would say, and never tire of saying, 'Tchaikovsky's music is in abominable taste', and indeed, though much of it is, Rimsky might have realized that his own music could share honours with Tchaikovsky's on this count. Nevertheless, Rimsky was proud to exhibit in his work-room a large silver crown Tchaikovsky had given him for the *première* of the *Capriccio Espagnol*. Tchaikovsky had attended the dress rehearsal and had so admired the brilliance of the music that he presented Rimsky with this token of homage the next day.

Rimsky was an Anglophile. He had learned English during his term as a naval officer, and though I cannot say how well he spoke it, I first heard the language from his lips. He often expressed himself in little English asides. Thus, one day a young composer had come to show him a score, but in his nervous excitement lost it in a droshky. Rimsky groaned disappointment in Russian, but whispered to me in English, 'The heavens are merciful.'

Rimsky did not mention me in his Autobiography for the reason that he did not wish to show me any mark of deference; he had many pupils and was always careful to avoid favouritism. My brother Goury *is* mentioned because he had sung in a cantata which I composed for Rimsky and which was performed in his house. After this event Rimsky wrote my mother a charming letter in appreciation of our talents.

Rimsky attended my first two *premières* with me. The first of these pieces, the Symphony in E Flat, is dedicated to him (the manuscript is still with his family). It was performed in St Petersburg on 27 April 1907; I remember the date because my Uncle Ielatchitch presented me with a medal commemorating it. Rimsky sat next to me and, from time to time, made critical remarks: 'this is too heavy; be more careful when you use trombones in their middle register'. As the concert took place at noon, and as the audience was not a paying one, I cannot say whether the applause I heard signified a success. The only bad omen was Glazunov, who came to me afterwards saying, 'very nice, very nice'. The Imperial Kapellmeister Varlich, a general in uniform, conducted the performance. My second *première*, *Le Faune et la bergère*, conducted by Felix Blumenfeld later the same year in one of Belayev's Russian Symphony Concerts, must have irritated Rimsky's conservatism, however, incredible though that may now seem. He found the first song 'strange', and my use of whole-tone progressions suspiciously 'Debussy-ist'. 'There, you see,' he said to me after the performance, 'I have heard it, but if I were to hear it again in a half-hour I would have to make the same effort of adjustment all over again.' At this time, Rimsky's own 'modernism' was based on a few flimsy enharmonic devices.

The *Chant funèbre* for wind instruments that I composed in Rimsky's memory was performed in a concert conducted by Blumenfeld in St Petersburg shortly after Rimsky's death. I remember the piece as the best of my works before the *Firebird*, and the most advanced in chromatic harmony. The orchestral parts must have been preserved in one of the St Petersburg orchestral libraries; I wish someone in Leningrad would look for the parts, for I would be curious myself to see what I was composing just before the *Firebird*. Alas, the only homage I have paid Rimsky since then was my conducting of his tone poem *Sadko** (not the opera; the tone poem is a more interesting work than the opera), the one work of his which I thought worth resurrecting.

*

*In New York, in 1935.

I no longer possess any of Rimsky's letters to me, though I must have had fifty or more in Oustiloug. I regret this very much as he had sent me many delightful cards from Lago di Garda, where he spent his summers. I have no manuscript either, though he gave me the first fifty pages of his *Snow Maiden* score. In fact, I have no autograph of his at all — which information is for the benefit of the person who regularly sends me registered letters from somewhere in Brazil begging for an autograph of Rimsky's.

CUI

R.C. Did you know César Cui in your Rimsky-Korsakov years?

I.S. I must have known him very early in my life for he was a great admirer of my father's and probably a guest at our home. My father had sung in some of Cui's operas and I remember being sent to Cui in 1901 with a special invitation to an opera performance celebrating my father's Jubilee — my father's wish to pay Cui a mark of attention. But though I saw Cui frequently at concerts I do not remember him dressed otherwise than in a military uniform — trousers with a stripe on the side, and a tunic which on special occasions had a little balcony of medals. Cui continued to lecture at the Military Institute in St Petersburg until the end of his life. He was said to be an authority on fortifications. Indeed, I suspect he knew more about them than about counterpoint, and the impression in my mind of Cui as a kind of Clausewitz is as strong as the impression of the musician. He was stiff and military personally, too, and one felt half-inclined to stand at attention when talking to him. He could be seen at concerts and other musical functions in St Petersburg almost regularly, in spite of his age, and the musicians of my generation came to stare at him as at a great curiosity.

Cui was rabidly anti-Wagner, but he had little to advance in Wagner's stead — a case of 'more substance in our enmities than in our love'. Nor could I take his orientalism seriously. 'Russian music', or 'Hungarian', or 'Spanish', or any other of the national nineteenth-century kind is, all of it, as thin as local colour and as boring. Cui did help me to discover Dargomizhsky, however, and for that I am grateful. *Russalka* was the popular Dargomizhsky opera at the time, but Cui considered *The Stone Guest* the better work. His writings drew my attention to the remarkable quality of the recitatives in the latter, and though I do not know what I would think of this music now, it has had an influence on my subsequent operatic thinking.

I do not know whether Cui had heard my *Firebird*, and though I think he was present at the first performances of the *Scherzo fantastique* and *Fireworks*, I recall no hint of his reactions to these pieces reaching my ears.

ARENSKY

R.C. And Anton Arensky?

I.S. Arensky was a composer of the Moscow school – in other words, a follower of Tchaikovsky. I – as a pupil of Rimsky-Korsakov, and for that very reason – could not know him well. And, in all that concerned Arensky, Rimsky was, I thought, unjustifiably harsh and unkind. He criticized Arensky's music captiously and unnecessarily, and a comment about it, which he allowed to be printed after Arensky's death, was cruel: 'Arensky did very little, and that little will soon be forgotten.' I attended a performance of Arensky's opera *Dream on the Volga* with Rimsky. The music was dull indeed, and Arensky's attempt to evoke sinister atmosphere with the bass clarinet was horse-opera farce. But Rimsky's exclamation to me that 'the noble bass clarinet should not be put to such ignominious use' must have been overheard several rows in front of us, and later, of course, throughout the theatre.

Arensky had been friendly, interested, and helpful to me, however, and in spite of Rimsky I always liked him and at least one of his works – the famous piano trio. He meant something to me also by the mere fact of his being a direct personal link with Tchaikovsky.

TANEYEV

R.C. And Serge Taneyev?

I.S. I saw Taneyev from time to time – as often, that is, as he came to St Petersburg, for he too was a Muscovite. He was a Tchaikovsky disciple also, and he sometimes took Tchaikovsky's classes for him at the Moscow Conservatory. Taneyev was a good teacher, and his treatise on counterpoint – one of the best books of its kind – was highly valued by me in my youth. I could respect Taneyev as a composer, especially for certain passages in his opera *The Oresteia*, and I admired him greatly as a pianist. But the same hostility prevailed on the Rimsky-Korsakov side and poor Taneyev was very unjustly treated in St Petersburg. I might add that Taneyev was held in some awe by us for an extra-musical reason: he was widely acknowledged to be the best friend of the Countess Tolstoy.

LIADOV

R.C. What were your relations with Anatol Liadov – especially after you had accepted the *Firebird* commission he had failed to fulfil?

I.S. Liadov was a darling man, as sweet and charming as his own *Musical Snuff Box*. We called him 'the blacksmith', but I can't think why unless it was because he was so soft and gentle and so very unlike a blacksmith. He was a small man with a sympathetic, squinting face and few hairs on his head. He always carried books under his arm – Maeterlinck, E. T. A. Hoffmann, Andersen: he liked tender, fantastical things. He was a short-winded, pianissimo composer and he never could have written a long and noisy ballet like the *Firebird*. He was more relieved than offended I suspect when I accepted the commission.

I liked Liadov's music, especially the piano pieces, *Kikimora* and the *Baba-Yaga*. He had a good harmonic sense and he always presented his music well instrumentally. Perhaps I was even somehow aware of the *Musical Snuff Box* when I composed a similar piece of my own, the 'ice-cream' wagon *Valse* in my second suite for small orchestra. I often accompanied Liadov to concerts, but if we were not together and he happened to see me in the hall he would always invite me to come and follow a score with him. I do not know if he had heard the *Firebird* in later years, but I am sure he would have defended it if he had. He was the most progressive of the musicians of his generation and he had championed my first pieces. Early in Scriabin's career, when the larger public's resistance to that composer was still general, someone referred to Scriabin in Liadov's (and my) presence as a fool, whereupon Liadov said: 'I like such fools.'

*

When I think of Liadov I remember another composer, and since it will not occur to you to question me about him, I will mention him myself. Joseph Wihtol, composer and teacher – he had collaborated with Rimsky-Korsakov in one or two works and was a colleague of Liadov's in that horrible musical prison, the St Petersburg Conservatory – was kindly like Liadov and very helpful to me. He was a jovial man, with round face and round hands like a cat's paws. He later lived in Riga, and when I visited that city on a concert tour in 1934 his affection and hospitality to me were princely.

SCRIABIN

R.C. What were your associations with Scriabin, both in St Petersburg, and later, when Diaghilev had become interested in him? Did he have any influence on you?

I.S. I do not remember my first meeting with Scriabin, but it must have been in Rimsky-Korsakov's house, for we often encountered each other there in the years of my tutelage with Rimsky. But he was personally so maladroit and his way of treating me and Rimsky's other pupils *von oben bis unten* was so detestable that I never wished to cultivate his company. Rimsky disliked him too; in fact, whenever he mentioned Scriabin to me he referred to him as 'the narcissus'. Rimsky did not value Scriabin's gifts as a composer very highly either: '*mais, c'est du Rubinstein*' ('Anton Rubinstein' being at this time a term of abuse equivalent to *merde*).

As a pupil of Taneyev, Scriabin was better grounded in counterpoint and harmony than most of the Russians – very much better equipped in these respects than, say, Prokofiev whose gifts were perhaps more brilliant. His own ground was derived in part from Liszt, which was natural for the age. I had nothing against Liszt, but I did not like Scriabin's way of continually arguing a Chopin-Liszt line as against a German tradition. I have elsewhere described his shock when I expressed my admiration for Schubert. The marvellous Schubert F minor Fantasia for piano four-hands was for Scriabin *la musique pour les jeunes demoiselles*. But most of his musical opinions were no better than that. I last saw him in Ouchy shortly before his death: his father was Russian Consul in Lausanne and I had gone to Lausanne to have my passport signed. Alexander Nicolaevitch had just arrived there. He talked to me about Debussy and Ravel, and about my own music. He had no insight at all: 'I can show you how to make their kind of French grimace. Take a figure of open fifths, relieve it with augmented $\frac{6}{3}$ chords, add a tower of thirds until you have dissonance enough, then repeat the whole thing in another "key": you will be able to compose as much "Debussy" and "Ravel" as you wish.' He did not tell me all that he told others about my own music, namely, that he, too, was horrified by *Le Sacre*; but as he had not been able to follow either *Petroushka* or the *Firebird* it was my fault to have been surprised.

Scriabin's vogue in St Petersburg began about 1905. I attributed it more to his phenomenal abilities as a pianist than to whatever new qualities there were in his music, but no matter the reasons, there *was* a sudden and very considerable interest in him, and he was hailed, at least in *avant-garde* circles, as an 'original'.

*

To answer your question, perhaps I have been influenced by Scriabin in one very insignificant respect, in the piano writing of my Études, op. 7. But one is influenced by what one loves, and I never could love a bar of his bombastic music. As for Scriabin's short career with Diaghilev, I know only why it was short: Scriabin was 'morbid'. Diaghilev had mistakenly assumed the contrary, and had decided to take him to Paris, telling me, 'I will show Scriabin's music to Paris'. The show, whatever it was, did not succeed.

Scriabin was literary-minded. Villiers de l'Isle Adam, Huysmans, the whole company of the 'decadents' were his rages. It was the age of Symbolism, and in Russia he and Konstantin Balmont were its gods. He was a follower of Mme Blavatsky, too, and a serious and well-considered theosophist himself. I did not understand this, for in my generation Mme Blavatksy was already very *démodée*, but I respected his beliefs. Scriabin was an arrogant-looking man with thick blond hair and a blond *barbiche*. Although his death was tragic and premature, I have sometimes wondered at the kind of music such a man would have written had he survived into the 1920s.

PROKOFIEV

R.C. What are your personal memories of Prokofiev, and what did you think of each other's music?

I.S. I met Prokofiev in St Petersburg in the winter of 1906-7. He was only seventeen or eighteen at the time, but he had been given part of a concert in Walter Nouvel's 'Evenings of Contemporary Music' series in which to play a group of his piano pieces. His performance was remarkable – but I have always liked his music hearing him play it – and the music had personality. I do not know if Rimsky was there, though I do remember from a conversation with him about Prokofiev that he regarded him very sceptically. But it was Liadov, not Rimsky-Korsakov, who had been Prokofiev's protector.

I did not know Prokofiev well until several years later, in Milan, during the war. Diaghilev was busy introducing him to the Futurists and to 'leftist' circles in general. Diaghilev wanted him to mix, to exchange ideas with other artists, but the attempt failed as it always did thereafter because Prokofiev was full of splinters, as he says about his music in a letter to me, with people who were more cultivated than he was – and a good many were that. On this Milanese visit *Le Sacre du printemps* was his only subject of conversation. He adored *Le Sacre* and was for many years quite unable to recover from the effect of it.

Prokofiev was the contrary of a musical thinker. He was, in fact, startlingly naïve in matters of musical construction. He had some technique and he could do certain things very well, but more than that, he had personality; one saw that in his every gesture – biological personality let us call it.

His musical judgements were usually commonplace, however, and often wrong. An example of the latter comes to mind in relation to *Petroushka*. He was once seated beside me at a performance of that work when, in the fourth tableau, at the climax of the Russian dances, he turned to me and said, 'You should have ended here'. But it is obvious to any perceptive musician that the best pages in *Petroushka* are the last.

Prokofiev was always very Russian-minded and always primitively anti-clerical. But in my opinion these dispositions had little to do with his return to Russia. The latter was a sacrifice to the bitch goddess, and nothing else. He had had no success in the United States or Europe for several seasons, while his visit to Russia had been a triumph. When I saw him for the last time, in New York in 1937, he was despondent about his material and artistic fate in France. He was politically naïve, however, and had learned nothing from the example of his good friend Miakovsky. He returned to Russia, and when finally he understood his situation there, it was too late. A few weeks before his death a friend of mine in Paris received a letter from him inquiring about me, and this touched me very much.

*

I do not know what he liked of my music beyond the Russian pieces, and especially *Le Sacre*, *Renard*, *Noces*, but I doubt if he knew very much of what I had written in the 1930s, and I am quite sure he would not have liked it if he did. The fact that we were not really in accord musically did not seem to matter. We were always on very good terms, there was never any incident between us, and I believe he liked me as much as he did any musical friend. But one could see Prokofiev a thousand times without establishing any profound connexion with him, and we rarely discussed music when we were together. I used to think that Prokofiev's depths were engaged only when he played chess. He was a master player and he played with all the celebrities, as well as with my wife, Vera.

Diaghilev had believed at first that Prokofiev would develop into a great composer, and he held to this belief for several years. Then, finally, he confided to me that he was beginning to think him 'stupid'. I have a letter from Diaghilev about Prokofiev:

Grand Hotel, Rome,
8 March 1915

Dear Igor, Many new questions, but first of all Prokofiev. Yesterday he played in the Augusteum, and with some success, but that is not the point. The point is, he brought me about one-third of the music of his new ballet. The subject is a St Petersburg fabrication; it would have been good for the Mariinsky Theatre ten years ago, but is not for us. The music, as he says, does not look for Russianism, it is just music. Precisely, just music, and very bad. Now we have to start all over again, and for this we have to be kindly with him and keep him with us for two or three months. I am counting on your help. He is talented, but what do you expect when the most cultivated person he sees is Tcherepnine who impresses him with his *avant-gardisme*(!) He is easily influenced and it seems to me he is a much nicer person than we suspected he would be after his arrogant appearance in the past. I will bring him to you. He must be changed entirely, otherwise we will lose him forever. ...

Of Prokofiev's Diaghilev ballets I preferred *Chout*, though the *L'Enfant prodigue* by Balanchine was the most beautiful choreographically. But I do not wish to criticize Prokofiev: I should be silent if I could say nothing good about such a man. Prokofiev *had* merits, and that rare thing, the instant imprint of personality. Nor was he cheap – facility is not the same thing as cheapness. Only, alas, he would not have understood Mallarmé's reply to a man who had congratulated him upon making such a clear speech: 'Then I will have to add some shadows.'

*

Prokofiev's letters to me were very affectionate. It is hard to reproduce their tone in English, but I think this example gives some idea of the character of his correspondence:

> *c/o Haensel and Jones,*
> *33 West 42nd St., New York,*
> *10 December 1919*

Dear Stravinsky,

I tell you the following with pleasure. Yesterday your *Pribaoutki* were performed for the first time in America. Vera Janacopulos sang, a very talented singer.* Her approach to them was most loving and she sang them beautifully except perhaps for *Uncle Armand* which is too low for her voice. The success was very great and all four songs were repeated. Lots of people in the audience laughed, but gaily, not indignantly. I sat next to Fokine and we bawled 'bravos' as loud as we could. The instrumentalists played well, and performed their tasks with interest. Only the viola and the bass may have been angry about it. The flautist, who has already played the *Japanese Lyrics*, was so sure of himself, no difficulties could frighten him. I went to the rehearsals and tried to explain what was not clear to them. Personally I like most: 1. *Uncle Armand*. The oboe and clarinet are like the gurgle of a bottle emptying. You express drunkenness through your clarinet with the skill of a real drunkard;

*I knew her well.

2. The whole *Natashka*, but especially the last five bars with the delightful grumbling of the winds; 3. *The Colonel*, entirely, but especially the oboe twitters and the climax on the words 'paea propala', etc.; 4. Many things in the last song, but the coda above all: the clarinet's G-A natural and the English horn's A flat are most excellent and most insolent.

I send you my cordial greetings and best wishes. I shall be very happy to hear from you,

Yours,
S. PROKOFIEV

Portraits Mémoires

VALÉRY

R.C. Your long friendship and admiration for Paul Valéry are well known. Would you tell me what you remember of him and also what you now think of his work?

I.S. I met Paul Valéry for the first time in 1921 or 1922: while only half recalling the date and the occasion (a reception by the Princess Edmond de Polignac, I think) I do remember the meeting. Valéry was small, about my own height in fact, which for some reason surprised me. He was quick, quiet (he spoke in rapid, *sotto voce* mumbles), and extremely gentle. He seemed a terrible dandy at first sight because of his monocle and *boutonnière*, but that impression dissolved as soon as he began to talk. Wit and intelligence were in everything he said, though not merely in what he said: they were manifest in his whole person. This was to be expected of Valéry, of course; what I did not expect, however, but was delighted to discover in him that first day, was a truly joyful sense of humour. By the time of parting we had already attained a high state of personal sympathy, and we were ever after natural friends.

Now that I have begun to force my memory about Valéry, I wonder I did not know him earlier. I had read *Monsieur Teste* before the 1914 war. I remember that I mentioned the book to Gide and that Gide responded with an encomium about its author. Ravel had also talked to me about Valéry in those years, and C. F. Ramuz too, though somewhat later, in Switzerland during the war. And we had many mutual

friends (Misia Sert, for example) at whose homes we ought
to have encountered each other. But whatever kept us apart,
we never failed to make up the gaps, and in the later 1920s
and in the 30s up to my departure for America, we saw each
other so regularly that we might be thought to have formed
a 'circle'. When I left Europe in September 1939 to give
the Norton Lectures at Harvard, I counted Valéry of
all my friends the one whose wisdom I would most sorely
miss.

Valéry was a deep source of intellectual and moral support to me on two important occasions in my life. One of
these concerned the Harvard lectures, *The Poetics of Music*,
as I call them. I had asked him to read and criticize my
manuscript. I was anxious to have his comments on its
literary style, especially since I had written the lectures
not in my own language but in French; I was not quite confident about some of the 'writing'. Accordingly, I read my
manuscript to him in a country house near Paris, sometime
in the late summer of 1939. He suggested various changes
in the phrasing and order of words, but to my great relief
endorsed the style of the lectures without reservation.

My other 'professional' call on him came at the time of
the first performance of my, and André Gide's, *Persephone*.
From my conversations with him I felt he had understood
my views on the tedious subject, 'music and words'. Not
that these views were difficult or obscure, or even original;
Beethoven had already expressed them, in sum, in a letter
to his publisher: 'Music and words are one and the same
thing.' Words combined with music lose some of the rhythmic and sonorous relationships that obtained when they
were words only; or, rather, they exchange these relationships for new ones – for, in fact, a new 'music'. They no
doubt *mean* the same things; but they are magical as well as
meaningful and their magic is transformed when they are

combined with music; I do not say that a composer may not try to preserve or imitate effects of purely verbal relationships in music. I have done precisely that myself, in instances where the verse form is strict or where the metre of the verse has suggested a musical construction to me (in the sonnet *Musick to Heare*, for instance). But this approach implies something of what is meant by the phrase 'setting words to music', a limited, pejorative description that is certainly as far from Beethoven's meaning as it is from mine.

Gide understood little or nothing of all this, however; or, if he understood, disagreed. (That Gide understood nothing whatever about music in general is apparent to anyone who has read his *Notes on Chopin*.) He had expected the *Persephone* text to be sung with exactly the same stresses he would use to recite it. He believed my musical purpose should be to imitate or underline the verbal pattern: I would simply have to find pitches for the syllables, since he considered he had already composed the rhythm. The tradition of *poesia per musica* meant nothing to him. And, not understanding that a poet and musician collaborate to produce *one* music, he was only horrified by the discrepancies between my music and his.

I turned to Valéry for support, and no arbiter could have given me more. I do not know what he said to Gide. But to me he affirmed the musician's prerogative to treat loose and formless prosodies (such as Gide's) according to his musical ideas, even if the latter led to 'distortion' of phrasing or to breaking up, for purposes of syllabification, of the words themselves. (But what kind of music did Gide expect of me?) And when *Persephone* was finally performed, at the end of April 1934, Valéry continued conspicuously to support me by attending all the performances, a fact I much appreciated – especially since his *Semiramis*, produced for

the first time only a week after *Persephone*, must have occupied a good deal of his time.

Shortly before the *Persephone première* I composed a statement of my views on the relations of text and music and on
the musical syllabification of a text. This manifesto, as it was
published in the Paris *Excelsior*, concluded with the words:
'. . . a nose is not manufactured: a nose just *is*, thus, too,
my art'. After the *première* I received the following letter
from Valéry:

The French Academy,
2 May 1934

My dear Stravinsky, I could not get to you Monday evening
to tell you of the extraordinary impression the *Persephone*
music made on me. I am only a 'profane listener', but the
divine *detachment* of your work touched me. It seems to me
that what I have sometimes searched for in the ways of
poetry, you pursue and join in your art. The point is, to
attain purity through the will. You expressed it marvellously
well in the article yesterday which I immensely enjoyed.
LONG LIVE YOUR NOSE.

Sincerely yours,
PAUL VALÉRY

Valéry knew little enough about music. But he knew that
he knew little and therefore did not utter banalities of the
type one so often hears from literary people. He made a
point of attending performances of my works, and this
touched me. I have a distinct recollection of him at the
first presentation of my *Dumbarton Oaks* Concerto in Paris;
my painter son Theodore made a drawing of him at the time
as a present for me.

*

The Valéry who most interests me at present is one whose

very existence most critics would deny: the religious. Valéry's nature *was* in some way religious, no matter how essentially non-religious his writings. Like Shaw, he had been the friend of a nun, of several nuns, in fact, and he had had doctrinal discussions with them. He was not susceptible to any religious orthodoxy, of course, nor, I think, was he even potentially a believer. When he had discovered the fallacy in the argument that the existence of absolute moral values must presuppose a Superior Being, when he saw that 'absolute' and 'Superior' represented an analytic contradiction, he did not look further, and instead of Valéry the theist we have Valéry the moralist. Nevertheless, he had thoughts that I would call religious, and these thoughts are revealed in the plays, especially in *My Faust*. If *Waiting for Godot* is religious, then so, certainly, is *The Only One*. And the Devil in *Luste* who says, 'I fell, but I fell from the top', is the Devil of the Scriptures and no mere personified idea. Valéry is even able to make this Devil invoke God, as when Mephisto says, 'No one has ever talked to me like this before. At least ... not for a long time.' And Valéry's finest line describing him, 'I am all the peril that is needed to make a Saint', is not the line of a pure moralist; nor is Faust's description of him, 'The Other', as 'Anything one likes, whatever one likes may be him', nor Mephisto's own self-description: 'I don't know how to think and I've got no heart ... all I know is my job.' Neither did Valéry in conversation with me display the sceptical temperament for which he was so famous, though in the religious-literary atmosphere of between-the-wars Paris, with, on the one hand, Gide and his Protestant manias, and on the other, Claudel and his Wagnerian-Catholic ones, I would have welcomed it.

*

Valéry is not one of the great innovators of our age, as

Joyce was, for example, or Webern, or Klee. He had been altogether too fascinated by the processes of creation. And, he worshipped intellect too much – indeed, to the point of valuing himself more as an intellectual than as a poet. The result of this Teste-ism was his contentment with *epistamenos*, with 'knowing how', at which point he would stop. Valéry's philosophical arguments are more rhetorical than philosophical, in my opinion, even when he is dealing with a pure philosophy such as Descartes's. I am even tempted to assert that Valéry's having written so much about poetry is responsible for dissipating his writing of poetry – though the examples of other poets contradict such an assertion.

I have never *seen* a Valéry play. I am therefore inclined to regard them all as collections of dialogues to be read. (The didactic dialogue on mind in *The Only One* is certainly 'to be read'.) And reading them, I somehow continue to hear all the characters speaking in Valéry's voice. I read, and heard, *My Faust* this way in the last spring of the war, not suspecting, of course, that I would never again hear Valéry's living voice. Very soon after came the news of his death. I grieved for him. His loss was a personal one.

ROLLAND

R.C. How did you come to know Romain Rolland?

I.S. At the beginning of the 1914 war, before the scandal of his *Au dessus de la mêlée*, he wrote asking me to contribute a statement to a book he was then preparing – an indictment of German 'barbarism'. I replied as follows:

Mon cher confrère! I hasten to answer your appeal for a protest against the barbarism of the German armies. But is 'barbarism' the right word? What is a barbarian? It seems to me that by definition he is someone belonging to a conception of culture new or different from our own; and though this culture might be radically different or antithetical to ours we do not for that reason deny its value, or the possibility that this value might be greater than our own.

But the *present* Germany cannot be considered as a manifestation of 'new culture'. Germany, *as a country*, belongs to the old world and the culture of the country is as old as that of the other nations of Western Europe. However, a nation which in time of peace erects a series of monuments such as those of the Siegesallee in Berlin and which, in time of war, sends her armies to destroy a city like Louvain and a cathedral like Rheims is not barbarian in the proper sense nor civilized in any sense. If 'renewal' is what Germany really seeks, she might better start at home with her Berlin monuments. It is the highest common interest of all those peoples who still feel the need to breathe the air of their ancient culture to put themselves on the side of the enemies of the *present* Germany, and to flee for ever the unbearable spirit of *this* colossal, obese, and morally putrefying Germania.

IGOR STRAVINSKY

PS. Throughout these terrible days – to which we are the living witnesses – your appeal *L'union fait la force* has been our one encouragement.

Shortly after sending him this letter I made his acquaintance on, of all places, a *lac des quatre Cantons* excursion boat. I was with my wife and children enjoying a day's outing when a tall, spectacled gentleman, evidently doing the same thing, came up to me and shyly introduced himself as my correspondent. I was immediately taken by his personal charm and intellectual honesty, and though his literature – *Jean-Christophe* and *Beethoven the Creator* – were and are exactly what I most abhor, these books have not obstructed my feeling for the man.* I saw him occasionally after that in company with Claudel and Jules Romains, if I remember correctly, at Ramuz's home near Lausanne. Later, he composed an enthusiastic article about *Petroushka* after hearing it at a concert in Geneva. I wrote to thank him for this criticism and we became friends.

FALLA

R.C. What do you remember of Manuel de Falla?

I.S. Sometime in 1910, at Cipa Godebski's, I was introduced to a man even smaller than myself, and as modest and withdrawn as an oyster. I took him, Manuel de Falla, for an *homme sérieux*; in fact, his nature was the most unpityingly religious I have ever known – and the least sensible to manifestations of humour. I have never seen anyone as shy. In the course of a party in his honour following a performance of *El Retablo de Maese Pedro* at the home of the Princess de Polignac (that curious American woman who looked like Dante and whose ambition was to have her bust next to Richelieu's in the Louvre), it was suddenly noticed that Falla himself had disappeared; he was found sitting alone in the darkened room of the theatre holding one of Maese Pedro's puppets. I was always surprised that a man as shy as Falla could bring himself to appear on a stage at all. He did conduct, however, and play the harpsichord – in his concerto, a piece I admire and have conducted myself. In fact, the last time I saw Falla was at a performance of this concerto in London in the 1930s.

* Since writing this I have come upon a remark of Rilke's about Rolland which coincides with my own feelings. Rilke found Rolland a 'sympathetic personality' (letter of 21 March 1913 to M. von Thurn und Taxis), but *Jean-Christophe* was 'indescribably thin, and the scene has been rightly placed in Germany because of the length and the sentimentality' (letter to the same of 10 April 1913) – a remark which, by the way, is almost the only attempt at humour I know of in Rilke.

Falla was always very attentive to me and my work. When, after the *première* of his *Tricorne*, I told him that the best music in his score was not necessarily the most 'Spanish', I knew my remark would impress him. And he did grow, though his material was so small he could not grow very far. I thought of him as the most devoted of all my musical friends. Whereas, for instance, Ravel turned his back on me after *Mavra* – indeed, the only later work of mine he ever noticed at all was the *Symphony of Psalms* – Falla followed me in all my later music. His ear was very fine, and I think his appreciation was genuine.

HAHN

R.C. Do you have any recollection of Reynaldo Hahn?

I.S. I saw him quite often, always in company with Marcel Proust. Diaghilev needed him and therefore staged his *Dieu bleu*; he was the salon idol of Paris, and salon support was very useful to Diaghilev at that time. After the war, how-ever, Diaghilev dropped him for the very reason that he had once found him important – his salon reputation. Hahn was an enthusiast of *Le Sacre du printemps*, as indeed almost everyone in Paris had become – except for Debussy, who persisted in calling it '*une musique nègre*', and the few con-servatives, who were calling it '*massacre du Printemps*' – and he remained a partisan of my music up to *Pulcinella* which, however, promptly turned him into an enemy. He was a thin, elegant man with motherly manners. Here is a New Year's note from him:

Paris,
1 January 1914

My dear friend, I thank you sincerely for your telegram, and I wish for this year the continuing development of your young glory. I enclose an article of mine that mentions your fascinating personality. You have had in me an admirer 'from the first hour'. But, do not think me a flatterer: I am too pedantic and, I dare say, too meticulous in my feelings to burst without restraint as some do, or to resign myself hypocritically as some others do. I avow my admirations and my true preferences, and I honour whoever is to be honoured. I admire you and esteem you very highly: you are a great musician.

As for my music, I beg of you to think as little good of it as you wish, but believe in my feelings of sincere friendship and profound artistic sympathy.

REYNALDO HAHN

GORODETSKY AND BALMONT*

.c. What do you recollect of the authors of your first song texts, Sergei Gorodetsky and Konstantin Balmont?

.s. I knew Gorodetsky well in 1906–7 when I was composing the music to his songs. We did not 'collaborate' in them, however, and after hearing them at a concert in St Petersburg, he confided to me that 'the music is very pretty, but it really does not interpret my texts accurately, since I describe a time-to-time ringing of long, slow bells and your music is a kind of jingle bells'. He was a tall, blond, sickle-nosed man who was later a good friend to my wife Vera in Tiflis during the revolution.

I did not meet Balmont though I saw him at one of our concerts in St Petersburg: he had bright red hair and goatee, and he was dead drunk, which was his normal condition from the day of his birth to his death. But I was never close to any Russian literary group, and in fact the only Russian literary intellectuals I ever did know – Merezhkovsky, for instance, and Prince Mirsky – I had met in Paris.

* See *The Poets of Russia 1890–1930* by Renato Poggioli, Harvard, 1960.

Balmont lived in Paris, but I did not encounter him there. His poetry is more significant than Gorodetsky's, and slightly less faded, though as a nature poet, he was easily overshadowed by the revolutionaries, and especially by Alexander Blok. His *Zvezdoliki* ('The Star-Faced One') is obscure as poetry and as mysticism, but its words are good, and words were what I needed, not meanings. I couldn't tell you even now exactly what the poem means.

BERNERS

R.C. What are your recollections of Lord Berners?

I.S. I met Gerald Tyrwhitt – he was not yet Lord Berners – in Rome in 1911. He had introduced himself to me as a friend of my St Petersburg friend Klukovsky. I found him droll and delightful. I saw him often after that and on every trip to Rome during the 1914 war. His remarks about music were perceptive; and though I considered him an amateur, but in the best – literal – sense, I would not call him amateurish, as we now use the word. When we knew each other better, he began to come to me for criticism and advice in his composition. I have often looked through his scores with him at the piano, or listened to them together with him in the theatre, and I thought his *Wedding Bouquet* and his *Neptune* as good as the French works of that kind produced by Diaghilev, though whether or not this could be construed as a compliment I cannot say.

I have already told how Lord Berners aided me when, on my way from Rome to Switzerland in 1917, I was detained by Italian border police and accused of trying to smuggle a plan of fortifications – in fact, my portrait by Picasso – out of the country. I suddenly thought of Lord Berners because of some Mandorlati figs he had given me to eat on the train; a policeman had confiscated the figs and begun to split them open with his sabre, in search of I know not what contraband. I contacted Berners at the British Embassy, and had the portrait sent to him to be forwarded to me in Switzerland as an official paper.

After the war Berners returned to London. I was a guest of his on each of my English visits. I remember with special pleasure an October week-end in the late 1930s in Faringdon, his country home near Oxford, where one slept in a crystal bed, walked in deep meadows, rode roan horses, and sat by brick fireplaces in Hepplewhite chairs. Faringdon's atmosphere was not exclusively traditional, however. Meals were served in which all the food was of one colour pedigree; i.e., if Lord Berners's mood was pink, lunch might consist of beet soup, lobster, tomatoes, strawberries. And outside, a flock of pink pigeons might fly overhead, for Lord Berners's pigeons were sprayed with (harmless) cosmetic dyes; my wife Vera used to send him saffron dye from France, and a blue powder which he used for making blue mayonnaise.

Lord Berners knew of my interest in old English music and once promised to present me with the complete works of Purcell. I think if he were to visit my home today nothing would please him more than the discovery that my library contains more old English music than any other kind.

Faringdon House,
Berkshire,
9 January 1919

Cher ami, Do you know that I have been bombarding you with letters and postcards from Rome for many months with no result? The Swiss border is a bad joke, and I suppose you have received nothing. In any case, I've had no answer. Meanwhile, however, I saw Carlo Ponti in Paris who gave me news of you. He was full of enthusiasm about the *Ragtime* which you had played him. I was a few days in London, also, where I saw Diaghilev and the Ballet several times. We celebrated the New Year together. I think he will stay in London until March and then go to Monte Carlo. I also saw Lady Cunard and Beecham, who talked about you a great deal. Beecham would like to play *The Nightingale* – has he told you about it? He is always very much in the clouds.

Recently I've written three small pieces for orchestra – *Chinoiserie*, *Valse sentimentale*, and *Kasatchok* – and they are to be played in Manchester on 8 March. I am pleased about this performance because, for the moment, Manchester has the best orchestra in England and the conductor will do them very well.

I expect to stay in England until March, and then go back to Rome.

Did you know that I had changed my name and am no longer Tyrwhitt? My aunt – or rather my uncle – *à héritage* – died. Unfortunately I inherit only the title, with a lot of taxes to be paid.

I would so much like to see you. I beg you to write me a little note and tell me what you are doing just now.

Your very devoted,

BERNERS

ROYAUTÉ

R.C. You must have met many of the Kings and Queens of Europe at gala performances in the early Diaghilev days?

I.S. No, for I contrived to avoid their official courtesies when I could. I do remember a few such confrontations, however, and among these the most impressive was my presentation to Queen Alexandra in her box at Covent Garden after a performance of the *Firebird* in 1912. I had tried to escape this also, but Diaghilev begged me to go, and Lady Ripon promised to be present and to help me. The Queen looked like a birthday cake – she wore a tall wig and was very rosily made up. She smiled at me but said nothing; as she was quite deaf, however, and as this affliction of hers was universally known, any compliment about my music would not have been in order. Most likely the poor woman had not the vaguest notion who I was or what I was doing there.

I knew Alfonso XIII of Spain rather better than this. As a balletomane who hardly ever missed a performance of our company in Madrid he often invited Diaghilev and me to his *loge*. I remember a *soirée* he gave for the dancers and artists of our troupe in some private rooms of the theatre where we were playing. I was seated between Queen Maria and the Queen Mother. I spoke German with the latter, and French with the two sovereigns, though the King himself did not remain at the table but walked about helping to serve us. (Harold Nicolson's description, in *People and Things*, of the solemn annual ceremony in which Alfonso had to wash the feet of a group of beggars gathered from the streets has curiously reminded me of this evening.) Alfonso was a kind man, but he was given to uttering the most awful *sottises*: '*Mon cher, il faut que vous composiez une musique pour les coupoles des églises russes,*' which is the sort of remark the Russian Grand Dukes used to make. He wore a medallion portrait of the Emperor Charles V on his chest which invited all who looked at him to compare the family features of the ancestral and the living king.

I also remember being presented to Queen Marie of Romania, King Carol's mother, the day after a concert in Bucharest in which I played my piano concerto; I think it was in 1925. The Queen had sent me an invitation which my Romanian friends considered to be indeclinable. Accordingly I went to the Royal Palace where I was escorted to an anteroom and left in the presence of several ladies-in-waiting, who were very eager to hear about Paris and kept asking me questions. One of them wanted to know what I thought was the most interesting thing in that city. I said the '*marché aux puces*' but the word '*puces*' seemed to shock them a good deal and they were silent. (I still wonder what *unanständig* meaning that word might have had in Romanian?) The Queen was both beautiful and a bluestocking: she had been an author herself, like that other Romanian queen, Carmen Sylva. She was most gracious to me and she even sent me to her bedroom to show me her fine collection of ikons.

But for a few chance meetings and one luncheon with the present Queen Mother of Belgium, who wanted to commission a violin concerto from me, and a brief presentation to the Queen of Holland at The Hague in 1952, these are all the queens of countries I have known.

Some Musical Questions

The song people praise is always the latest thing.
TELEMACHUS, trans. W. H. D. Rouse

R.C. For whom do you compose?

I.S. For myself and the hypothetical other. Or rather, this is an ideal achieved by only a very few composers. Most of us write for an audience, as, for example, Haydn: '... You ask me for an opera buffa. ... If you intend to produce it on a stage in Prague ... I cannot comply with your wish because all my operas are far too closely connected with our personal circle (Esterházy) and moreover they would not produce the proper effect which I calculated in accordance with the locality.' And, in another letter: 'I have to change many things (in a symphony) for the English public.' But this does not mean that an artist compromises himself when he considers an audience and its tastes. *Hamlet* and *Don Giovanni* were written for real audiences while, at the same time, the authors of these masterpieces had certainly first composed for themselves and the hypothetical other.

PATRONAGE

R.C. Most of your music was composed on commission. Has this circumstance affected the course of your art; that is, have the nature or specifications of a commission ever helped to determine your musical direction, or perhaps imposed a limitation on the musical substance? Would you comment on the role of the commission in contemporary music in general?

I.S. The trick, of course, is to choose one's commission, to compose what one wants to compose and to get it commissioned afterwards, and I myself have had the luck to do this in many instances. But, to reply to your question, I attribute hardly any influence on the direction or the substance of my music to the circumstances of commissions. Though Diaghilev had confronted me with Pergolesi's music, suggesting and finally commissioning me to write a ballet based upon it, and though this circumstance did undoubtedly lead to a new appreciation of eighteenth-century classicism on my part, I consider that I created the possibility of the commission as much as it created me, and that *Pulcinella*, though it may seem to have been an arbitrary step at the time, was an entirely logical step for me.

But, while I minimize the importance of commissions in relation to my own art, I believe that most new music is influenced, and even to some extent predetermined, by them. A certain kind of product *is* expected – however free the terms of a commission may seem to be. For example, a piece of music commissioned for performance by an American symphony orchestra is expected to be performable after four to six hours of rehearsal, to be standard in instrumentation, in length, and, since these standards tend to suggest others, standard in style – i.e., somewhere between Schoenberg and Stravinsky, but domesticated. The composer cannot stray very far from this pattern, e.g., produce a two-minute piece requiring thirty-five hours of rehearsal and twenty extra instruments and written in a style of such originality that the conductor's contract will be cancelled if he plays it. (This particular set of conditions is almost exactly reversed in the major radio stations of West Germany. Funds and rehearsal time for new music are abundant there and – this is my point – the styles of the new music, for better or worse – that is not the point – are, from a performing point of view, of a corresponding complexity.)

I do not say that a composer cannot write personal and original music in these conditions; I do say that, inevitably, conditions create patterns.

*

Probably the most significant difference between the role of the commission today and in the past is the question of utility. Or, at any rate, I imagine that music was commissioned in the past to satisfy an *actual* need. The commissions of a Renaissance Duke, of the Church, of an Esterházy or Diaghilev were of this sort. Actual, i.e., commercial, uses for new music of a high, i.e., non-commercial, quality do still exist, of course – the new concerto for a violinist, the new symphony for the Philharmonic, etc. – but whether the music is really needed for itself and not for some adjunctive value, namely, PUBLICITY, is often difficult to determine. I doubt, for example, that some of the commissioners of my own later music have paid what they have paid just for their musical pleasure. But this is still utility – no matter the motive. In the main, however, the need for new cantatas, string quartets, symphonies, is wholly imaginary, and commissioning organizations, like the Ford and the Rockefeller Foundations, are really only buying up surplus symphonies as the government buys up surplus corn. In fact, the need for such music is so hopelessly non-actual that the commissioners are now obliged to try to buy the need for the symphony as well as the symphony.

Great, i.e., immortal, music creates its own need; whether or not it happened to be commissioned should be a private economic fact of interest only to the composer. Webern's songs with instrumental accompaniment were not commissioned nor did they meet any demand; no performing organization was capable of presenting them at the time they were written. In fact, this music which is so consequential at present is a perpetual embarrassment to the whole idea of commission-for-use. None the less, even Webern could compose music on commission. Thus his *Symphony* for the League of Composers; it probably scandalized the League, and everybody else, but that couldn't have mattered to Webern.

But while the composer is guided by his genius (if he has any, and if he hasn't he doesn't matter), what guides the commissioner? I have just seen a list of composers recently awarded commissions of several thousands of dollars by one of the Foundations. As I know music and, also, some of the music of some of these composers, I think the Foundation concerned would have been wiser and kinder if it had *fined* some of these people the same amount of money, for money will not enrich their music, nor discourage the fulsome ideas of 'success' and 'career' such people pursue and believe to be theirs by the compliments of reviewers who automatically complimented their sort of trash. I have had my own experience with commissioners, too, a brush with Anti-maecenas himself – a scion of grocery stores and sciolist of 'modern art' – who would have commissioned *The Rake's Progress* from me, had I agreed to his condition that he should sit in judgement while I played my music to him at the piano.

Do you remember Sigismondo Malatesta's letter to Giovanni de'Medici asking for an artist to beautify the newly plastered walls of the Tempio Malatesta with frescoes? In Pound's version, Sigismondo wishes to promise the painter, whoever he may be, that he:

> . . . *can work as he likes,*
> *or waste his time as he likes,*
> *never lacking provision.*

That should be read by anyone who intends to commission an artist.

*

..c. Has music ever been suggested to you by, or has a musical idea ever occurred to you from, a purely visual experience of movement, line, or pattern?

.s. Countless times, I suppose, though I remember only one instance in which I was aware of such a thing. This was during the composition of the second of my *Three Pieces* for string quartet. I had been fascinated by the movements of Little Tich whom I had seen in London in 1914, and the jerky, spastic movement, the ups and downs, the rhythm – even the mood or joke of the music – which I later called *Eccentric*, was suggested by the art of this great clown (and *suggested* seems to me the right word, for it does not try to *approfondir* the relationship, whatever it is).

Incidentally, these pieces were not influenced by Schoenberg or Webern, as has been said – at least not to my conscious knowledge. I knew no music by Webern in 1914, and of Schoenberg only *Pierrot lunaire*. But, though my pieces are perhaps thinner in substance and more repetitive than music by Schoenberg and Webern of the same date, they are also very different in spirit, and mark, I think, an important change in my art. In spite of the obvious recollection of *Petroushka* in *Eccentric*, it seems to me these *Three Pieces* look ahead to the *Pièces faciles* for piano duet of one year later, and from the *Pièces faciles* to my so aberrant 'neo-classicism' (in which category, nevertheless, and without knowing it was that, I have managed to compose some not unpleasing music).

..c. How did you happen to use the *Jambe en bois* melody in *Petroushka*?

.s. A hurdy-gurdy played it every afternoon beneath my window in Beaulieu (near Nice) and since it struck me as a good tune for the scene I was then composing, I wrote it in. I did not think whether the composer might still be living or the music protected by copyright, and Maurice Delage, who was with me, was of the opinion that the 'melody must be very old'. Then, several months after the *première* someone informed Diaghilev that the tune had been composed by a Mr Spencer, a gentleman still very much alive and resident in France. Since 1911, therefore, a share of *Petroushka's* royalties has gone to Mr Spencer or his heirs. I do not cite this to grieve about it, however: I *should* pay for the use of someone else's property. But I do not think it fair that I have to pay, as I must, a sixth of all royalties deriving from purely musical (non-staged) performances of *Petroushka*, even of excerpts, such as the *Russian Dance*, to the co-author of the libretto.*

The *Jambe en bois* incident might have had a sequel years later with the 'Happy Birthday' melody in the *Greeting Prelude* I wrote for Pierre Monteux's eightieth birthday (a piece I had already sketched out in 1950 for a project that did not materialize). I must have assumed this melody to be in the category of folk music, too, or, at least, to be very old and dim in origin. As it turned out, the author was alive, but, graciously, did not ask for an indemnity.

*The injustices of copyright laws and non-laws would add a complicated chapter to my 'life' and demand a reinterpretation of some of my composing activity. Those who imagine that my works make me rich do not realize that everything I composed before 1931 (I became a French citizen in 1934, and this citizenship extended authors' rights retrospectively for three years) was and is unprotected in the United States: the United States and the U.S.S.R. failed to sign the Berne copyright convention. I do not receive performance rights for the *Firebird*, which, as one of the most popular pieces of music composed in this century, would have made me a 'millionaire' (though, of course, for the good of my soul, I do not aspire to be any such thing).

The *Firebird*, *Petroushka*, and *Le Sacre du printemps* were pirated in the United States and have been performed there free for the last thirty-five years. I tried to protect the music I composed after these three ballets by having an American editor sign my compositions – a humiliating

R.C. To what extent does your Russian music, especially *Renard* and *Les Noces*, make use of folk melody?

I.S. There is no conscious use of folk melody whatever in *Renard*, and only one of the themes of *Les Noces* is folk derived; and it is not really a folk melody but a workers'

melody, a proletarian song. This theme, incidentally, was given me by my friend Stepan Mitusov at least ten years before I made use of it in the final tableau of *Les Noces*. Excellent collections of Russian folk music by Tchaikovsky and Liadov, and a more or less good one by Rimsky-Korsakov, had been published; all of these were familiar to me, of course, and while I did not actually turn to folk music as source material, I was undoubtedly influenced by it. The song 'Down St Peter's Road' in *Petroushka* (St Petersburg was called simply 'Peter' in the peasant villages – 'Are you going to Peter?') was taken from Tchaikovsky's collection. There are also three folk melodies in the *Firebird*, the two 'Khorovod' themes

---

expedient, though Albert Spalding, who kindly gave his name, was so obviously not a real editor. This stratagem covered only those less frequently performed works of the 1920s, however, which it would not pay a pirate to copy. When I became an American citizen in 1945 I prepared new versions of almost all the music I had composed before 1931. These versions vary from complete re-writings, like *Petroushka* and the *Symphonies of Wind Instruments*, to the mere correcting of printers' errors – as in the case of the *Capriccio* and *Symphony of Psalms*. But the three popular and lucrative early ballets are still far more commonly played in the old, pirated editions.

I like a story about Schoenberg and an early piece of his that was also unprotected. Someone suggested to him that he change the score, re-write a minim as two tied crotchets, for instance, so that the piece could be copyrighted as a new version. Schoenberg's reply was: 'I can't change anything – it's perfect already.'

and

and the theme of the *Finale*

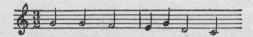

which had a dotted rhythm in the original. I do not remember which of the three collections supplied which themes, however.

The opening bassoon melody in *Le Sacre du printemps* is the only folk melody in that work. It came from an anthology of Lithuanian folk music I found in Warsaw, and not from Borodin or Cui as some critics have suggested; the anthology was a recent publication. And, to my knowledge, none of my Russian songs – *Pribaoutki*, the *Four Russian Peasant Choruses*, the *Four Russian Songs*, the *Berceuses du chat* – contains folk material. If any of these pieces *sounds* like aboriginal folk music, it may be because my powers of fabrication were able to tap some unconscious 'folk' memory. In each case, however, the syllables and words of the songs dictated the music. The *Balalaika* in my *Pièces faciles* is also my original melody, like a folk song, of course, but not directly borrowed. One other work of mine, not 'Russian' and therefore not in your category, borrows extensively from folk music. All the themes in my *Norwegian Moods* were taken from a collection of Norwegian folk music my wife had found in a second-hand book store in Los Angeles – and not from Grieg as some writers on my music have stated!

Some Musical Questions

.c. What prompted you to arrange the *Star-Spangled Banner*?

s. I undertook the arrangement at the suggestion of a pupil – a composer, rather, who visited me twice a week to have his works recomposed – and partly because I was obliged to begin my concerts during the war with the *Star-Spangled Banner*, the existing arrangements of which seemed to me very poor. My version was composed in Los Angeles on 4 July, 1941, and performed shortly after that by an orchestra and negro chorus conducted by my pupil's son-in-law. After this performance I sent the manuscript to Mrs F. D. Roosevelt for a war-fund auction, but my major seventh chord in the second strain of the piece, the part patriotic ladies like best, must have embarrassed some high official, for my score was returned with an apology. I then gave it to Klaus Mann, who soon succeeded in selling it for a similar purpose. I performed it myself for the first time with the Boston Symphony Orchestra in the winter of 1944. I stood with my back to the orchestra and conducted the audience, who were supposed to sing but didn't. Though no one seemed to notice that my arrangement differed from the standard offering, the next day, just before the second concert, a Police Commissioner appeared in my dressing-room and informed me of a Massachusetts law forbidding any 'tampering' with national property. He said that policemen had already been instructed to remove my arrangement from the music stands. I argued that if an *Urtext* of the *Star-Spangled Banner* existed, it was certainly infrequently played in Massachusetts – but to no avail. I do not know if my version has been performed since. It ought to be, for it makes the linear and harmonic best of the material, and is certainly superior to any other version I have heard. (The compliment to myself in this comparison is very small indeed.)

ELECTRONIC MUSIC

R.C. Have you any further observations to make about electronic 'music'?

I.S. I would still repeat the criticisms I made of it two years ago – namely, I do not see why a medium so rich in sound possibilities should sound so poor; and, though shape and composition are more in evidence and the liaisons more convincing in the newer pieces, the impression of desultoriness is still a main impression. At the same time the newer electronic music has more direction – a fact I attribute to the clearer division between those who are trying to create a new and purely electronic sound and those who are trying to transform existing sounds, instrumental and otherwise; some attractive results have been attained on both sides of this split. Now, however, with the appearance of the R.C.A. synthesizer the whole electronic music experiment up to the present can only be regarded as a pre-natal stage in its development.

Also, many composers have now begun to see a use for electronically produced sound, mixed or used adjunctively with traditional instrumental sound – though no one, I think, has been entirely successful in bridging the modulatory ground between the two. I myself am interested in this problem of bringing together the live and the mechanical. In fact, my first idea, in 1917, for the instrumentation of *Les Noces* was to use mechanical instruments, player pianos, together with ordinary orchestral instruments – an idea I abandoned only because I did not know how to coordinate and control both elements.

Perhaps the real future of electronic music is in the theatre. Imagine the ghost scene in *Hamlet* with electronic 'white noise' entering the auditorium from several directions (Berio's *Omaggio à Joyce* is perhaps a preview of this kind of thing). But this very theatricality – which electronicians will object to as more for the effect of another art than for the thing itself – exposes another problem. 'Concerts' of electronic music are, in fact, more like séances. With nothing to look at on the stage – no exhibition of orchestra and conductor, but only conduit-speaker boxes and, suspended from the ceiling, mobile reflectors – what is the audience to look at? Surely not at anything so arbitrary as the 'symbolic' colours and pictures of the San Francisco 'Vortex' experiment?

I have uncovered a Diaghilev letter that should be of at least historical interest in the discussion of 'Futuristic' music, *musique concrète*, and electronic music. It is dated Rome, 8 March 1915, and was sent to me at the Hotel Victoria, Château d'Oex, Switzerland. It is naïve, of course, but not more so than the 'Futuristic' composers themselves; and it is a good example of Diaghilev's flair.

... now to something else, and much more important. An idea of genius has come to my mind. After having thirty-two rehearsals of the *Liturgie*, we have concluded that absolute silence is death ... and that aerial space is not absolute silence and cannot be. Silence doesn't exist and couldn't exist. Therefore, dance action must be supported not by music but by sounds, *id est*, by filling the ear harmonically. The source of this 'filling' should not be recognizable. The changes of these harmonic junctures, or liaisons, must not be remarked by the ear – one sound merely joins or enters another, *id est*, there is no obvious rhythm whatsoever, because one does not hear either the beginning or the end of the sound. The projected instruments are: bells wrapped round with cloth and other material, aeolian harps, guzli,* sirens, tops, and so on. Of course all this has to be worked out, but for that purpose Marinetti proposes we get together

* The goat plays this instrument in *Renard*.

for some days in Milan and discuss it with the leader of their 'orchestra', and examine all their instruments. Also, he guarantees that at this time he will bring Pratella to Milan so he can show us his newest works which are, according to him, *formidables*. We could do it between the 15th and 20th of March.

Telephone me at Naples, Hotel Vesuvio, if you can come to meet us in Milan. You will see many new Futuristic studios; from there we will go together to Montreux. I urge you very strongly to come – it is very important for the future. I will send you some money for the trip immediately. As for the concert of Prokofiev in Geneva, he can give it as a benefit for the Serbs if he is busy on the 20th. Then, until we meet soon,

je t'embrasse,   SERIOSHA

PS. Compose *Noces* quickly. I am in love with it.

VARÈSE

R.C. Some of this might be a description of the music of Edgar Varèse? What do you make of Varèse?

I.S. There is nobility in his noise and he himself is a noble figure in our music (how much more honest to have kept his long silence than to have written the apish music of so many others). And it is useless to remark, as many do, that his music is limited and repetitive, and that after he had done the one kind of thing he had nowhere to go. The point is he *had* done the one thing. I have never heard *Amériques* and *Arcana* (they *look* as though the shadow of *Le Sacre* had fallen over them), but I do know and greatly admire *Ionisation*, *Octandre*, *Density* 21.5, and *Intégrales*, and I consider Varèse's present activity – tape-recording the sound of New York City – of the highest value and not merely as documentation, but as material of art.

WEBERN

.c. Have you changed your mind in any particular about Webern?

s. No; he is the discoverer of a new distance between the musical object and ourselves and, therefore, of a new measure of musical time; as such he is supremely important. But Weburn's importance is now recognized even by the matinée idols. A celebrated conductor who recently performed one of the two pieces by him that could be called popular conceded in an interview that 'Webern does have an influence on music', a statement comparable in politics to Eisenhower's discovering communists in China.

Webern the man has now begun to emerge, too, with the publication of his letters to Berg, Humplik, and Jone. The Webern of the letters is, first of all, profoundly religious, and not only institutionally (extraordinary, though, that he should compare the six movements of his second cantata to a Kyrie, a Gloria, a Credo, a Benedictus, a Sanctus, an Agnus Dei), but in the simple holiness of his feeling towards each of God's *essents* (a flower, a mountain, 'silence') as well. Music is a mystery to him, a mystery he does not seek to explain. At the same time, no other meaning exists for him but music. He stands before the Parthenon friezes and marvels at the sculptor's 'conception' which he compares to his own 'composition method . . . always the same thing in a thousand different ways' (in another letter: ' . . . the meaning is always the same however different the means'). He never explains beyond that, and he even admits, in one letter, to being severely tried by the necessity of explanation: 'I am sometimes . . . tortured by teaching.'

He is like a village in that his world does not extend beyond his village – indeed, he makes *my* world seem a million miles away. His manners and address are also both *villageoises* and . . . priestly. He contains no word of technical jargon (to Berg: 'art must be simple') and no aesthetics ('I don't understand what "classic" and "romantic" mean'). He is infinitely patient and, of course, he takes infinite pains* but composing is entirely natural to him. He does not have a rebellious heart – indeed, he accepts without criticism the musical tradition to which he was born – nor has he any conception of himself as a radical composer; he was what he was wholly apart from the so-called *Zeitgeist*. This Webern will embarrass 'Webernists'. They will blush for their master's 'naïvety' and 'provincialism'. They will cover his nakedness and look the other way. And this turning away will coincide, too, with a reaction against his music (in favour of Berg's; I hear everywhere now that Webern's series are too symmetrical, that his music makes one too conscious of twelves, that *la structure sérielle chez Berg est plus cachée*; for me, however, Berg's music, compared with Webern's, is like an old woman about whom one says 'how beautiful she must have been when she was young'). Webern was too original – i.e., too purely himself. Of course the entire world had to imitate him, of course it would fail, of course it will blame Webern. No matter, though. The desperate contrivance of most of the music now being charged to his name can neither diminish his strength nor stale his perfection. He is a perpetual Pentecost for all who believe in music.

*

R.C. Would you analyse your own composing process in any part of one of your more recent pieces – in, for example, the little *Epitaphium*?

I.S. I began the *Epitaphium* with the flute-clarinet duet (which I

---

* That his music cost him terrible birth pains I have no doubt. The few musical examples in the letters indicate how deeply he had been concerned in his later music with the relation of note values to musical substance (and tempo, metre, beat), and how this problem alone involved him in several stages of re-writing.

had originally thought of as a duet for two flutes and which can be played by two flutes; the piece was written to be performed in a programme with Webern's songs, op. 15, which use the flute-clarinet combination). In the manner I have described in our previous conversations I heard and composed a melodic-harmonic phrase. I certainly did not (and never do) begin with a purely serial idea and, in fact, when I began I did not know, or care, whether all twelve notes would be used. After I had written about half the first phrase I saw its serial pattern, however, and then perhaps I began to work towards that pattern. The constructive problem that first attracted me in the two-part counterpoint of the first phrase was the harmonic one of minor seconds. The flute-clarinet responses are mostly seconds, and so are the harp responses, though the harp part is sometimes complicated by the addition of third, fourth, and fifth harmonic voices. (The harp in this piece, as in all my music, must be pinched *près de la table* to produce the sound I want; incidentally, the deep bass notes of the harp are, I think, the most beautiful on the instrument.)

Only after I had written this little twelve-note duet did I conceive the idea of a series of funeral responses between bass and treble instruments and, as I wanted the whole piece to be very muffled, I decided that the bass instrument should be a harp. The first bar of the harp part was, however, written last. As I worked the music out, it became a kind of hymn, like Purcell's *Funeral Music for Queen Mary*. There are four short antiphonal strophes for the harp, and four for the wind duet, and each strophe is a complete order of the series — harp: O, I, R, RI; winds: O, RI, R, I.

*

I *have* discovered new (to me) serial combinations in the *Movements* for piano and orchestra, however (and I have discovered in the process, too, that I am becoming not less but more of a serial composer; those younger colleagues who already regard 'serial' as an indecent word, in their claim to have exhausted all that is meant by it and to have gone far beyond, are, I think greatly in error); and the *Movements* are the most advanced music from the point of view of construction of anything I have composed. No theorist could determine the spelling of the note order in, for example, the flute solo near the beginning or the derivation of the three F's announcing the last movement simply by knowing the original order, however unique the combinatorial properties of this particular series. Every aspect of the composition was guided by serial forms, the sixes, quadrilaterals, triangles, etc. The fifth movement, for instance (which cost me a gigantic effort – I rewrote it twice), uses a construction of twelve verticals. Five orders are rotated instead of four, with six alternates for each of the five, while at the same time, the six 'work' in all directions, as though through a crystal.

Now that I have mentioned my new work I should say, too, that its rhythmic language is also the most advanced I have so far employed; perhaps some listeners might even detect a hint of serialism in it, too. My polyrhythmic combinations are meant to be heard vertically, however, unlike those of some of my colleagues. Though parallels are not equivalents, look at Josquin for a parallel, that marvellous second *Agnus Dei* (the three-voice one) in the *Missa l'Homme armé*, or at Baude Cordier's *pour le deffault du dieu Bacchus*,*

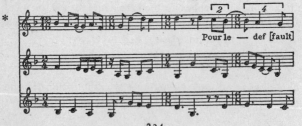

or, for even more remarkable examples, at the Cyprus Codex.

Each section of the piece is confined to a certain range of instrumental timbre (another suggestion of serialism?), but the movements are related more by tempo than by contrasts of such things as timbre, 'mood', character; in a span of only twelve minutes, the contrast of an *andante* with an *allegro* would make little sense; construction must replace contrast. Perhaps the most significant development in the *Movements*, however, is their tendency towards anti-tonality – in spite of long pedal-point passages such as the C of the first ending, the clarinet trill at the end of the third movement, and the string harmonies in the fourth movement. I am amazed at this myself, in view of the fact that in *Threni* simple triadic references occur in every bar.

FILM MUSIC AND FILMS

R.C. Have you ever considered writing music for films?

I.S. Yes, several times, and in two instances I had even begun to compose, not 'film music', which is aural erethism, an emotional counterpart to scenery, but music for film use; my *Four Norwegian Moods* was originally intended for a film about the Nazi invasion of Norway, and my *Scherzo à la Russe* began as music for another war film, with a Russian setting. Neither score differed in any way from its present concert form, however, though I re-orchestrated the *Scherzo* for the Paul Whiteman band later; I could conceive of music for films only as incidental music, which is what these pieces are. That this conception is quite wrong from the film industry's point of view I am well aware, but it is as far as I will go, and I can probably count myself fortunate that none of the proposals Hollywood has made me ever reached a contractual stage.

I do enjoy negotiating with film people, though, for only

rarely do they try to obscure their motives with nonsense about art. They want my name, not my music – I was even offered $100,000 to pad a film with music, and when I refused, was told that I could receive the same money if I were willing to allow someone else to compose the music in my name. The classical Hollywood story is not mine but Schoenberg's, however. The great composer, who earned almost nothing from his compositions, was invited to supply music for *The Good Earth*, at a fee that must have seemed like Croesus's fortune to him, but with impossible artistic conditions attached. He refused, saying, 'You kill me to keep me from starving to death.' Incidentally, Schoenberg's *Accompaniment to a Cinematograph Scene* is by far the best piece of real film music ever written, an ironic triumph if there ever were one, for the film itself was imaginary.

I first saw a moving picture in St Petersburg in 1904. (I am certain of the date as it was shortly after Tchekov's death, an event that impressed me, though the fact of his illness was well known, and though I was never a great admirer of his – to my taste – too intellectualized literature.) I remember waiting a long while in a small, crowded room and then seeing a film that proved to be an advertisement for Swiss chocolate. A woman stood by a table pouring hot chocolate into a cup, and a child then swallowed the contents of the cup. That was all. The whole performance lasted no longer than a Bagatelle by Webern, and the cup and the liquid trembled terribly. A second short film was shown, too, a conflagration in a Swedish match factory.

My real interest in films began in 1912 with the first Chaplins – at any rate, I seem to remember seeing a Chaplin film then, in Nice, in company with Michel Larionov, but if that is not accurate I am positive I saw a Chaplin film with Diaghilev in Santander, in 1915. I also remember *Les Mystères de New York*, in Lausanne, I think in 1912. This was one of the first of the 'to be continued next week' serialized adventures, and though it was the most shameless *chyepouha*, the insidious secret of films is such that I was there again each next week.

Chaplin was an event in my life, as he was in Diaghilev's. His so prodigal inventiveness was a continual amazement to me; but I was touched also by the moral point of each Chaplin episode, as well as by the moral of the whole film. (For example, the lunch scene on the tempest-driven boat where he tries to impale a single *petit pois* rolling about his plate like the ball in a pin machine. The Chaplin touch is in the moral ending: when finally he picks up the pea with his fingers, a lady looks on in disgust.) I met Chaplin in Hollywood in 1937 and we became friends. I had concerts there at the time, and he came with me to my rehearsals. For me, Chaplin *is* Hollywood, in its brief age of art.

Film music is significant, in many ways, of course, but not as music, which is why the proposition that better composers could produce better film music is not necessarily true: the standards of the category defeat higher standards. Still, I must express my respect for the craftsmanship of the many good musicians employed by the films, especially the arrangers, who are often responsible for more than the word 'arranger' would seem to imply; in fact, it is said that in Hollywood Haydn would have been credited as the composer of the *Variations on a theme by Haydn* and Brahms as their 'arranger'.

*

Teaching makes of art a virtue.
THE LORD OF SUGAWARA
(in the Bunraku play by Chikamatsu)

R.C. Why did you never become a teacher?

I.S. I have very little gift for teaching, and no disposition for it: I am inclined to think that the only pupils worth having would become composers with or without my help (though I am not sure that I would say the same thing in the same way about Berg and Webern in relation to Schoenberg). My instinct is to recompose, and not only students' works, but old masters' as well. When composers show me their music for criticism all I can say is that I would have written it quite differently. Whatever interests me, whatever I love, I wish to make my own (I am probably describing a rare form of kleptomania). I regret my inability, however, and I am full of veneration for Hindemith, Krenek, Sessions, Messiaen, and those few other composers who possess the teacher's gift.

R.C. Your remarks about 'virtuosi' (in the first volume of our 'conversations') might easily be misunderstood. Would you describe the kind of performer you mean?

I.S. I mean, of course, the false virtuosi, the virtuosi without *virtù*, for the term is no longer prestigious; but I should have distinguished between past and present examples, and in the present between the true and the false. Whereas the virtuosi of other eras collaborated closely with new music in exploring new instrumental possibilities and extending technique, the virtuosi of today are inclined to pronounce the most interesting new music – no matter how often 'lesser' performers play it – unplayable. But true virtuosi do still exist. They are the exceptional instrumentalists – the flute player in Rome (Gazzelloni), the clarinettist in Paris (Deplus), and others, who really have attained new instrumental and musical powers through their performances of new music. They are unknown, of course, but their value to music is greater than that of their famous colleagues.

I would define the false virtuoso as that performer who plays only nineteenth-century music, even when it is by Bach and Mozart; or, as the kind of performer who should begin his recitals with the encores, since they are what he plays best.

PERFORMANCE AND INTERPRETATION

R.C. Would you comment on any recent performances of Haydn, Mozart, or Beethoven you may have heard?

.s. A few days ago I was exposed to a Toscanini recording of Beethoven's first symphony. The *Adagio molto* introduction was played not adagio but andante, in an undivided beat of four and badly played from the very first chord which was not unanimous. The *Allegro* was also an absurdly fast Rossini-like tempo that obliterated phrase accents and articulations, except in the little G minor episode (cellos, basses, and oboe), where even Toscanini must have sensed something wrong – for a moment his pace slackened almost to the right tempo. And Toscanini's ambition throughout the movement seems to have been to create climaxes, whether or not they coincided with Beethoven's own climaxes and, especially, Beethoven's own scale of climax. The second movement was also badly played. At one place in the development section the strings performed strict demisemiquavers after dotted notes. Then, a few bars later, the winds doubly shortened these demisemiquavers (as indeed they were right so to do).* The strings hearing themselves corrected followed suit in the next statement of this rhythm. But can Toscanini have failed to hear such a thing? In any case, he did not hear that the ritardando he applied to the beginning of the recapitulation was insufferably gross, that the whole minuet and trio were so absurdly fast as to make no sense at all, and that the last movement was not only too fast but too slick as well, so that the finest passage in the symphony – the dozen bars

* On the other hand, Beethoven's seventh symphony has been ruined by shortening both the dot and the subsequent note in every performance I have heard:

     soon becomes

or so which open the development (bars 96–108) – was reduced to insignificance.

I am not a *doryphore*, nor have I grievances against Toscanini other than those just stated. I submit, however, that these remarks are the sort that music critics should make about Toscanini's or anybody else's performance of Beethoven's first symphony; and, until they (the critics) are able to discern such realities of musical performance ('discern' and 'criticize' have the same root, by the way) they have no right to utter the hieratic nonsense about interpretation they do in fact utter.

Two weeks ago I witnessed a concert of three symphonies, one by Haydn, from the first Salomon series, Mozart's A major (K. 201), and Beethoven's second. I love the Haydn for the different lengths of its sentences, but it was stifled by tempi too fast and too slow – the *Andante* was played adagio and both allegros were played prestissimo: the natural respiration of the music was everywhere frustrated and the performance was unreal – pulsation is the reality of music. Next day, however, the reviewers' only comment was that the strings had sounded like 'velvet' – though Haydn's strings should sound like strings and not like velvet. But the word 'interpretation' was saved for the Mozart. Now, the interpretative ground of this little symphony is (a) beat: the first movement should be in cut, i.e. 2/2 time and the last movement in 3/8, the bars divided in half; and, (b) style. That is all the interpretation possible; the word is a myth. But the really extraordinary event of the concert was the introduction to the Beethoven, for the conductor gave the first note of the symphony, the demisemiquaver, as a down-beat. His purpose, of course, was to make the orchestra attack together, but the character of the second note, and, indeed, of the whole introduction was thereby destroyed. One preparatory up-beat is enough to accomplish a clean attack, but, as this conductor's beat was like hot plasticine, he naturally could not, by a simple motion, cause the whole orchestra to feel a subdivision of demisemiquavers. Concerning this, however, the reviewers said nothing.

*

R.C. What is academicism in music?

I.S. Academicism results when the reasons for the rule change, but not the rule; the academic composer is therefore concerned more with the old rule than with the new reality – though by 'rule' I mean something nearer to 'principle'; a rule, in the simple sense, is a mere means of conformity in an imitative exercise.

If the real end of academicism is knowledge itself, as I think it is, then, academically speaking, I know very little. Though I have worked all my life in sound, from an academic point of view I do not even know what sound is (I once tried to read Rayleigh's *Theory of Sound* but was unable mathematically to follow its simplest explanations). My knowledge is activity. I discover it as I work, and I know it while I am discovering it, but only in a very different way before and after.

R.C. How do you think the development of information theory in music might affect your art?

I.S. I have always been interested in the theory of games (since a childhood reading of Cardano, in fact) but this has not meant anything to me as a composer or even helped me at Las Vegas. I realize that choice is an exact mathematical concept, and that I ought to be looking beyond the particular example for the process that generated it (even though the particular example is all that matters to me). I realize, too, that a really comprehensive information theory can explain 'inspiration' – or, anyway, the equation of its components – and, indeed, almost everything else about my processes of musical communication. But though I am confident these explanations would enlighten me, I am even more confident they would not help me to compose. My attitude is merely proof that I am not an intellectual, and therefore problems of explanation are of no very great interest to me. To borrow G. E. Moore's example – 'I do not see how you can explain to anyone who does not already know it, what "yellow" is' – I do not see any means of explaining why I have chosen a certain note if whoever hears it does not already know why when he hears it.

R.C. What does 'creation' mean to you?

I.S. Nothing. The word was already badly overloaded when psychologists made it their propaganda term for what was no more than a change in methodology: a child's scribble is not an 'act of creation', nor is our intestinal function, as Freud thought, since animals do as much and animals cannot create; the word, which to Coleridge meant the noblest operation of imagination, is now horribly debased. Only God can create.

R.C. And 'modern'?

I.S. The only sense in which I think 'modern' can now be used must derive from, or so I imagine, a meaning similar to that of the *devotio moderna* of Thomas à Kempis. It implies a new fervour, a new emotion, a new feeling. It is 'romantic', of course, and it suffers (*paschein*, to suffer, is also the root of pathos, incidentally) for it cannot accept the world as it is. 'Modern' in this sense does not so much mean or emphasize the appearance of a new style though, of course, a new style is part of it. Nor is it brought about merely by its innovations, though innovations are part of it too.

This is very far from the popular association of the word with all that is newest and most shocking in the world of sophisticated unmorality. I was once introduced to someone at a party with the recommendation, '*Son* Sacre du printemps *est terriblement moderne*', '*terriblement*' meant 'terribly good', of course. And Schoenberg's *bon mot*, 'my music is not modern, it is just badly played', depends on the same popular association of the word, though Schoenberg himself, according to my meaning, is a true, archetypal 'modern'.

CHROMATICISM

R.C. You often associate 'pathos' with chromaticism. Do you really believe in an innate connexion?

K.S. Of course not; the association is entirely due to conventions, like those of *musica riservata*; artists believe not in innate qualities but in art. Nevertheless, 'chromatic' and 'pathos' are connected, and the first musical use of chromatic, in the *misura cromatica*, was meant to indicate a rhythmic change for expressive, i.e., pathetic, purposes. I prefer to use chromatic in a limited sense, and in relation to diatonic. But we have acquired the habit of looking for *our* (post-Wagnerian) chromaticism in old music, with the result that contexts are grossly distorted. For example, in his setting of the funeral sentence *In the midst of Life we are in Death*, at the words 'Art justly displeased', Purcell avoids the conventional cadence and composes one that was certainly intended, in one sense, to displease his audience; but the cadence pleases *us* in another sense, far more than the conventional one would have done. In fact, though, our whole approach to sixteenth-century music is apt to be slanted towards a chromaticism that was really no more than a tiny development. Willaert's *Quid non ebrietas* quartet,* though it is not so much chromatic as modulatory, was the only work of its kind by Willaert (how I would like to have known Willaert, this little man – you remember Calmo's description – who restored Venice to its musical glory), and

---

*Thanks to Professor Lowinsky it need no longer be called the 'Chromatic Duo'.

so were Lasso's *Alma nemes* and Hans Leo Hassler's *Ad Dominum cum tribularer* unique chromatic works by these masters. And, though I do not know music by Stefano Rossetti and Matthias Greiter other than the chromatic pieces Lowinsky has printed, the fact that only these pieces have gained attention proves my point.

*

Incidentally, I should like to hear someone learned in both sixteenth- and seventeenth-century music discuss a notion of mine, based roughly on a few examples, that the century of chromatic development from Clemens non Papa through Rore and Wert to Marco da Gagliano, Luzzaschi, Macque (the beautiful seconda Stravaganza), and Gesualdo, etc., exceeds in sureness of harmonic movement and in the use of dissonance the chromaticism of the operatic composers of the seventeenth century – always excepting Purcell. In fact, not until Bach do we find music as advanced, in our sense – the Bach of the chorale preludes and, if he wrote it, of the *Kleines harmonisches Labyrinth* – as the motets and madrigals of the late sixteenth-century masters.

*

But we cannot experience the full power of Gesualdo's or any sixteenth-century master's chromatic expression precisely because we are unable to hear it contrasted with the customary diatonic music which was its background (and because our ears have been corrupted by later music). Huizinga remarks the greater contrasts of all things in the late Middle Ages, and though his period is earlier than ours, the contrast between chromatic and diatonic might be added to his list. '... Illness and health presented a more striking contrast; the cold and darkness of winter were more real evils. Honours and riches were ... contrasted

more vividly with surrounding misery. ... The contrast
between silence and sound, darkness and light, like that
between summer and winter, was more strongly marked
than it is in our lives. The modern town hardly knows silence or darkness in their purity, nor the effect of a solitary
light or a single distant cry.'

'Chromaticism' means something different to each and
every composer today.

*

R.C. You often say you cannot 'think' about composing before
you actually start work.

I.S. I do not try to 'think' in advance – I can only start to work
and hope to leap a little in my spirit.

R.C. What piece of new music has most interested you in the last
year?

I.S. Stockhausen's *Gruppen*. The title is exact: the music really
does consist of groups, and each group is admirably composed according to its plan of volume, instrumentation,
rhythmic pattern, tessitura, dynamic, various kinds of highs
and lows (though perhaps the constant fluctuation of highs
and lows, a feature of this kind of music, is its very source of
monotony). Also, the music as a whole has a greater sense of
movement than any of Stockhausen's other pieces (I have
not yet heard *Zyklus**), though I do not think the form is
more successful than that of the *Zeitmasse*. Historically, I
suppose, the chief significance of *Gruppen* is in its post-serial
inventions, but as my own chief interest in music is still
note-against-note counterpoint, and as Stockhausen's is in
pattern and shape, I may be excused for remarking the ex-
terior aspects.

The question of the three orchestras has aroused much

* The score of which is very Cage-y, though very attractive to look
at, too – one almost wishes it didn't have to be *translated* into sound but
were a kind of hand-drawn photo-electric sound (after a spectrum).

comment. Actually, when the orchestras play separately or overlap, their roles are very marked, but in the tutti sections they simply sound like one orchestra, and this is true of all poly-orchestral music whether it is by Schütz or Mozart or Charles Ives, or anyone else. (It may not be true of Stockhausen's new *Carree*, however.)

The problem of the three conductors is more complicated. If I were to blindfold three conductors and start them beating 60 to a beat, they would not be together at the end of even ten bars. Therefore, when the metronomic indication for one orchestra is 70, for the second 113.5, and for the third 94, these tempi are unattainable with any exactitude by merely human conductors. What, in fact, happens is that the conductors follow each other, juggle, and adjust. Incidentally, this is also why I would rather listen to than conduct one of the orchestras in *Gruppen*: the business of synchronizing with the other conductors and of concentrating on the details of one's own orchestra makes the whole very difficult to hear.

Stockhausen's orchestra is full of remarkable sounds. Let me cite only a few places: the 'cello and bass music at bar 16, for example; the solo guitar music at bar 75, and the music three bars before bar 102. But perhaps the most exciting sounds in the whole score are near the beginning – the pizzicato third orchestra at bar 27, the third orchestra at bars 63 to 68, and especially the brass trills and fluttertongues at bars 108 to 116.

The rhythmic construction of *Gruppen* is, I think, of the greatest interest. For example, the following bar,*

* The musical example opposite is used by permission of Universal Edition, Vienna, the copyright owners.

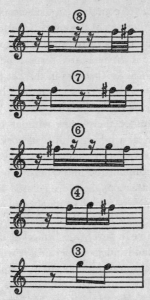

which means that without showing the actual rhythmic relation of the notes they should sound in this order:

R.C. Does the orchestral player or chorus singer in certain types of new music understand his own role in the composition? For instance, when he plays one of the parts in the bar from Stockhausen's *Gruppen* you have quoted, is he not performing a merely mechanical job which, in fact, a mechanical agent might perform better?

I.S. Just how much do you think the choral singer understood of his 'role' in the structure and composition of, say, the fourteenth-century motets in Dr Apel's collection? Much new music does appear to contain a large mechanical element, of course, but whether or not the effort to perform it is mechanical depends on the performer and his experience.

For example, I have heard several performances of Webern's *Variations for Orchestra* in the last few years but I have never been able to answer those critics of it who maintained that the players were unable to understand the inter-relationships of their roles without the score. Recently, however, at a rehearsal of that work in Hamburg I actually did observe musicians listening to each other, and not only for the line of the music but for its every nuance as well. The conductor, therefore, ceased to be the usual puppeteer and became a kind of monitor in a large work of cooperation.

At the same time, a purely mechanical element does exist in music today and it might be better if it were isolated and relegated to mechanical means. I am in sympathy with Milton Babbitt when he says that he is 'depressed by the sight of duplicative' – Mr Babbitt has his own vocabulary – 'orchestral musicians'.

R.C. Is any musical element still susceptible to radical exploitation and development?

I.S. Yes, pitch. I even risk a prediction that pitch will comprise the main difference between the 'music of the future' and our music, and I consider that the most important aspect of electronic music is the fact that it can manufacture pitch. Our mid twentieth-century situation, in regard to pitch, might perhaps be compared to that of the mid sixteenth century, when, after Willaert and others had proved the necessity of equal temperament, the great pitch experiments began – Zarlino's quarter-tone instrument, Vincentino's thirty-nine-tones-to-the-octave archicembalo, and others. These instruments failed, of course, and the well-tempered clavier was established (though at least three hundred years before Bach), but our ears are more ready for such experiments now – mine are at any rate. I had been watching the Kuramatengu play in Osaka one afternoon recently and had become accustomed to the Noh flute. Later, in a restaurant, I suddenly heard an ordinary flute playing ordinary (well-tempered) music. I was shocked, music apart – I think I could keep the music apart anyway – by the exprive poverty of the *tuning*.

1912 – AND AFTER

R.C. Do you see any similarities between the present (post-war) years of musical 'exploration' and 'revolution' and the era before the First World War; and, if so, do you then foresee a decline from this 'radical exploratory' movement – a decline into formulation, such as the late 1920s and 1930s might be considered to have been in relation to the prewar years?

I.S. I can hardly assess a development to which I myself am still contributing, but the richest musical years in this century do now seem to have been those immediately before the 1914 war, and, specifically, 1912, for to that date belong *Pierrot lunaire*, *Jeux*, the *Altenberg Lieder*, and *Le Sacre du printemps*.*

* *Le Sacre du printemps* is usually dated 1913 but it was completed a full year before its performance.

The *Altenberg*, or *Ansichtskarten Lieder*, though still relatively unknown, are one of the perfect works composed in this century and worthy of comparison with any music by Webern or Schoenberg up to the same date. Incidentally, they seem to me to approach Webern very closely in form, instrumentation and, despite their Wagnerism, sensibility. What exquisite pieces they are, especially the passacaglia ... '*Hier tropft Schnee leise in Wasserlachen. . . .*'

Since I have already expressed my reservations about *Jeux* – I consider the musical substance too poor for the musical working-out – perhaps I should now say why I value it. *Jeux* discovers a whole new

The stage following the summit of 1912 was also wonderfully rich and even more protean, though it could be considered something of a decline in originality and explosive force, at least from *Le Sacre* and *Pierrot*. Webern's songs with instruments belong to this period, and so does *Wozzeck*, and Schoenberg's *Serenade* and *Five Pieces*, op. 23, and my own *Renard*, *Noces*, *Soldat*, and the *Symphonies of Wind Instruments*. This is still the period of exploration and discovery, however. Your so-called period of formulation came only in the later 1920s, with the establishment of so-called 'neo-classicism' – Schoenberg's, Hindemith's, and my own. During the fifteen years from 1930 to 1945, however, these three 'neo-classic' schools were ascendant and the fact that they can be called schools is already an indication of the onset of formulae. The Schoenberg, or, as it is now called, the dodecaphonic school, for all its great merits, was obsessed by an artificial need to abnegate any suggestion of triadic 'tonality' – a very difficult thing to do. And, curiously, its music was heavily founded in the most turgid and graceless Brahms.

As for my imitators, my 'school' if you prefer, their trouble was that they imitated not so much my music as my person in my music. They were noted for their rhythms, their ostinatos, their 'unexpected' accents, their diatonic 'lines', their 'dissonances', and for their final C major chords with B natural or A in them. The characteristics of the Hindemith school were its interminable 9/8 movements, its endless fourths and its fugues with subjects thirty-two

world of nuance and fluidity. These qualities are French, even peculiarly French perhaps, but they are new. The work's influence on Boulez is therefore natural (and natural too is its lack of influence on me, for its free-beat, loose bar-lines are worlds apart from my rarely-rubato, strong-bar-line music). I would still call *Jeux* decadent, though I mean that only in relation to my own development.

bars long. Other schools existed, of course – the Broadway, the Appalachian, the Neo-Neanderthal (Orff), the *arrière-garde*, etc. – but these three were principal and paramount.

All three schools had come to a stalemate, however, when at the end of the war in 1945 a new period of exploration and revolution began precisely with the rediscovery of the masterpieces of 1912, and the music of Webern in general. Boulez's cantatas are representative of this new music of the immediate post-war. They derive from the Webern cantatas in substance and style but are more complex in texture. (In fact, with them the ideal of a thin, neo-classic line disappears.) In this new period of exploration the only significant work so far is Boulez's *Le Marteau sans maître* (1954).

The next work in this succession, it is already apparent, must utilize musico-electronic means, exploit acoustical mirror effects, and mix composed with improvised elements. But enough of soothsaying: I am a composer myself and I must cultivate my own garden.

STEREOPHONY

R.C. What does stereophony mean to you, both as composer and performer, and would you comment on the use of it in present recording technique?

I.S. Our two ears are about six inches apart, whereas the stereo microphones which hear a live orchestra for us are sometimes as much apart as sixty feet. We do not hear live performances stereophonically, therefore, and stereo – instead of giving us 'the best seat in the house' – is, in fact, a kind of non-existent, omnipresent seat. (Nor is it a seat in the orchestra, for an orchestra doesn't sound stereophonic to itself.) I say this not to criticize stereo, however, but to question the meaning of 'high fidelity'. Fidelity to what? But though stereo may be unreal in my sense, it can be in

another sense ideal, and as such it has important consequences. For one thing, it is a challenge to existing concert
halls; how can we continue to prefer an inferior reality (the
concert hall) to ideal stereophony?

The stereo principle that the *distance* between the speakers
is the 'microphone', instead of the microphone itself, is
still too imperfectly demonstrated by most recordings I have
heard, where I have been more conscious of the switch from
one speaker to another than of the space between. This
ping-pong effect, in certain kinds of music – Wagner's, for
example – can be a disturbing distortion, indeed. Wagner's
musical-acoustical idea in Bayreuth was to fuse the orchestra, to bring it as close together as possible. Stereophonic
separation, with its illusion of orchestral space, is therefore
quite alien to his musical intentions. But any purely harmonic music – music that depends on fusion and balance –
will suffer from too much focus on its individual parts. In
principle, of course, stereophonic recording should be able
to fuse and balance, but in practice we often feel as though
we are being made to follow the equivalent of an 'Arrow'
score,* that is, to jump to the violins on their entrance, or
swerve in an acoustical spotlight towards the trombones on
theirs.

On the other hand, distortion of this sort does not ruin
certain kinds of polyphonic music, for the very reason that
this music is poly-phonic, i.e., can be heard from different
aural perspectives. Some polyphonic music does not depend
on round harmonic balances, and we are even grateful when
bits of interior construction are suddenly exposed, or when
details of part-writing are brought into relief.

Stereophony also enables us to hear the true effect of
many kinds of 'real' stereophonic music, Mozart's *Notturno*

* An American edition of orchestral scores in which arrows are used
to guide the reader to what is purported to be the leading part.

for four orchestras, for example, or the *cori spezzati* of the Venetians, music in which the stereophony has been composed rather than engineered. I would also include in this category most of Webern, for a work like his orchestral *Variations*, op. 30, seems to me to exploit the 'distance factor' and to anticipate the new stereophonic idea.

Stereophony has already influenced composed music, too. At one level this amounts to the exploitation of the stereo effect (the stereo fault, rather) by 'building' it 'in', i.e., creating distance and separation by re-seating the orchestra, etc. (When I listen to this sort of music, I find myself *looking* in the direction of the sound, as I do in Cinerama; 'direction' therefore seems to me as good a word as 'distance' to describe the stereo effect.) Stockhausen's *Gruppen* and Boulez's *Doubles* are examples of this influence. At another level, composers will soon come to see that stereo obliges them to construct a more interesting 'middle dimension' in their music.

I cannot contribute very much on the subject of present stereophonic recording techniques, but I do know something about the difficulties conductors experience in satisfying the demands of stereo microphones during recording sessions. Stereophonic separation used to require a separation of orchestral and choral performers, and the various groups of separated instrumentalists and singers are sometimes greatly handicapped in hearing each other; also, solo singers or groups of singers, or perhaps an especially resonant drum, must sometimes be isolated by panels, which makes ensemble playing almost impossible.

In spite of all my reservations about stereo, however, I know that when I am accustomed to it – to its much greater volume and dynamic range, to its really remarkable ability to clarify orchestral doublings (which were probably better left in the dark), to its ability to create the distance between a close instrument and a far-away instrument – I shall be unable to listen to anything else.

TRADITION

Thou bearest not the root, but the root thee.

ST PAUL

R.C. Do you have a special theory of, or meaning for, tradition?

I.S. No, I am merely very prudent with the word, for it now seems to imply 'that which resembles the past' – the reason, incidentally, why no good artist is very happy when his work is described as 'traditional'. In fact, the true tradition-making work may not resemble the past at all, and especially not the immediate past, which is the only one most people are able to hear. Tradition is generic; it is not simply 'handed down', fathers to sons, but undergoes a life process: it is born, grows, matures, declines, and is reborn, perhaps. These stages of growth and regrowth are always in contradiction to the stages of another concept or interpretation: true tradition lives in the contradiction. *Notre héritage n'est précédé d'aucun testament* (Our heritage was left to us by no will).*

This is, I think, 'true'. At the same time, however, the artist feels his 'heritage' as the grip of a very strong pair of pincers.

* René Char.

Three Operas

THE NIGHTINGALE

ITS PREMIÈRE

R.C. Your *Autobiography* contains very little information about the *première* of the Nightingale, nor do other sources describe the event more fully – which is curious if only because the *Nightingale* followed the so sensational *Sacre du printemps*. What do you remember of the performance and its reception, and why was the production so quickly eclipsed?

I.S. To answer the second question first, the *Nightingale* was introduced only a few weeks before the 1914 war, and during the war the Diaghilev company was too reduced in means to mount anything as complicated as an opera that for only forty-five minutes' playing time required three sets and many costly costumes. The eclipse, as you call it, must be attributed to budgetary rather than artistic reasons.* The present neglect of the *Nightingale* is in part due to the fact that it must be performed in a double bill, and suitable companion pieces have been difficult to find (when I conducted it myself at La Scala in the 1920s – a performance efficiently prepared by Toscanini, incidentally – the other half of the

---

* Since these remarks were made I have conducted the *Nightingale* in Los Angeles. I now find that Act I, in spite of its very evident Debussyisms, *vocalisés à la Lakmé*, and Tchaikovsky melodies too sweet and too cute even for that date, is at least operatic, whereas the later acts are a kind of opera-pageant ballet. I can only attribute the musical style of the later acts – the augmented seconds, parallel intervals, pentatonic tunes, orchestral devices (tremolos, muted brass, cadenzas, etc.) to the great difficulty I experienced in returning to the opera at all after five years, and especially after *Le Sacre du printemps*.

bill was . . . *Hansel and Gretel*!). Diaghilev programmed it with ballets, however; and with *Petroushka*, especially, it went very well. Diaghilev always wanted to stage opera as he had staged the *Nightingale* – that is, as opera-ballet, with dancers miming the sung roles, while the singers themselves were nicely out of sight in the orchestra pit.

The *première* was unsuccessful only in the sense that it failed to create a scandal. Musically and visually, the performance was excellent. Monteux conducted capably; the singers – particularly 'Death' and the 'Nightingale' – were good; and, scenically, thanks to Alexander Benois who designed the costumes and sets, it was the most beautiful of all my early Diaghilev works. Boris Romanov composed the dances, and Alexander Sanin was the *metteur en scène*. The opera was sung in Russian; and that is all I remember about the *première*.

*

As to its reception, the 'advanced' musicians were genuinely enthusiastic – or so I thought. That Ravel liked it, I am certain, but I am almost as convinced that Debussy did not, for I heard nothing whatever from him about it. I remember this well, for I expected him to question me about the great difference between the music of Act I and the later acts, and though I knew he would have liked the Mussorgsky-Debussy beginning, he probably would have said about that, too, 'Young man, I do it better.' On my last trip to Russia I remember reading a remark in my diary – I kept a diary from 1906 to 1910* – written when I was composing the first act of the *Nightingale*: 'Why should I be following Debussy so closely, when the real originator of this operatic

* Left in a steel safe which was part of my grandfather's Biedermeier desk, a piece of furniture which might still be in our house in Oustiloug – together with my manuscripts and letters. Incidentally, all my music before *Petroushka* was written at this desk.

style was Mussorgsky?' But, in justice to Debussy, I must own that I saw him only very infrequently in the weeks after the *Nightingale*, and perhaps he simply had no opportunity to tell me his true impressions.

The *Nightingale* was staged in a great hurry. In fact, I was still composing the music only a few months before the *première*. The London performances were probably better than the Parisian, because the singers and dancers would have had more time with their parts. I immensely enjoyed them, at any rate, thanks also to the generosity of Sir Thomas Beecham.* I should record the fact, too, that at the outbreak of war Beecham helped me with a payment of money which enabled my mother to return to Russia from Switzerland (by boat from Brindisi to Odessa).

But, rather than attempt to describe the staging of the original *Nightingale*, I will publish Alexander Benois's letters to me covering that period. Benois was in Russia and I in Switzerland during the latter stages of the opera's planning and composition. My wife was ill with tuberculosis and we moved to Leysin – to be near the sanatorium. I could not meet Benois, therefore, which was a misfortune, though it produced these letters. Benois was the conservative of the company, and Diaghilev tended to favour Roerich, not Benois, as the *Nightingale*'s designer. I had great respect for Benois, however, and insisted that he decorate my opera. Benois' ideas *were* followed, and his suggestions in the fourth letter are, in fact, an exact 'in colour' account of the actual staging.

* I think it was on this trip, though it may have been the year before, that I met Frederick Delius. He had come to Covent Garden to attend a performance of our Ballet. Beecham introduced him to me, and he paid me compliments for *Petroushka*, but, as I spoke almost no English, and he but little French, the conversation did not develop. Thirty-seven years later, I visited his famous orange farm, D. H. Lawrence's would-have-been Utopia, in Florida.

St Petersburg,
September 1913

Dear Igor Feodorovitch,

My dear friend, how sad that we are living so far apart. It seems to me that we could do great things together! But this way nothing will happen. And all the others are dispersed, too. Serge is the Devil knows where. After discussing the Bach ballet with me in Baden, he was to have come to see me in Lugano and to have brought Ravel with him. But I have heard nothing from him, and since he has disappeared without a note, I am inclined to believe those charming gossipers (their news has probably reached you too) who say that Vaslav married a Hungarian millionairess and Serge, in his grief, has sold the company to an impresario. Have you any news of our dissolute genius Serge? Valetchka,* who went to Paris (cursing his fate, poor fellow), also does not know anything.

Besides the staging of the Goldoni I must also start to prepare *The Possessed* for the spring season, and all this in addition to writing my *History of Painting*. I am passionately interested in the *Nightingale*. When do you think it will be ready for its run? I do not give up hope of doing it myself. It would be a creative aphrodisiac for me. I believe that Roerich would achieve something miraculous with it, but some details Roerich would probably not do, and just these details would interest me enormously.

My dear friend, write to me again, and soon. I promise to answer without delay, and if you want some information I will be glad to help you. I embrace you and I kiss the hand of dear Catherina Gabrielovna, to whom my wife sends her most cordial greetings.

Your loving,

ALEXANDER BENOIS

* Walter Nouvel.

Dear Igor Feodorovitch, I was in Moscow and found your letter only on my return. The news about Nijinsky's marriage struck me like a thunderbolt. When did it happen? None of our friends is here in town at the moment, and I know of no one who can give me any information about it, since I do not want to talk to a stranger like Svetlov.* I saw Serge and Vaslav almost on the eve of Vaslav's departure for Argentina, and there was no hint then about the coming event. Nijinsky was very attentively studying Bach with us, preparing the Bach ballet. Is it possible that he had no idea of it then? Be kind and tell me one thing: was it a complete surprise for Serge, or was he prepared for it? How deep was his shock?† Their romance was coming to an end, and I doubt that he was really heartbroken, but if he did suffer I hope it was not too terrible for him. However, I imagine he must be completely bewildered in his position as head of the company. But why can't Nijinsky be both a ballet master and a Hungarian millionaire?‡ The whole story is such a phantasmagoria I sometimes think I have read it in a dream and am an idiot to believe it.

I am sorry to be unable to fulfil your request completely, but listen why: the two theatres have become rivals, and all connexions between them are broken. The gossip I hear about it has been contradictory and I do not know what to believe. Some people say everything in the Free Theatre is perfect: that there is plenty of money; that each invention

* A well-known balletomane.
† I had been with Diaghilev in the Montreux Palace Hotel when the news of Nijinsky's marriage came, and I had watched him turn into a madman who begged me and my wife not to leave him alone.
‡ Benois evidently thought Nijinsky had married a Hungarian heiress.

is more amusing and ingenious than the one before; that two of the subscription nights are already sold out (this, it seems, is true), etc., etc. ...

Some people are delighted by Mardzhanov, but others say he is impossible, etc., etc. I personally think that, in any case, it will last at least two years and that they will be able to stage the *Nightingale*,* but I would not promise it absolutely. I think also that they will do a mixture, some interesting things and much *merde*. The Moscow public will swallow it all, good and bad alike, of course, since Moscow knows no better and will devour anything. I am very impatient for the opening, however, because a venture as naïve as *that* must at least result in something refreshing.

I am longing for the *Nightingale*, especially after seeing Mitusov, who gave me his impressions after Warsaw.†

I embrace you. As soon as I have something more definite I will write you. I kiss Catherina Gabrielovna's hand and send you best wishes. With love,

ALEXANDER BENOIS

3   *St Petersburg,*
                                       1 January 1914

Dear Igor Feodorovitch, I write in a hurry as I am just leaving for Moscow. For the last two hours I have looked everywhere for your letter with the description of the sets (and the enumeration of the characters), and cannot find it. I could start to study the play and just now comes this delay. I beg you, send me immediately a second copy, and also a

* The *Nightingale* was produced at the Imperial Theatre in 'Petrograd', January 1916, staged by Meyerhold and decorated by Golovine.

† I had been with Mitusov in Warsaw to discuss the *Nightingale* libretto. I was on my way from Russia to Switzerland, where I finished the composition of the opera.

detailed libretto. I beg you not to insist on the colours. I have my own ideas, and I think the result will be good. The hall in the castle will be pink with dark blue and black. But, my God, where is the music? Is it possible that I will have to work without this main source of inspiration and without your personal promptings?

Goodness, the train!!! I embrace you cordially.

Your,

ALEXANDER BENOIS

PS. Write to me c/o Moscow Art Theatre, Kammergersky Drive. *Come!*

4   *Moscow,*
15 February 1914

Dear Igor Feodorovitch, Although your so obstinate silence shows that you do not wish to talk to me at all, I am obliged to bother you to clarify a few points. (I flatter myself, however, and hope that the real reason for your silence is not a change of your feelings towards me, but circumstances which have enveloped you as much as they have me.)

The hall of the Emperor will be white with blue.* On the other hand there will be a lot of pink and green in the costumes. But what keeps me from finishing the sketch of this setting and of the set in this tableau in general, is this: what am I do with the procession? You wanted a palanquin and you wanted the Emperor 'inserted' in the throne.† A marvellous idea! But how do you visualize the following combination: the throne is carried by a whole crowd of people, including eight small children; the throne is put on a scaffold, and then the Emperor appears, surrounded closely

---

* *Sic.* See letter 3.

† My idea was to have the Emperor fixed on his throne like a doll. (I.S.)

by dignitaries who hold five parasols above *Him*! You wanted a palanquin, but every procession has one, and *this* is new.

In general, I am constructing the procession as follows:

seven female dancers dressed in gold;

seven female dancers dressed in silver;

one male dancer and one female dancer very luxuriously costumed, and with them three dancers; monsters, and two white boys with swords, and five black boys with swords; all this party participating in a symbolic pantomime.

After this comes the court (the chorus is already on the stage):

first appear two white-costumed mandarins;

then – two grey-costumed mandarins;

then – a totally black Grand Master of the Court;

then – the Chief Chamberlain with the Nightingale.

Then comes the throne, and finally, His Majesty, whom nobody could see until this moment because of the parasols hiding him.

The procession closes with two soldiers who take a standing position at the foot of the throne. (The same kind of soldiers can walk in front, or be ready on the stage in the beginning.)

Do you see now what I mean? But perhaps you want something quite different. The final word is with you, but for God's sake, send me this word immediately, or everything will go to hell. Until I have your exact instructions I shall not start the definitive work.

Perhaps an even more important question concerns the last act. How do you see it yourself? And, first of all, I beg you to send me the details of the staging immediately, and the libretto itself, which I ask you to mark with the basic tempi. This is supremely important (the music will explain what I shall not understand in the text). I would prefer to have the piano score, but probably it is far from finished.

How can we see each other to discuss all this? I wanted to come to Berlin for a meeting but now it is simply impossible. Think only how many days will be wasted, and just now, when every hour is precious. Is it absolutely impossible for you to come here?

Now, about the décor of the third act. I imagine it like this: in front is a kind of antechamber, separated from the bedroom by a big curtain (covering the whole stage: red, yellow, gold, and black). This curtain is first drawn back and we see a majestic bedroom at night and in moonlight. The curtains are then closed and at the end again opened for us to see a Sacrum Cubiculum in all its splendour (many windows, a gigantic bed, etc.). What do you think of it? Perhaps you have conceived it quite differently? I implore you to answer.

I kiss Catherina Gabrielovna's hand and wish with all my heart happiness for the newborn baby,* the mother and the happy father. I am burning with impatience to embrace you. One of these days I expect to hear Kussevitsky conduct *Le Sacre du printemps*. I embrace you.

ALEXANDER BENOIS

PS. Write me in St Petersburg, 31 Admirals' Canal, and on the envelope write 'in case of absence please forward the letter immediately'. But the best thing to do, my dear, would be to answer the main points by telegram. If you are in agreement with all: '*Approuve tout*'; if not, then in a few words: '*Emperor en palanquin*'; '*Trône en scène*', etc. Something of this kind. For God's sake, hurry with an answer.

*My daughter, Maria Milena.

5   *St Petersburg,*
                         14–17 February 1914

Dear Igor Feodorovitch, I am in a great rush, for which reason I will limit myself to business and avoid speaking about my artistic feelings.

It is already a whole week that I have been living with the sounds of *Le Sacre du printemps* in my ears. It started in Moscow and continues now in St Petersburg. I am longing to hear it again, and am sad when I think that for a long time I shall be unable to hear this music, about which I cannot even say if it is good or great, because I am still completely bewildered by it. Nor do I know if Kussevitsky conducted it correctly. However, we have our impressions of it.

The success, alas, was rather big, in spite of the hundred people who walked out after the first part. I say 'alas' because the audience applauded in advance, in defiance of Paris, and also because *that* audience applauds Bach, Beethoven, Wagner, Rachmaninov, and Stravinsky all equally. (Do not carry your head too high, and do not draw conclusions, but I love the first of these names and very much dislike most of the others.) A success with such an audience is nauseating. I am very glad that Nurok liked it, however; and that the Rimsky-Korsakov clan hissed it violently is also a consolation.

I babble too much. Business! Business! My dear, what about the following combination: in the beginning, a huge bedroom with a few windows flooded by moonlight; ghosts (Serge does not want ghosts but why not have them sitting on the bed or showing their ugly faces through the curtain of the bed – I do not yet know myself exactly how to do it); a bed with a canopy; a catafalque through which 'Death' leaves (not through the window; the catafalque must melt in front of you – is such a trick possible?). Day breaks during the Nightingale's song. Then, with the bird's last notes, the courtiers, thinking the Emperor dead, ceremoniously close the curtains (the courtiers walk on stage, single file).

The next scene, the court, is in front of the stage curtain, so that when the curtain goes up the bedroom can be flooded by sunlight for the Emperor's '*Bonjour à tous*'. Apropos this finale, I thought the ending of the *Sacre* perhaps too abrupt – lacking in the feeling of finality. People who saw the stage performance say that it is even more noticeable there. I am afraid such a thing can happen again; but, of course, you must know better. Do not listen to that monster Serge, who has a mania to cut and will cut until nothing is left. I await your confirmation of the plans, or any changes that have to be made.

The set for the second tableau is already done, and whether it is good or bad I cannot say because I have no time to look at it again.

Anna Karlovna* had a sore throat and could not be present at the *Sacre*. She sends you and dear Catherina Gabrielovna, whom we both love with all our hearts, our greetings and best wishes.

Devotedly yours,

ALEXANDER BENOIS

PS. My family all praise the *Nightingale* sets, but how can one believe one's family?

PPS. I know nothing about the Free Theatre beyond what has been written in the newspapers. I hear, however, that Mardzhanov found another idiot willing to give money and that he wants to ruin this new idiot by introducing spectacles of dramatic action.

Sanin will stay with Suhodolsky and will stage operettas, probably. Since I came back from Moscow, where I did the décors and sets for Goldoni's *Tavern Keeper*, I am so deep in

* Mme Benois.

the *Nightingale*, I have no time to read or to learn anything. I see no one, and I have had no conversation with anybody.

I embrace you devotedly, dear Igor Feodorovitch, and again wish you everything that is good. And, once more, please give my greetings to your charming wife.

6 *St Jean de Luz,*
Hotel de la Porte,
23 July 1914

My dear friend, your letter puzzled me so much I have gone around composing answers to it for the last five days, but I cannot manage a single one. I really do not like Kozma Prootkov,* or rather, I do not understand the gigantic importance he assumes in Russian literature and in Russian life. Kozma Prootkov is funny, foolish, clever, and from time to time extremely talented, but the book never shows a really strong sense of humour, or the real art of laughter of Gogol and Dostoyevsky. At any rate, I do not see real wit in Prootkov's too long and naïve – in the bad sense – salad of parody. So, in my opinion, it is not worthwhile spending time on Prootkov, and I think it would be better to forget this 'manual for Russian schoolboys', this copybook for our *Satirikon* and *Boodilnik*.† Laughter must be different now, funnier and more terrible. Nevertheless, I read the book from the first page to the last (by the way, I thank you for it, because it gave me great pleasure, nevertheless). Your

* Under this imaginary name, three well-known Russian poets of the 1860s, Alexei Tolstoy and the brothers Jemchooshnikov, wrote a book of humorous and nonsensical verse that was very popular in Tsarist Russia. I had proposed a collaboration with Benois to make a comic piece for the theatre, a kind of *Renard*, to some verses and a little play from Kozma Prootkov.

† Russian humorous magazines.

rapture over it perplexed me and I wished with all my heart to feel the same. Alas, this did not happen, and I was left a cold fish. I decided to be frank and to tell you the truth, but my truth is not absolute, and I would be unhappy indeed if my opinion were to disconcert you. Perhaps you find something where I see only emptiness. If so, start work. Though I hold to my opinion, I am sure that Kozma Prootkov as seen by Stravinsky will start to live a new and wonderful life. Also, I am sure that listening to your music (and I believe in every note) I shall be able to catch your feelings and create something worthy of your music — or, at least, something that will not spoil it. But perhaps you should choose another painter, for instance, Sudeikine, who is under-rated and who, more swiftly than I, will find response in his soul to what Jemchooshnikov and Tolstoy fabricated.

My dear, I am very worried about the impression this 'cold-water' letter will make on you and your muse, but cold water is not so bad if it comes at the proper time and if you have a towel handy. If my douche was mistimed and you catch cold, please forgive me, dear.

With love and kisses for you both,

ALEXANDER BENOIS

PERSEPHONE

R.C. Your autobiography did not reveal the circumstances of your collaboration with André Gide. To what extent was *Persephone* in fact a collaboration? And, as Gide was one of your first acquaintances in Paris, would you describe him as you knew him?

I.S. Gide is a complicated subject in any case, and he was not less so personally. He had to be prised open, like an oyster, and the priser had to remember not to put his fingers in the wrong place, for, like an oyster, he could bite. If I were to hear someone else describe him I think I could comment on the accuracy of the description, but for me to talk about such a man myself is difficult indeed.

We met for the first time in 1910, in Misia Sert's rooms at the Hotel Meurice. I knew him by reputation, of course: he was already an established writer, though his fame was to come much later. After that I saw him from time to time at ballet rehearsals. Whether he came to those of *Le Sacre du printemps*, however, I do not know. (But I was too busy with *Le Sacre* to be aware of anyone besides Debussy and Ravel, who were not then on speaking terms and who sat on opposite sides of the house; I took my place directly behind Monteux to avoid a show of partiality for either of the feuding composers. Debussy, incidentally, was very amiable about *Le Sacre* at the rehearsals, which made his later, negative attitude all the more surprising.)

Some months after *Le Sacre* Gide approached me with a project to compose incidental music for his translation of

Antony and Cleopatra. I replied that the musical style would depend on the style of the whole production, but he did not understand what I meant. Later, when I suggested that the production be in modern dress, he was shocked – and deaf to my arguments that we would be nearer Shakespeare by inventing something new, and nearer him in every way than he was, veristically, to Antony and Cleopatra. I still believe, by the way, that the music in Shakespeare's plays should be Shakespearean, i.e., period music, and that even Purcell's Shakespearean pieces should be performed only with a style of production appropriate to the period; and, of course, 'modern' music is justified only in 'modern' versions of the plays. (Sound effects – electronic music – are something apart; I am talking about musical style.)

As for *Persephone*, I hardly think it can be called a collaboration. The only parts of the libretto we had actually worked on together were the children's choruses; I wished to repeat the music here and asked Gide to compose additional verses (as, later, I was to ask Auden for a second set of choruses in Act I, scene 2, of the *Rake*).

His *Persephone* was an early work and quite unknown to me. Madame Ida Rubinstein had asked me to read it and to meet Gide to discuss the possibility of a collaboration based upon it. A dance-mime role would have to be created for her, of course, but we understood that to be the only stipulation. (Mme Rubinstein was an actress and a woman of great wealth. I had known her since my arrival in Paris in 1910, and I attended the first performance of Debussy's *Le Martyre de Saint Sébastien* with her and d'Annunzio, in her box. She was also an 'original', as she proved in her eighteenth year by hiring a private train to take her from St Petersburg to Moscow. She had commissioned Bakst to arrange the flower beds of her Paris garden so that all the flowers were in trays and the whole garden could be changed every few weeks. I often saw Gide at her Paris home.) Gide came to Wiesbaden to see me in 1933. We read his original *Persephone* together and decided at once on the device of the speaker and on the three-part form. Gide reconstructed and rewrote the original book after this meeting.

These are some of the letters I received from Gide during our 'collaboration':

I

1 bis rue Vaneau,
Paris VII,
20 January 1933

My dear friend, Ida Rubinstein has asked me to write to you. She has been seduced by an idea, which I have just submitted to her, for a symphonic ballet. She says that if it seduces you also, you will agree to work with me for her. The thought of attaching my name to your name in a work that has been close to my heart for a very long time fills me with extreme pride and joy. A word from you would call me to Berlin or elsewhere to talk to you about it – and the sooner the better. I will dine Monday the 23rd at Ida's with Sert, who is very enthusiastic and who would like to do the settings. I could join you Wednesday. It does not matter where.

A word from you or a telegram to Ida Rubinstein or to me would tell us where to telephone you Monday evening between nine and ten o'clock (don't forget the difference in time, and what is the number?).

This moment Ida Rubinstein telephones me to say that you expect to reach the south of France soon where I could then join you. And perhaps you will come through Paris, which would save my coming to Berlin.

Amicalement, and full of hope,
ANDRÉ GIDE

My dear friend,

First of all, let me tell you of the excellent impressions I
have brought back with me from our meeting in Wiesbaden.
I told Mme Rubinstein that our understanding was perfect.
Without exaggeration, I am sure that we will find in her our
best support in the struggle with even the most exacting designer, whoever he may be. She is extremely pleased with
what I told her about the way in which you understood the
subject as the celebration of a mystery, and that you want to
remove from the libretto what I was at first tempted to put
in: episodic bits – as though for a kind of *divertissement*. I am
now working in this direction.

I will send you an edition of the Odyssey (in translation)
that contains the Homeric hymns. It is the last of these
hymns (to Demeter) which inspired me, and I do not doubt
that you will find in it the same extraordinary exaltation
which I found myself when I read it the first time. All my
efforts will be towards maintaining the nobility of this
exaltation throughout my text.

As you will feel for yourself, the subject itself is halfway
between a natural interpretation (the rhythm of the seasons;
the corn falling in the soil must die to be resurrected through
the sleep of winter) and a mystical interpretation; this
way the myth is connected at the same time with both the
ancient Egyptian cults and Christian doctrine.

I was much moved by what you said to me in Wiesbaden:
that it will be interesting to mark and to fix the change of
seasons, and the feeling of the seasonal cycle is indispensable
to our melodrama. But this idea of starting with the Autumn
(however seductive it may be as an idea for beginning the descent of Proserpina into Hell) cannot be maintained. It
would be cheating the Greek myth too outrageously, and
you will see why when you read the Hymn to Demeter.

Proserpina has nothing to do with Autumn. (Besides, the Greek year had only three seasons.) She is the purest personification of the *Spring*.

The plan of the first scene will follow in two days. It consists of recitation, dances, and songs. Mme Rubinstein says it is impossible for the chorus to dance or for the dancing nymphs to sing. Therefore, it will probably be necessary to place the chorus in the orchestra pit or to one side of the stage front: this will have to be studied. What is most important to me is to know, after my plan, how much time this first scene will take.

> Very attentively and cordially yours,
>
> ANDRÉ GIDE

3

> *Grand Hotel,*
> *Le Lavandou,*
> *Var,*
> *24 February 1933*

My dear Igor, This short note to welcome your return to Voreppe which you said would be on the 25th. I am working 'like a dog' for you. By now you should have received the sketch of the first scene. I consider the text as definitive only in so far as it suits you. The same with the second scene, which I gave to be typed today and which you will receive very soon (in one or two days).

The part of the speaker (Eumolpus, the founder and first officiating priest of the Eleusinian mysteries) should be played by a baritone, the part of Pluto by a bass, the bass-est bass possible, and the chorus by women's voices only. As you will see, I decided, at your invitation, to exclude everything anecdotal. Even the character of Eurydice. I fear that this scene (the meeting with Eurydice), completely episodic as it is, will make it too long. I could add this scene, however, if the text seems to you too short for the musical development, as it now seems to me.

Madame Rubinstein seems to be very pleased. I want you to be pleased, too, and I will listen with attention to all your criticisms, remarks, suggestions, etc.

Wishing you fruitful work, I am, full of hope and expectations.

Very affectionately yours,

ANDRÉ GIDE

4   *1 bis rue Vaneau,*
Paris VII,
8 August 1933

My dear Igor, Excuse this delay. I found your letter yesterday evening coming back from a small trip in Belgium.

Encore is written (in poetry) either with or without the final *e*, depending on the requirements of the rhythm and the rhyme. I propose – *ad libitum* – for the second verse: *Parle encor Parle encor, princesse Perséphone*, which is better than my previous proposal.

Parle-nous, parle-nous encor Perséphone

is perfectly possible without *e* (and so would satisfy your wish for two syllables) but the verse would have only eleven feet because we do not count the final syllable as a foot if it is a silent 'e'.

It seems to me that according to the musical indication you gave me *Parle encor Parle encor, princesse Perséphone* would work perfectly.

Happy to know you are working well. I shake your hand.

Amicalement,

ANDRÉ GIDE

*

There are at least two explanations for Gide's dislike of my
Persephone music. One is that the musical accentuation of
the text surprised and displeased him, though he had been
warned in advance that I would stretch and stress and otherwise 'treat'* French as I had Russian, and though he understood my ideal texts to be syllable poems, the haiku of
Bashō and Busōn, for example, in which the words do not
impose strong tonic accentuation of their own.† The other
explanation is simply that he could not follow my musical
speech. When I first played the music to him at Ida Rubinstein's he would only say '*c'est curieux, c'est très curieux*',
and disappeared as soon afterwards as possible. He did not
attend the rehearsals, and if he was present at any of the performances *I* did not see him. A play of his was then being
staged in the Petit Théâtre des Champs-Élysées, but this
shouldn't have prevented him from hearing at least one performance of *Persephone*. Shortly after the *première* he sent me
a copy of the newly published libretto with the dedication
'in communion'. I answered that 'communion' was exactly
what we had not had; his last letter to me is in reply to that.

* I will admit, however, that my habits of musical accentuation have
misled meaning in at least one instance. The line *Ego senem cecidi* in
Oedipus Rex accented on the *ce*, as I have it, means 'I fell the old man',
whereas it should be accented *Ego senem cecìdi* and mean 'I killed the
old man'. This can be corrected in performance, but remains awkward.

† Since making these remarks I have witnessed an instance of word
treatment similar to my own in the Kanjinchō play (Kabuki Theatre).
Here, in the famous catechism scene between Togashi and Benkei, a
verse dialogue I did not have to understand to enjoy as music, the
verbs are syncopated, I am told, held over the bar lines, so to speak,
and the syllables grouped into rhythmic quantities that tend to obscure
sense.

1 bis rue Vaneau,
28 May 1934

My dear Stravinsky,

    I hope, none the less, you will not put in doubt my affection for you and my admiration for your work, because I did not attend the rehearsals of your, of our, *Persephone*! Or do you harbour some other grievance against me that I do not know of?

    As I have no grievance of any kind against you, I will continue in my ardent friendship for you.

ANDRÉ GIDE

    We did not meet again after *Persephone*, but I do not think we were really angry with each other even then. Indeed, how could anyone be angry for long with a man of so much honesty?

*

If I could distinguish between Gide's talent and his writing, it would be to proclaim a preference for the latter, though the writing, too, is very often like *eau distillée*. I considered the *Voyage au Congo* the best of his books, but I did not care for either the spirit or the approach in his fiction: he was not grand enough as a creator to make us forget the sins of his nature – as Tolstoy can make us forget the sins of *his* nature. However, as he seldom talked about his work my relations with him were smooth in this respect.

    Though Gide was not a conspicuously loving critic he was at least inside the art he criticized. And his criticism could and did illuminate. His limitation, I thought, was his 'reason': all he did or said had to be reasoned, with the result that he lacked enthusiasm and could find no sympathy for all the vast unreasonableness in man and art. 'It is better to reason,' he would say, 'than to make an enthusiastic mistake.' That he had wit is evident from his reply when asked to name the greatest French poet: '*Hélas, Victor Hugo.*' And verbal precision such as he had is always enviable; I would have esteemed him if only for that. But he was at his best in company, with Valéry, or Claudel, or Ramuz, for then the conversation would always revert to the French language, and on this subject he was without peer.

Gide was fascinated by Pushkin, and he would sometimes call on me in my Paris apartment to talk to me about the Russian poet and indeed about everything Russian. He called on me in Berlin, too, in October 1931, an occasion I also remember because of Hindemith's having bravely chastised the Berlin Radio Orchestra for its bad playing of my new violin concerto. Apart from Pushkin and Russia his favourite conversational subject was religion. I had returned to the Orthodox Church in 1926 (I became a Communicant then for the first time since 1910 and composed my first religious work, an *a cappella Pater Noster**) and was not a good quarry for his proselytizing Protestantism, but I have more respect for him and his views than for some of the Catholic Pharisees who ridiculed him.

*

I do not know how to describe him in appearance. He was quite undistinguished and he must have wished to become even more so by dressing like a *petit bourgeois*. And the one physical characteristic of his I can remember is also negative.

* I composed the *Pater Noster* and, later, an *Ave Maria* and a *Credo*, for use in the Russian Orthodox Church. In accordance with liturgical tradition, and in view of the Eastern Church fiat prohibiting the use of musical instruments (even of pitch pipes), the music is a simple harmonic intonation of the words. I heard the *Pater Noster* for the first time in the Russian Church in the rue Daru, Paris, by surprise, at the funeral of a Beliankin cousin. In 1949 I prepared a Latin version of all three pieces, revising the *Ave Maria* somewhat in the process.

When he spoke, only his lips and mouth moved: his body and the rest of his face remained perfectly immobile and expressionless. He also smiled a little smile which I thought ironic and which may or may not have been – though I thought it was – a sign of inner torment. But if I had not known so much *about* Gide wouldn't I have been more open with him myself?

THE RAKE'S PROGRESS

R.C. How did you come to choose the 'Rake's Progress' as the subject, and W. H. Auden as the librettist, of your opera? How much of the plot and how many of the characters, the scenes, and the sequences of musical numbers were conceived and planned by you together with Auden? What are your present thoughts about the style and construction of the opera?

I.S. Hogarth's 'Rake's Progress' paintings, which I saw in 1947 on a chance visit to the Chicago Art Institute, immediately suggested a series of operatic scenes to me. I was, however, readily susceptible to such a suggestion for I had wanted to compose an opera in English ever since my arrival in the United States. I chose Auden on the recommendation of my good friend and neighbour Aldous Huxley: at that time all I knew of his work was the commentary for the film *Night Train*. When I had described to Huxley the kind of verse opera I wished to write he assured me Auden was the poet with whom I could write it. Accordingly, in October 1947, I wrote to Auden telling him of my 'Rake's Progress' idea. He replied as follows:

> *7 Cornelia Street,*
> *New York 14, N.Y.,*
> *12 October 1947*

Dear Mr Stravinsky,

Thank you very much for your letter of October 6th, which arrived this morning.

As you say, it is a terrible nuisance being thousands of miles apart, but we must do the best we can.

As (*a*) you have thought about the Rake's Progress for some time, and (*b*) it is the librettist's job to satisfy the composer, not the other way round, I should be most grateful if you could let me have any ideas you may have formed about characters, plot, etc.

I think the Asylum finale sounds excellent, but, for instance, if he is to play the fiddle then, do you want the fiddle to run through the story?

You speak of a 'free verse preliminary'. Do you want the arias and ensembles to be finally written in free verse or only as a basis for discussing the actual form they should take? If they were spoken, the eighteenth-century style would of course demand rhyme but I know how different this is when the words are set.

I have an idea, which may be ridiculous, that between the two acts, there should be a choric parabasis as in Aristophanes.

I need hardly say that the chance of working with you is the greatest honour of my life.

Yours very sincerely,

WYSTAN AUDEN

PS. I hope you can read ¦my writing. Unfortunately, I do not know how to type.

I then invited him to come to my house in California where we could work together. On 24 October I received the following telegram from him:

MANY THANKS FOR WIRE AND GENEROUS OFFER SHAMEFACEDLY ACCEPTED SUGGEST LEAVING NEW YORK NOVEMBER TENTH IF CONVENIENT FOR YOU. WYSTAN AUDEN.

He arrived at night carrying a small bag and a huge cow-skin rug, a gift for me from an Argentine friend. My wife had been anxious that our only extra bed, a studio couch, might not be long enough for him, but when we saw this big, blond, intellectual bloodhound on our front porch (before an hour had elapsed, however, we knew he was going to be a very gentle and lovable bloodhound, however super-intellectual) we realized that we hadn't been anxious enough. He slept with his body on the couch and his feet, covered by a blanket pinioned with books, on a nearby chair, like the victim of a more humane and reasonable Procrustes.

Early the next morning, primed by coffee and whisky, we began work on the *Rake's Progress*. Starting with a hero, a heroine, and a villain, and deciding that these people should be a tenor, a soprano, and a bass, we proceeded to invent a series of scenes leading up to the final scene in Bedlam that was already fixed in our minds. We followed Hogarth closely at first and until our own story began to assume a different significance.

Mother Goose and the Ugly Duchess were Auden's contributions, of course, but the plot and the scheme of action were worked out by the two of us together, step by step. We also tried to coordinate the plan of action with a provisional plan of musical pieces, arias, ensembles, and choruses. Auden kept saying, 'Let's see, now . . . ah, ah, ah . . . let's see . . . ah . . . ah. . . .', and I the equivalent in Russian, but after ten days we had completed an outline* which is not radically different from the published libretto.

*

Auden fascinated and delighted me more every day. When we were not working he would explain verse forms to me, and almost as quickly as he could write, compose examples;

* See Appendix, p. 291.

I still have a specimen sestina and some light verse that he scribbled off for my wife; and any technical question, of versification, for example, put him in a passion; he was even eloquent on such matters.

The making of poetry he seemed to regard as a game, albeit to be played in a magic circle. The latter had already been drawn; Auden's task, as he considered it, was to redefine and be the custodian of its rules. All his conversation about Art was, so to speak, *sub specie ludi*.

I still remember some of the things he said on that first visit – though not, alas, his exact words. He was forever putting forth little Scholastic or psycho-analytic propositions: 'Angels are pure intellect', 'Tristan and Isolde were unloved only children'; Pelléas had 'alarming trichomaniac tendencies; the sign of a man's loss of power is when he ceases to care about punctuality' (Auden himself lived by the clock – 'I am hungry only if the clock says it is time to eat') 'and of the woman's, when she stops caring about dress'. These, too, were – so they seemed – part of the game.

I was puzzled at first by what I took to be contradictions in his personality. He would sail on steady rudders of reason and logic yet profess to curious, if not superstitious, beliefs – in graphology, for instance (I have a graphological chart with an analysis of his writing, the souvenir of an evening in Venice), in astrology, in the telepathic powers of cats, in black magic (as it is described in Charles Williams's novels), in categories of temperament (I was a 'Dionysian' if I happened to work at night), in preordination, in Fate. Another, though more apparent than real, contradiction in him was his display of good citizenship. However lofty his criticism of Society, he was almost too conscientious in fulfilling his everyday democratic duties. He would even serve on juries (I remember his having stalled one for two weeks: 'not for Justice, of course – I quite understood the point involved – but because the housewife jurists were motivated purely by revenge'). He was properly and justly outraged by us for our failure to vote.

Auden's mind was didactic, but it was also, for me anyway, happily heuristic. Few people have taught me as much, and after he left, books he had talked about from Groddeck to de Tocqueville began to appear in our library. Nor do I confine his influence on me to literature, for however good his literary criticism (and why haven't his pieces on Santayana, on Yeats, and on so many others, been collected?), he always seemed to me more profound as a moralist – indeed, he is one of the few moralists whose tone I can bear.

*

I recall only two events of his visit, apart from our work. One day he complained of pressure in his ears. We took him to a doctor who removed large wax globes from each ear. Auden was intrigued by this and kept referring to the 'extraordinary little creatures' that had been harbouring in his auditory canals. We also attended a two-piano performance of *Così fan tutti* together – an omen, perhaps, for the *Rake* is deeply involved in *Così*.

*

The following letters came from Auden after his return to New York:

7 Cornelia Street,
New York 14, N.Y.,
20 November 1947

Dear Mrs Stravinsky,

First, an account of my stewardship, I have

(*a*) Posted the letter to the Guggenheim Foundation.

(*b*) Called Miss Bean.

(*c*) Called Mr Heinsheimer.

The journey was a nightmare. The flight was cancelled; I was transferred to an American Airlines local which left at 7 a.m., stopped *everywhere* and reached New York at 4 a.m. this morning. The meals, as usual, would have tried the patience of a stage curate, so you can imagine what I felt, after a week of your luxurious cuisine. And finally, of course, I got back here to a pile of silly letters to answer – a job I loathe. The only consolation is the pleasure of my writing you this bread-and-butter letter (how do you say that in Russian?). I loved every minute of my stay, thanks to you both, and shall look forward with impatience to the next time we meet.

Greetings to Vassily, Das krankheitliebendes Fräulein, Popka, Mme Sokolov, La Baroness des Chats, etc.*

Yours ever,

WYSTAN AUDEN

PS. Could you give the enclosed note to the maestro?

(Enclosed note) – *Du Syllabiste* – *Au compositeur.*

Cher Igor Stravinsky,

Memo. Act I, Sc. 1,

Je crois que ça sera mieux si c'est un oncle inconnu du héros au lieu de son père qui meurt, parce que comme ça la richesse est tout à fait imprévue, et la note pastorale n'est pas interrompue par le douteur, seulement par la présence sinistre du villain. En ce cas, la girl possèdera un père, pas un oncle.

* Vassily was our cat; the 'illness-loving Fräulein' is our house-keeper, Evgenia Petrovna; Popka, our parrot – we had forty parrots and lovebirds at that time – was the special favourite of Evgenia Petrovna and a relationship alarmingly like that in Flaubert's *Félicité* existed between them; Mme Sokolov was the wife of the actor and a dear friend and neighbour; the Baroness was Catherine d'Erlanger, another friend and neighbour.

Êtes-vous d'accord? Je tiendrai silence pour oui,

WYSTAN AUDEN

PS. I can't tell you what a pleasure it is to collaborate with you. I was so frightened that you might be a *prima donna.*

Salut au 'making'

*

7 *Cornelia Street,*
New York 14, N.Y.,
16 January 1948

Dear Igor Stravinsky,

Herewith Act I. As you will see, I have taken in a collaborator, an old friend of mine in whose talents I have the greatest confidence.*

We are in the middle of Act II now, which I will send as soon as it is done.

I've marked places where cuts in the text can be easily made if you want to, but of course, don't hesitate to make cuts of your own.

With warmest remembrances to Mrs Stravinsky and everyone else.

Yours ever,

WYSTAN AUDEN

I was delighted with the first act, but afraid it might be too long.

Auden telegraphed:

* Chester Kallman, who, in fact, wrote the latter part of the first scene (after the aria 'Since it is not by merit'), and the entire second scene; the first scene of Act II to the end of Tom's aria 'Vary the song', and the entire second scene; the first scene of Act III (except for the off-stage lines of Tom and Shadow) and the card-guessing game in scene two. Auden, of course, wrote the rest.

24 January 1948

MANY THANKS FOR WIRE WILL MAIL ACT TWO
MONDAY DO NOT WORRY ABOUT EXCESSIVE LENGTH
WHICH CAN BE CUT AD LIB WHEN WE MEET HOPE
YOU COME IN MARCH BEFORE I LEAVE APRIL
SEVENTH. WYSTAN AUDEN.

*

7 Cornelia Street,
New York 14, N.Y.,
28 January 1948

Dear Igor Stravinsky,

Voici Acte II. It seemed best to transfer the Auction
Scene to Act III, as that is where the time interval occurs.
Have made a few slight alterations in our original plot in
order to make each step of the Rake's Progress unique, i.e.:

Bordel   – *Le plaisir.*
Baba   – *L'acte gratuit.*
La Machine – *Il désire devenir Dieu.*

As I said in my wire, don't worry about length. Once you
have the whole material to look at, you can form your own
opinions and it won't be hard to make cuts and alterations.

Yours ever,

WYSTAN AUDEN

*

I saw him next in the Hotel Raleigh (in the 'Lily Pons
Suite', to be exact), Washington, D.C., on 31 March 1948.
He had shown the finished libretto to T. S. Eliot meanwhile
(Eliot had noted one split infinitive and one anachronism –
'alluvial', I think; 'fluminous' would have been the word
used in the Hogarth period). We spent the day working to-
gether, and I saw him again the following week in New
York, after a performance of the *St John Passion* in which
Hindemith had played the viola d'amore part.

*

7 Cornelia Street,
New York 14, N.Y.,
22 November 1948

Dear Igor Stravinsky,

I got back from Washington yesterday afternoon to find your letter. I enclose another verse which should, I think, come first. It is difficult in this metre to get an *exact* rhythmical identity – e.g., *who cares what* is slightly different from *far too soon*, but they are, I hope, near enough. In case you can't read my pencil on the score, here is the verse in printed CAPS:

SOON DAWN WILL GLITTER OUTSIDE THE SHUTTER
AND SMALL BIRDS TWITTER; BUT WHAT OF THAT?
SO LONG AS WE'RE ABLE AND WINE'S ON THE TABLE
WHO CARES WHAT THE TROUBLING DAY IS AT?

I'm very excited about what I hear of the music from Robert Craft. Very Mozartian, he says.

Yours ever,
WYSTAN AUDEN

Via Santa Lucia 22,
Forio d'Ischia,
Prov. di Napoli,
28 April 1949

The sirocco is blowing, which makes it a good day to write letters. Arrived after a *very* boring voyage just before Easter, when the Madonna ran down the street to meet her son, to the sound of explosions. Your photo is up in the kitchen. Hope that Act II is going well. I keep nagging at St Restituta about it.

Love to all,
WYSTAN

> *7 Cornelia Street,*
> *New York 14, N.Y.,*
> *24 October 1949*

Dear Igor,

Many thanks for your letter.

In order to distinguish Baba in character and emotion from the two lovers, it seems to me that her rhythm should be more irregular and her tempo of utterance faster. In writing her part therefore I have given any line of Baba's twice the number of accents as compared with the equivalent line of Anne's or Tom's. If you find I have given her too many lines, cuts are easy to make.

Much love to you and Vera, and come East soon.

> WYSTAN

> *7 Cornelia Street,*
> *New York 14, N.Y.,*
> *15 November 1949*

Dear Igor,

If you haven't yet composed the Trio in Act II, Scene 2, here is an alternative version of Baba's part where the rhymes fit the others, which you may prefer to what I sent you.*

Looking forward to hearing *Persephone* on Monday,†

> Love to you both,
>
> WYSTAN

* In fact, the original was kept.
† A concert conducted by Robert Craft in Carnegie Hall, in which Auden read a group of his poems.

BABA

I'm waiting, dear. . . . Have done
With talk, my love. . . . I shall count up to ten . . .
Who is she? *One* . . .
Hussy! . . . If I am found
Immured here, dead,
I swear . . . *Two* . . . I'll haunt you . . .
Three . . . You know you're bound
By law, dear . . . *Four* . . . Before I wed
Could I . . . *Five, Six* . . . have . . . *Seven* . . . then
Foreseen my sorrow? . . . *Eight, Nine* . . . *Ten* . . .
O never, never, never . . .
I shall be cross, love, if you keep
Baba condemned to gasp and weep
Forever.

*

7 Cornelia Street,
New York 14, N.Y.,
14 February 1951

Dear Igor,

Many thanks for your letter.

Delighted to hear that Act III, Scene 3, is nearly finished.
Mr Kallman and I are a bit worried about the directing.*
As you can imagine, we – as librettists – are as concerned
about the stage goings-on as you are about the singing.

If it can possibly be arranged, Kallman and I would like to
be present in an advisory capacity when rehearsals start.

Hope you have a lovely time in Cuba.

Love to all,

WYSTAN

* It had been settled that the *Rake* was to be produced at La Fenice,
Venice, in September.

Via Santa Lucia 14,
Forio d'Ischia,
Prov. di Napoli,
9 June 1951

Dear Igor,

Thank you for your letter of April. Everything still seems in a terrible muddle here and I hope that we aren't going to have a scratch performance with last-minute singers, designers, etc.

Mr Kallman, who has been proof-reading the vocal score in New York, writes me that in Act II, Scene 1 (p. 85), stage directions prior to no. 48, the stage direction now indicates that the broadsheet of Baba should be visible to the audience – the face, that is. Did you mean this, because there seem to be two serious objections:

(1) It is physically impossible to show the broadsheet in such a way that it is equally visible in all parts of the house. Those of the audience who can't see it will be irritated.

(2) More importantly, the revelation that Baba has a beard at this point will ruin the dramatic effect of the finale to Act II, Scene 2.

I know you must be frightfully busy, so don't bother to answer this, unless you violently disagree.

Looking forward to seeing you in Italy,

Love to all,

WYSTAN

[*Florence, October 1958*
Kyoto, April 1959]

APPENDIX

First Scenario for *The Rake's Progress* by Stravinsky and Auden

Place	Characters	Action	Number
ACT I, Sc. I Garden of Uncle's Cottage in the country.	Hero and Girl seated.	Pastoral, comme Theocritus, of love, youth, country, etc. (Perhaps mention Adonis here?)	Duet, ten. & sop.
Fine spring afternoon.	Uncle appears in doorway.	Blesses (to himself) the pair and looks forward to their marriage.	Trio, ten., sop., bass.
	Girl and Uncle enter cottage, leaving Hero solus.	Uncle summons Girl into house.	Piano recit.
		Hero walks about garden, humming melody of duo. His voice trails off into silence. Pause. He yawns.	
	Villain appears at garden gate. He whistles.	Hero turns around. An exchange of questions and enigmatic answers.	Orch., recit., ten. and bass.
	Uncle and Girl reappear from house.	Villain explains how his coach has stuck in mid. of lane. Uncle invites him in. Girl goes to fetch wine. They drink. Villain proposes toast to the Future and says he can foretell it. Girl asks him to tell hers.	Piano recit.
		He does so in the manner of a Baroque Delphic Oracle. Egged on by girl, reluctant Hero asks his future.	Bass aria with soli comments.

291

Place	Characters	Action	Number
ACT 1, Sc. 1 (continued)			
	Servant enters with Letter for Hero.	A brief silence. Villain whistles. (Villain: 'Read it.') Hero reads Letter announcing illness of Father. 'I must get to London.' Villain offers services.	Orch. recit., ten.
	Curtain	Ensemble in which Hero speaks of Father, Villain of inheritance, Girl and Uncle with foreboding of Future.	Quartet. sop., ten., bass, and bass.
		Orchestral Interlude ?	
ACT 1, Sc. 2. A Brothel. One table with two chairs. Centre backstage a grand-father cuckoo clock with an inscription, TEMPUS FUGIT.	Madam, Whores, and Roaring Boys. Enter Hero and Villain. Greeted with great deference by Madam, who escorts them to table.	They sing of the Love of War and the War of Love.	Chorus. *Marche militaire.*
		Villain: '*Ne vous dérangez pas, mes amis. Amusez-vous. Dansez.*' Hero: 'I want to go home. It is late.' Villain: 'Late? That is easy to change.' (Clock cries One. Clock cries Twelve.) They dance.	Piano recit.
		Villain to Hero: 'Let Madam see if you know your lesson.' He takes him through Catechism of Pleasure.	Gigue. Duet, ten. and bass. Comments by contralto.

292

Place	Characters	Action	Number
ACT I, Sc. 2 (continued)		'Now you are ready for confirmation. Your attention, Ladies and Gentlemen.' Villain introduces Hero as Virgin and rich. Hero sings Serenade of the conventional gallant.	Orch. recit. Orch. recit. Ten. aria.
		All applaud and make a rush for Hero. Madam: '*Va-t'en. Ce gosse est à moi.*' She leads Hero slowly out, singing him a nursery rhyme.	*Bruits choriques.* Contralto aria.
	Curtain	Villain whistles.	
ACT I, Sc. 3 Same as Sc. 1. Winter Night. Full moon.	Girl comes out of house dressed in travelling clothes.	She speaks of getting no letters, fears Hero has forgotten her and announces her intention to run away from home to London to find him.	Orch. recit. and sop. aria.
ACT II, Sc. I Hero's dining-room Morning.	Hero *en déshabillé* at breakfast.	Hero speaks of his debts, his boredom with the bachelor life he has been leading, and wonders what to do next. He yawns. Villain: 'I have a present for you.' He produces a miniature.	Orch. recit. and ten. aria.
	Enter Villain whistling.	Hero: 'Who is this Medusa?' Villain: 'Your wife-to-be.'	Piano recit.

Place	Characters	Action	Number
ACT II, SC. I (continued)		Hero: 'I'd rather marry a hedgehog.' Villain: 'You will change your mind when I tell you who she is.' He gives a list of her titles.	Orch. recit.
		Hero: 'Let me look again. No, I don't think I could.' Villain: 'You know nothing about Marriage. Let me tell you, while you dress.'	Piano recit.
		Gives a lesson in the choice of a wife. Hero gets more and more excited, and joins in.	Bass aria, turning into ten. and bass duet.
	Curtain	When he is ready, Villain cries, 'To Hymen's altar.' Exeunt with bravura.	
ACT II, SC. 2 Street outside Hero's front door.	Enter Girl. Footman at door.	She expresses her fear at her daring at being alone in the city. She knocks at door. Footman tells her Hero is not at home but expected soon. She comes downstage to a corner.	Orch. sop. recit.
			Piano recit. sop.
Dusk.	Procession of tradesmen.	Procession of tradesmen arrive with packages. She wonders fearfully what it means, and expresses her love.	Sop. aria.
	Hero and Ugly Duchess in sedan chair. Servants with torches.	Hero and Ugly Duchess arrive.	Marche comique.

Place	Characters	Action	Number
ACT II, SC. 2 (continued)	Girl, Hero, Ugly Duchess.	With a cry the Girl rushes forward, confronts Hero, and the fight is on. Girl: 'False one, what of your vows to me?' Hero: 'Let me explain. What shall I say?' Ugly Duchess: 'Who is this person?'	Trio – sop., mezzo, and ten.
	Curtain		
ACT II, SC. 3 (same as Sc. 1)	Hero and Ugly Duchess at breakfast.	Wife chatters about nothing; Hero answers with absent-minded grunts. Wife complains that he doesn't listen or care for her and bursts into hysterics. Hero gets up and puts tea-cosy over her head. Sudden silence. He returns to his chair. He yawns.	Mezzo aria with tenor monosyllables.
	Villain enters. Whistling.	Enter Villain wheeling fantastic apparatus, for making gold out of sea water. Hero: 'What on earth is that?'	Piano recit.
		Villain: 'Your fortune. Watch.' Villain pours water into machine and turns handle, explaining process. A nugget of gold drops out. He hands it to Hero. 'There you are.'	Comic orch. recit.
		He begins to suggest what can be done with absolute wealth. Hero joins in.	Ten. and bass duet.

Place	Characters	Action	Number
ACT II, SC. 3 (continued)		Villain: 'Well, will you go into business with me?'	Piano recit.
		Hero: 'Yes.' They shake hands.	
		Villain: 'Will you tell your wife?'	
		Hero: 'It's not necessary.' (Points to her.) 'I have buried her.' They exit with machine.	
	Curtain		
		Orchestral Interlude	
ACT II, SC. 4 (Same as previous scene, except that furniture, etc., is stacked as for an auction and covered with cobwebs. Ugly Duchess has not moved.) Afternoon.	Chorus of respectable citizens come to bid.	Chorus sing a moral, while they examine the things.	Chorus.
	Girl.	Enter Girl who runs from one group to another asking for news of Hero. They reply, 'He has disappeared, he ruined himself in a speculation, etc.',	Mezzo and chorus en chuchotant.
	Auctioneer and assts.	Auctioneer enters, mounts dais, starts selling lots of fantastic objects.	Ten. aria.

Place	Characters	Action	Number
ACT II, Sc. 4 (continued)		Voices in Chorus bid: Lot I Lot II	Chorus bids.
		Lot III is the Ugly Duchess herself, labelled *Chose inconnue*. Auctioneer plucks tea-cosy off her head. She recognizes Girl and breaks into a tirade, blaming her for everything because Hero only loved her.	Mezzo aria leading to mezzo and sop. duet.
	Hero and Villain off-stage.	Hero and Villain are heard off, singing a street cry – Old Wives for Sale. Ugly Duchess (to Girl): 'Go to him if you want him, I don't.' Girl runs out. Chorus: *Quelle histoire.*	Ten. and bass in unison. Ensemble.
	Curtain		
		Orchestral Prelude	
ACT III, Sc. 1 A cemetery. Starless night.	Hero and Villain playing dice on a grave.	Hero: '*Je m'ennuie.*' Villain: '*Qu'est-ce que vous désirez maintenant? Le plaisir?*' Hero: '*Non.*' Villain: '*La gloire?*' Hero: '*Non.*'	Orch. recit.

Place.	Characters	Action	Number
Act III, Sc. I (continued)			
		Villain: '*La puissance?*' Hero: '*Non.*'	
		Villain: '*Quoi donc?*'	Ten. aria.
		Hero: '*Le passé.*'	
		Hero sings of lost innocence and love.	
		Villain: '*Joue, alors.*'	
		They play. Hero loses.	
	Girl (off).	Villain: '*Mon vieux, c'est fini.*' He whistles. The voice of the girl is heard in the distance, expressing her undying love for Hero.	Sop. aria (off).
		Hero: (in great excitement) '*Non. Il reste encore une chose. Le futur. Joue.*'	
		Villain: '*Je refuse.*'	
		Hero: '*Vous ne pouvez pas. Je le commande. Joue.*' A clock begins to strike twelve.	
		Villain: '*C'est trop tard.*'	
		Hero: '*J'arrête le temps. Écoute.*' The clock stops in the middle of its striking.	
		Villain sings with defiant despair of the future of a love that he can never have.	
		Hero: '*Assez. Joue.*' They play. Villain loses.	Orch. recit.

298

Place	Characters	Action	Number
ACT III, SC. 1 (continued)		Hero: 'Eh bien. Siffle.' Silence. 'Siffle!!' Silence. 'Siffle!!!' Villain sinks into the grave. The clock finishes its striking. Hero: 'Let it strike. Le temps ne m'effraye plus. Pour l'amour il n'y a pas de passé ou de futur, il n'y a que le présent. Amant et aimé, je suis l'Adonis, le toujours jeune.'	Bass arioso.
	Curtain		
ACT III, SC. 2 Bedlam	Hero. Chorus.	Hero: 'Levez-vous, mes amis, couronnez-vous de fleurs. Vénus, reine de l'amour, me visitera.' Chorus: 'Elle ne viendra jamais.' Hero: 'Elle m'a fait sa promesse.' Chorus: 'Elle ne la tiendra pas.'	Ten. solo and chorus.
	Hero and Chorus of Madmen.	They dance, mocking him. Hero sinks his face in his hands.	*Danse choquante.*
	Enter Keeper and Girl.	Keeper (to Chorus): 'Allez-vous en.' (Chorus retire.) (To Girl): 'Le voilà. N'ayez pas peur. Il n'est pas dangereux. Seulement, il s'imagine l'Adonis. Entrez dans son jeu et il sera satisfait.'	Piano recit.
	Exit Keeper.		

299

Place	Characters	Action	Number
ACT III, Sc. 2 (continued)		Girl: *S'approche du Héro et l'appelle par son nom. Il lève la tête.*	Orch recit., ten.
		Hero: 'At last, *Venus*, *tu es arrivée. Je t'ai attendue si longtemps. Ces types – là m'ont dit que tu m'as oublié. Monte à ton trône.*' (He leads her to his chair and kneels at her feet.)	
		'*O Vénus, ma vraie déesse, pardonne-moi mes péchés. J'ai dédaigné ton amour en chassant les ombres stupides. Mais maintenant le sanglier est mort et tout est changé. Je sais que je t'aime comme tu m'aimes. Pardonne-moi, je t'implore.*' Girl: '*Si tu m'aimes il n'y a rien à pardonner.*'	Ten. aria, then ten. and sop. duet.
		Both: '*L'amour change – chaque enfer particulier a l'Elysée mutuelle.*' Hero: '*Laisse-moi placer ma tête à tes genoux. Je suis fatigué et je veux dormir. Chante, Vénus, chante à ton enfant.*'	Orch. recit.
		Girl sings a lullaby. Hero falls asleep.	Sop. aria.
	Enter Keeper with Uncle.	Uncle (to Girl, *tout simplement*): 'The tale is ended. I have come to take you home.'	Piano recit.

Place	Characters	Action	Number
ACT III, SC. 2 (continued)		Girl (to Hero, *aussi très simplement*): '*Adieu. Dors tranquillement.*' *Le Héros s'éveille brusquement.*	
	Exeunt Keeper, Uncle, and Girl.	Hero: '*Où es-tu, Vénus? Où es-tu? Les oiseaux chantent, les fleurs s'ouvrent. C'est le printemps. Viens. Vite. Je veux coucher avec toi.*' '*Holà Achille, Hélène, Orphée, Platon, Eurydice, Perséphone. Où est ma Vénus? Vous l'avez volée pendant que je dormais. Où l'avez vous cachée?*'	Orch. recit.
	Re-enter Chorus.	Chorus: '*Il n'y avait personne ici.*' Hero: '*Mon cœur se brise. La mort approche. Pleurez, mes amis, pleurez pour moi, l'Adonis le toujours jeune, l'Adonis que Vénus a aimé.*' Chorus: '*Nous pleurons pour Adonis, le jeune, le beau, que Vénus a aimé.*'	Fugal chorus.
	Curtain		
Epilogue	Before the Curtain.	Hero, Girl, Villain, Wife, and Uncle sing a moral, THE DEVIL FINDS WORK FOR IDLE HANDS TO DO.	Quintet.

FIN